AF553946

THE AKAS

LAND AND PEOPLE

THE AKAS

LAND AND PEOPLE

Gibji Nimachow

The Akas : Land and People

Edition : 2027

ISBN 978-81-311-0332-6

Published by :
COMMONWEALTH PUBLISHERS (P) LTD.
4831/24, Govind Lane,
Ansari Road, Darya Ganj,
New Delhi - 110002
Ph. : 23272541, 23242541
e-mail : commonwealthpublishers2016@gmail.com

Distributed by :
ARJUN PUBLISHING HOUSE
4831/24, Govind Lane,
Ansari Road, Darya Ganj,
New Delhi - 110002
Ph. : 23272541, 23242541
e-mail : arjunbooks2001@gmail.com

Laser Typesetting by :
Dimple Computers
Delhi

Printed at :
Milan Enterprises
Delhi

To

My Aou (Father) and Ain (Mother)

Shri Lisang Nimachow and

Late Lame Nimachow

ACKNOWLEDGEMENTS

I take this opportunity to express deep sense of regards and thankfulness to my Supervisor, Prof. R. C. Joshi, Dean, Faculty of Environmental Sciences, Department of Geography, Rajiv Gandhi University, Itanagar for his constant suggestions and guidance in completing this noble work. He has been always a source of inspiration for my research work. I also express sincere thanks to Prof. R. S. Yadava, Department of Geography, BHU, Varanasi for taking initiative and encouraging me to carry out this research work. My special thanks go to the faculty members of the Department of Geography, RGU for their kind help and arrangements in my academic works.

I am thankful to the respondents in general and the village experts in particular for their co-operation in the conduct of field survey as well as filling up of the questionnaires smoothly. My grateful thanks go to Mr. Govardhan Nimasow, Mr. Nichow Khabisow, Mr. Nizam Thasusow, Mr. Lukhi Delusow, Mr. Lambu Sagrosow, Mr. Pario Sidasow, Mr. Mahabu Desisow, Mr. Miali Sidisow, Mr. Sherdopla Dibisow, Mr. Thasu Aglasow, Mr. Biga Nimasow, Mr. Lagon Degio and Mr. Bazi Sopung for narrating various myths, rituals and other important socio-cultural activities of the Akas.

I express love, regards and gratitude to my adorable *Paa* and *Maa* Shri Lisang Nimachow and Late Lame Nimachow. My sincere thanks also go to relatives namely Mr. Serphow Nimachow (uncle), Mr. Ronjeet Nimachow, Mr. Subhash Nimachow, Mr. Raji Nimachow, Mr. Japtow Nimachow (brothers), other family members, the villagers of Palizi and all the Aka populace for helping me in the collection of various relevant materials, statistical data, and carrying out the field survey.

I must be thankful to my friends namely Mr. Ramda Jidusow, Mr. Amit Kr. Tamang, Mr. Leki Norbu, Mr. Hui Tag, Mr. Kamu Desisow and Ms. Wachom Rabasow for their kind help in various works leading to the completion of the research work in appropriate time. My special thanks and love go to Dr. Tasi Kaye and his family members for helping me to carry out this work.

I sincerely express special thanks to Commonwealth Publishers, New Delhi for bringing out this work into a book form within a short and right time.

Finally, my heartfelt love to wife Oyi Dai Nimachow, *Akho* Kuthru Nimachow (son), Ms. Yamum Pasing (sister-in-law), and Ms. Sanchimo Nimachow (sister), for being a part of me even through the tears and thorns.

The views expressed in the book are of the author and the works of other scholars are cited with proper references in the text. For any error and inaccuracies in the analysis or facts the author takes the responsibility and welcomes constructive suggestions to improve the same.

Dr. Gibji Nimachow

CONTENTS

1 CONCEPTUAL FRAMEWORK

Introduction

The term 'tribe' has been derived from a Latin word '*tribus*', which refers to a group of families or communities, linked by social, economic, religious, or blood ties, and usually having a common culture and dialect and a recognized leader. Generally, 'tribe' is used for a "socially cohesive unit, associated with a territory, the members of which regarded themselves as politically autonomous....." (Mitchell 1979). An ideal type of tribe is characterized as a socially homogenous unit having its own dialect, political and cultural institutions and territory which isolates the tribe from the outside influences.

The term 'transition' has been derived from a Latin word '*transitio*' (as transit), which refers to a passing or change from one place, state, condition, etc. to another. The term 'transition' has been used as a synonymous to change. All the societies are characterized by change, continuity and transformation. The tribals constitute about 7% of the total Indian population and have attracted the attention from various corners. Social scientists and other researchers apart, the official administration and non-official agencies established contact with the tribals to induce their respective programme. Under the circumstances the tribal communities have not been spared from the conditions of persistence and change. A study on transition is concerned about the significance of 'place' and 'time' or geography and history in the human activities and behaviour. Indeed, according to the conditions, demands and exigencies of the time and place, what is today may become different tomorrow. Transitional study includes the functional and structural changes taking place on the society. It may be studied either for a particular tribe, which may be a study on that tribe from a time period up to the present context or a comparative study between two or more tribes. The change of whatever order and quality attributed to culture attract the social scientists to study the causes and consequences in tribal society. Both, the originality and change in tribals depict positive and negative aspects. Some changes and developments sound healthy, whereas part of attachment to traditional mode of living and some of the results of change sound unhealthy or lead to problem for the tribals.

In the present study the concept of transition is used in terms of both physical as well as cultural elements. The physical elements includes physiography of the earth's surface (relief, drainage, location, situation, etc.), climatic (the atmosphere including sunrays), and biotic elements (plants and animals and man). Cultural transition may be perceived in terms of the change in land use pattern, economy, dress, food habits, rituals, religion, etc. In this study an attempt has been made to study such changes among the Akas during different time periods i.e. post independence, statehood and 2000 onwards in connection to the society, economy and culture. It has been found that the tribal people as an underdeveloped communities are more prone to transition, continuity of change and transformation. In this age of science and technology, globalization process has brought people of different society very close. In this process needs, desires and expectations are changing very fast. Thus, it is almost impossible to survive in isolation. In this research, the trend of social, economic and cultural changes of the tribal people is very significant in contemporary world.

In all living creatures change is inevitable. One culture may foster change faster than another while some cultures may be selective in their response to factors of change. Like any other tribe, the Akas of Arunachal Pradesh are also changing very fast in respect of their social, economic, political and cultural spheres of life by the influence of different forces of change. As development is necessary for any society in the contemporary world, change is essential for attaining any kind of development in a society. The traditionalized institutions, relationships, views, attitudes, outlook and the value system of the Akas have considerably changed in the recent few years under the influence of some self-generating factors and extraneous forces. Plenty of research works have been done to assess the status of tribal transitions viz. Vyas and Mann (1980), Gohain (1994), Parihar (1989), Balan (1992), Nair (1993), Kuppuswamy (1989), and Singh (1994). Though such works have been done from the national and regional perspectives but only a few works have been done to find out the transition occurring in the tribal people of Arunachal Pradesh. In order to address such important issues on tribal transitions, the present theme has been selected by the researcher for a comprehensive study of the social, economic and cultural changes taking place among the Akas of Arunachal Pradesh. The study aims at to fill such gap in a very meaningful and worthwhile manner.

Objectives

(i) To identify the geo-environmental background of the area.

(ii) To study the traditional social aspects and demographic characteristics/dynamics of the Aka society during the recent past.

(iii) To reveal the cultural milieu of Aka society and changes taking place due to the commencement of the various developmental activities.

(iv) To study the linkages and dependency on the forest resources.

(v) To analyze and interpret the changes taking place in infrastructure and economy.

Study Area

Aka, a small tribal group inhabits in the sub-Himalayan region of Arunachal Pradesh (India). According to a myth

Dzuw Buslou Aou (Hrusso)/Saslon (Koro) was their ancestor who is said to have originated from the sky and the earth. According to Hesselmeyer (1868) the *Hrussos* do not pretend to be aborigines of the country they now inhabit. But, the history of their migration to this area is veiled in mystery. They have a legend that they came to their present homeland from the plains where their ancestors lived in Partabgor on the banks of the Giladhari river, north of Bishnath and were ousted from there by Krishna and Boloram. Pratabgarh (a historical rampart), the Giladhari river and Viswanath are all in the Darrang District of Assam south of the Kameng region. The legend seems to convey unambiguously an historical truth that the Akas were once settled in the plains of Assam and they migrated from there to the northern hills as a result of a feud. Another Aka legend, quoted by R. S. Kennedy (1914) briefs that 'the Akas first settled near Bhalukpong, where on the right bank of the Bhareli river, their two chiefs, Natapura and Bayu built their respective capitals. Bayu demanded Natapura's beautiful wife as a sort of tribute and after a number of adventures the girl with a new born child arrived at Bayu's court. The child Arima grew up to be a great warrior and finally killed his own father by mistake. Overcome with remorse he migrated to the present locality of the Akas, it is from his children that the present Akas are descended'.

According to the village elders (Plate 1.1) migration is called as *Ghao – Khayiw etrii*. As per their narration mankind was born at *Bjiga-go-hutu – Ksum-go-nyetrii*, from this place human beings dispersed in different parts of the earth. The Akas had traversed a series of rivers, mountains, passes, places before settling down to the present location. The sequel of the places are "*Bjiga-go-hutu – Triimi-go-hutu – Muhuw-psiw Nyetrii – Triimiw-psiw Nyetrii – Muhuw-sutuw Nyetrii – Triimi-ghyiw Nyetrii – Tograda Nyetrii – Ghamada Nyetrii – Huwtsaye-piw – Druwyiye-piw – Dodum – Kamuphu – Dzumuphu – Vunyiphu – Luphophu – Dzuyiphu – Tako-suwo-husu – Lamalaghaphu – Notsugo – Kutso-ghaghye – Sani-ghbhz*".

PLATE NO. 1.1
VILLAGE ELDERS INTERACTING WITH THE INVESTIGATOR

(a)

(b)

(c)

(d)

(e)

(f)

(g)

(h)

(i)

Photo : (a) Village elder of Palatari (Nizam Thasusow), (b) Village elder of Buragaon (Nichow Khabisow), (c) Village elder of Palizi Village (Lt. Lame Nimachow), (d) Village elder and priest of Giziri (Thasu Aglasow), (e) Village elder of Jamiri (Sherdopla Dibisow), (f) Respondents of Kararamu village, (g) Village elder of Yangsey (Lagon Degio), (h) Village elder of Sopung (Bazi Sopung), (i) Young key informer of Palizi Village (Biga Nimasow).

An interesting observation noted in the narration is the use of term '*Ksum*' as the place of origin of mankind. The term is the name given to the Kameng River by them. Thus, it seems that they had migrated to the present location from the source of Kameng River which is situated at the northern parts of East Kameng district. By following this assumption it can be also observed that the *Kutsun* and *Kuvatsun* sections of Aka as cited by the earlier British writers were the early settlers of the area and they might had settled down to the plains of Assam, but later on due to conflicts and feuds arising out of powerful forces of new migrants they have receded back to their original place. However, this is an observation made because of the two different routes of migration recorded in the books as well as narrated by the village elders.

The migration routes mentioned in the available literatures mostly describes the inhabitants of two village viz. Jamiri and Buragaon while other villages were either unknown to them or the villages were inaccessible. The rest of the villages along with the *Koro* sub-tribes have a similar migration route from the northern part of the area which is indicated by the use of the term Kameng river and its source in their narrations. In fact, the name Aka has been given by the people of the plains in Assam, which means a painted, that may be because of the custom of painted forehead, nose and chin of this tribal group. Akas are settled in both West and East Kameng districts of Arunachal Pradesh. However, major share of the area falls under West Kameng district.

The area is located in between 27° 0' N to 27° 30′ N latitudes and 92° 30′ E to 92° 55′ E longitudes. It shares a state boundary of about 27.65 km with Assam towards the south. The location of the area is shown in Figure 1.1. The total geographical area is about 1262.21 Sq. km, which comprises of 38 (thirty-eight) villages namely - Balefu, Bana, Bhalukpong, Buragaon, Chijang, Dijungania, Elephant, Giziri, Gohaithan, Husigaon, Husugo, Jamiri, Janapam, Kadeya, Karangania, Kararamu, Khamsiri, Khuppi, Kichang, Morkha, New Kaspi, Palatari, Palizi, Pichang, Pochong, Prizin, Ramdagania, Sakrin, Saljipam, Sopung, Subu, Tania, Thissa, Thrizino, Thuluhui, Tippi, Yangsey and Yayong (Plate 1.2). Out of the total 38 settlements (Fig.1.2) the *Hrusso* sub tribes are inhabited in 29 villages (665 households) under West Kameng District. The *Koro*, a sub tribe is inhabited in the remaining 9 villages (197 households) of East Kameng District. The Aka villages are situated on the hilltops as well as in the plains of the river valleys. Site selection for the settlement is always guided by the availability of water and land for jhum cultivation. The area starts from Bhalukpong on the south to Buragaon on the north, Bichom on the west and Kitchang on the east. The Aka territory is bounded by the Mijis on the north, Sonitpur district of Assam on the south,

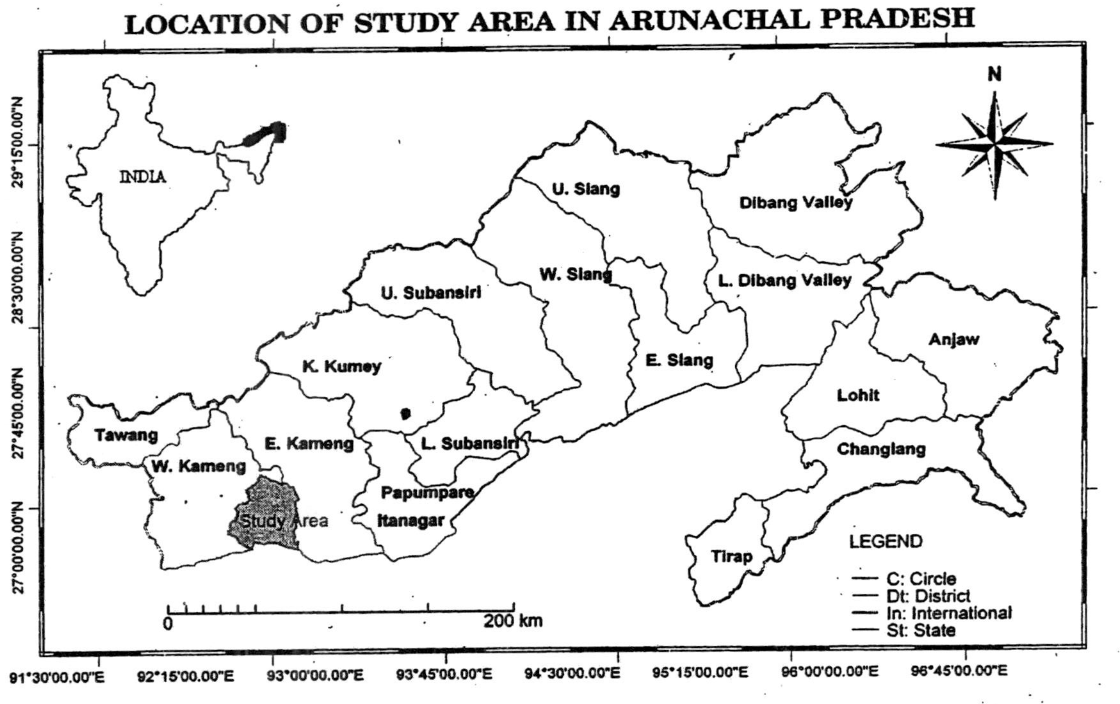

Fig. 1.1 : Location Map

the Nyishis on the east, and the Buguns, Sherdukpens and Monpas on the west and north-western part. While describing Akas, Mackenzie (1884) mentioned the Aka and *Hrusso* as synonymous and identified two clans, namely *Hazarikhawa* and *Kapaschors,* which in fact was the nickname given by the plains people to the *Kutsun* and *Kuvatsun* sections of the Akas respectively. However, R. Yusuf Ali, Deputy Commissioner, Kameng District (1971 Census), feels that this division of Aka society into two groups is rather a superficial over-simplification inherited from British writers whose contacts were limited mainly to the influential villagers of Jamiri and Buragaon, whose pattern was later assumed to apply totally to the entire tribe which now recognizes itself as *Hrusso* (Aka). He feels that this *Hrusso* groups have coalesced into their present distinct tribal entity by a much earlier fusion of at least three elements. Firstly, the migrants from Bhalukpong who achieved certain aristocratic supremacy and their version have been accepted from the British to the present day. Secondly, some earlier local groups probably identical with Mijis, thus explaining the otherwise unusual phenomenon of traditional inter-tribal inter-marriage, and thirdly some other groups whose tradition of migration and origin are from the East and the South-East.

But, according to the present study they are territorially divided into two sub-tribes namely *Hrusso* and *Koro*. Further, they are divided into a number of exogamous clans such as Nimasow, Parisow, Ramdasow, Tisasow, Libasow, Dususow, Dibisow, Jebisow, Sichisow, Khabisow, Sorisow, Borisow, Bolusow, Saksasow, Sidisow, Fomsow, Desisow, Regisow, Sasusow, Dipisow, Dajusow, Sagrosow, Rabasow, Nikhiwsow, Sidasow, Richisow, Aglasow, Delusow, Thasusow, Jidusow, Talingsow, Sanchasow, Jabosow, Khandusow, Sapun, Yanje, Thrisa, Degio, Yame, Netan, Chijang, Sopung, Tania, Mijuw, Dore, Badi, Jang, Ruzong, Drumbra, Tusa, Rumo, Dava and Tanio. The language spoken by the two sections of the tribe i.e. *Hrusso* and *Koro* is very much varied from each other. This might be due to the geographical isolation from their community brethren on the other side of the river or

PLATE NO. 1.2
SETTLEMENTS OF THE AREA

(a)

(b)

(c)

(d)

(e)

(f)

(g)

(h)

(i)

Photo : (a) A view of Palizi Village, (b) Thrizino, the headquarters of SDO office, (c) A view of Janapam hamlet, (d) A view of Buragaon, (e) A view of Karangania Village, (f) Close view of Buragaon, (g) A view of Subu Village, (h) A view of Balefu Village, (i) Close view of Palizi Village.

mountain. It is to be noted here that most of the local terms used in the study belongs to the *Hrusso* sub-tribe. However, some important terms of both the sections has been mentioned simultaneously wherever it seems necessary. Akas believe in *Nyezino (Hrusso)/Mene Alan (Koro),* meaning thereby the sky and the earth). They have a distinct feature of traditional dress, dialect, appearance, etc. and speak their own dialect which is affiliated to Tibeto-Burman family of language. They belong to Mongoloid stock with well built body structure of Mongoloid traits. They are fair in complexion and medium in stature with usually a flat nose, conspicuous cheek-bones, and black hair and usually brownish to pale blue eyes. They have scanty hair on the face as well as on the body. The total population of the tribe prior to the post independence period was very less say about 1000 approximately but, according to 1991 census the population of the Akas was 3,531, which increased to 5027 as per the recent household survey conducted for the area. Out of the total population, 3905 inhibits the three circles of West Kameng namely Thrizino (2598), Bhalukpong (290) and Jamiri (1017). The remaining 1122 person inhibits the Rechukrang circle of East Kameng district. There is a considerable increase in the literacy rate i.e. 62.32% as per the recent survey. The socio-economic life of the people is largely determined by the environmental conditions of their habitat. The family in the society comprises of the husband, wife(s) and their children. They are socially organized on the basis of a compact social group, through the village community and through the clan.

Marriage in the society is a socially sanctioned institution. Marriage can take shape in two ways, either by negotiation or by the romantic way of capture. The major festival is *Nyetriidow (Hrusso)/Sarok (Koro),* which means to clean the village from the evil influences, sufferings and natural calamities. Traditional jhum cultivation is practiced on a large scale basis because it is the only activity for their subsistence. Besides, they undertake some subsidiary means of sustenance, such as fishing, hunting and food-gathering to supplement the shortage of their food supply.

DATABASE

The topographical maps published by Survey of India (1971) have been used for the preparation of base map of the study area. The area has been traced out by using four topographical sheets viz. No. 83 $^{A}/_{11,}$ $^{A}/_{12,}$ $^{A}/_{15}$ and $^{A}/_{16.}$ The Satellite data (IRS – 1C LISS III) available in the Department of Geography, Rajiv Gandhi University has been used to have a synoptic view of the area. Available data from Census and Economics and Statistics Department has been collected and used for construction of suitable indices for preparation of variety of tables and thematic maps. Census data of 1971, 1981, 1991 and 2001 has been collected to meet the necessities of the research work. Data related to different species of flora and fauna were collected from Department of Forestry and

BASE MAP OF THE STUDY AREA

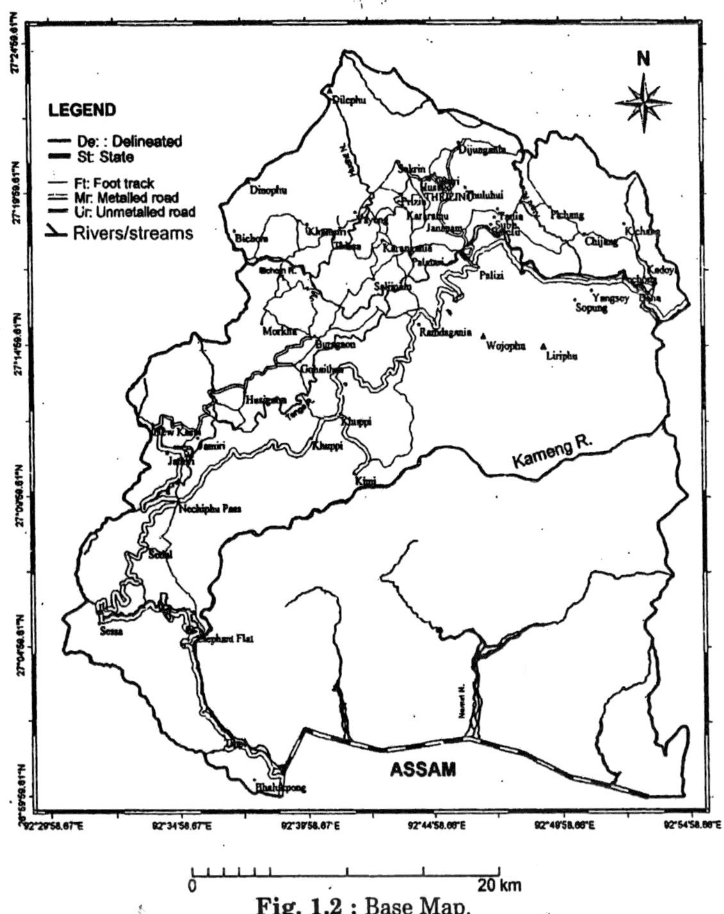

Fig. 1.2 : Base Map.

State Forest Research Institute, Itanagar. The climatic data have been collected from the Meteorology and Observatory installed at district and circle headquarters. Information data regarding the people, their economy and culture has been collected from the district statistics handbooks and few books available on the Akas of Arunachal Pradesh.

METHODOLOGY

The area inhabited by Akas as narrated by the elderly people of the area is demarcated on topographical map. The

Fig. 1.3 : Study area (IRS–1C LISS III).

boundaries are coinciding with watersheds, divides of rivers, administrative boundaries (districts and circles) and stream channels. Geographic Information System (GIS) software ILWIS 3.2 and 3.3 has been used for digitizing and computing various important maps such as Location map, Drainage density, Slope map, geology map, etc. As per the requirements of the research problem, suitable questionnaires were constructed for generation of primary data for specific and detailed study of the community. Cent per cent household survey of the 39 villages has been conducted for reliability of the information collected. Different data collected from the field were analyzed using SPSS 9.05 package for generating appropriate quantitative and qualitative results. Most of the research work is based on empirical survey through recording narrations of elders, photography, collection of specimens, etc. Primary and secondary data collected has been tabulated as per the aims and objectives of the study. Suitable maps and diagrams were prepared by applying variety of cartographic techniques. After tabulation, analysis and interpretation of the information collected through various sources has been chapterised to give the present shape to the work.

Literature Review

Literature Review has been made to reflect the salient aspects of social and economic development as perceived by various scholars in the different parts of the globe. Some of them are being mentioned as below:

Balan (1992) has mentioned that education is a powerful tool inextricably and inseparably connected with the economic growth and social change of the nation, particularly so in a society where majority are illiterates, living under stresses and strains, poverty, diseases, unemployment, moral dwarfs and spiritual bankruptcy. It has to play an indispensable and instrumental role in expediting the tempo of social change and development in all areas of the study giving priority to backward areas and people.

Gohain (1994) has stated that the change situation in India attracted attention of the social scientists and administrators at a much later stage. Probably this was because of the fact that when British administrators first started to take interest on the ethnography of the tribes they could think to be in a static condition, change, if any, is very slow as such changes are self-generating and not the resultant of any extraneous force. It is for reason that in all the earlier monographs on the tribes of North-East India we don't find any discussion about change.

Kuppuswamy (1989) has stated that social change simply means that there is some change in social behaviour, social structure and social and cultural values. The social system is undergoing some change in time. It is implied that it was in one state earlier and it is in another state now. When it is possible to set up criteria to measure these changes objectively it will also be possible to indicate the future state that is to predict, provided all other conditions are constant.

Parihar (1989) has mentioned about the importance of place and time or geography and history in the activities and behaviour of man as recognized by the Hindu thinkers and the Royal sage *(Rajarshi)* Bhisma's teachings that according to the conditions, demands and exigencies of the time and place (*Desa-Kala*) what is otherwise *Dharma* may become *Adharma* and what is *Adharma* may become *Dharma* for the time being.

Sinha (1962) mentioned about the social and economic life of the Akas as largely determined by the conditions of their habitat. The hilly tracts do not leave any other alternative to jhuming. The abundance of jungle further provides ample resource to practice the indigenous system. The over all result is that the Akas are still one of the main jhum cultivators among the tribes of India.

Mann and Mann (1989) has mentioned that the contemporary tribal culture can be classified under three heads that is traditional, transitional and changed. However, each category does not maintain complete exclusiveness, except in some rare cases. And this is supported by the fact that most of the tribal cultures are by now, exposed to alien influence which is intermittently or constantly impinging on them. How much force it can exert would depend among other factors, upon the barriers and stimulants. And the same may operate at the conscious as well as unconscious level.

Kar (1982) has mentioned about the Garos that Christianity and Christian missions have been an active agent of change among the Garos. During the British period, the Baptist Mission could implant, among others, the essence of modern democratic traditions into Garo society by organizing allied services on western models that could cut across clan membership or regional interests. A parallel authority structure with new bonds and values has thus emerged among the Garos modifying their age-old socio-cultural practices.

Soumen (1988) has mentioned that with every development of culture there is a corresponding development of religion. The process may be slow or fast depending upon the pace of development. But with a significant transformation of society with the emergence of new social forces, religion takes a completely new dimension. This is how theology comes in, replacing, to a large extent, the earlier need based (and so-called animistic) religion. That is why it is said that, agricultural revolution transformed mythology into theology and theology became an instrument of class rule in civil society.

Verrier (1968) has mentioned the origin of the Akas in the following lines. As per a *Hrusso* (Aka) tradition, long ago there was a man called *Awa*, who got married to *Jusam*, the beautiful daughter of the Sun and out of their union were born one son and one daughter named *Sibji Sao* and *Sibjim Sam* and they are regarded as parents of all mankind.

Chaudhari (1992) has stated that the Mundas have rejected a few of their non-sanskritic traditional beliefs and practices and have borrowed and imbibed the Sanskritic elements from neighbouring superior Hindu culture. So, there has been a change in Munda religion in its beliefs and practices and also in the festival cycle. They are also exposed to Sanskritic values and ideas.

Joshi (1997) has mentioned that when someone says that the tribals have a different culture and that culture must be preserved, it raises two questions: (i) Not only tribes many caste and regional groups have different cultures why to talk of preservation of tribal culture only? (ii) We, the non-tribal upper classes have changed our culture but we now want tribals to preserve their culture. I think,. it is tribals themselves who should decide whether they want to change or not. Our hegemony which was an impact on many tribal development programmes. We believe that we will develop them while preserving their culture.

Singh (1994) mentioned the agricultural practices of the Akas in the area. They practice slash and burn (Jhum) cultivation and supplement their economy through hunting and fishing. Some of them have also taken to terrace and sedentary cultivation. They are skilled in basketry, pottery and weaving. In addition to this, they are engaged in animal husbandry and services.

Raza and Ahmad (1990) stated that there is a need to understand the tribal urges and aspirations within the context of the regional millieux and as emanating from the overall framework of the intervention into the resource base of the tribal areas and its social and economic consequences.

Nair (1993) mentioned about the agricultural land use of the Arunachal Pradesh. The Akaland does not admit of animal traction. The shifting cultivation is an economic productive activity in which the forests are cut down, burnt and seeds are sown. The broadcast is the only practicable mode of agriculture. A clearing which becomes exhausted within a year or two is left fallow for 7 or 8 years.

Kholey (1997) has mentioned about the marriage laws of Aka society. In Aka society marriage is a socially sanctioned institution. Traditionally girls have neither choice nor voice regarding marriage. Cross cousin marriage, child marriage, sororate, levirate, marriage by elopement and capture, bride-price, polygamy are permissible and approved by the society.

Ghosh (1992) mentioned about the ritual dance of the Akas as *Nyetchi-Sao*. The two men put on wooden phallus. They are called the *Anh-Anh*. Two other men duck themselves with the hairy bark of the rambang plant and wear replicas of females private parts made from the tuberous root of banana. These two persons are called *Froh-Froh*. The male folk, followed by the priest, the two *Anh-Anh* and two *Froh-Froh*, starts towards the eastern side of the village making wild shouts and gestures and brandishing swords and spears in the air while the two *Anh-Anh* and *Froh-Froh* dancing all the time with erotic movement.

Gadgil and Guha (1992) mentioned about the resource use of the tribal people as in many areas the customary use of nature was governed by traditional system of resource use and conservation that involved a mix of religion, folklore and tradition in regulating both the quantum and form of exploitation.

Design of the Work

The book is divided into eight (8) chapters.

First chapter deals with the conceptual framework i.e. introduction, objectives, study area, methodology, sources of data and reference materials and design of the work.

Second chapter describes about the land i.e. location, physiography, drainage system, soil, climate, and different species of flora and fauna.

Third chapter deals with the people i.e. family, marriage system, traditional village council, literacy rate, status of women in the society, division of labour, population growth, natural increase, proportion of scheduled tribe population, fertility/crude birth rate, mortality/crude death rate, demographic transition, age sex distribution and sex ratio.

In fourth chapter the cultural milieu of Aka society and the undergoing changes taking place due to commencement of various developmental activities has been highlighted. This change includes house types, festivities, priesthood, religion and rituals, traditional attire and ornaments, food habits, dialect/language, tattooing and ethno medicine.

Fifth chapter deals with forest and economic life, forest and material culture, forest, food habits and ethnomedicine, significance of belief system in forest conservation and concept of sacred groves.

In chapter six a detailed interpretation of infrastructural development taken place from 1971 to 2006 is made. The infrastructural facilities include educational, medicinal, drinking water, banking, post and telegraph, transport and communication, power supply and market.

Chapter seven includes the analysis and interpretation of the various aspects of economy and the changes taking place. A detailed description of their economic activities i.e. agriculture, hunting, fishing, food gathering, basketry and weaving, barter trade, etc. is presented. An attempt is also made to incorporate secondary and tertiary workers also.

In chapter eight the whole study is summarized and desirable suggestions has been incorporated to have a synoptic view of the work as well as development of the area.

2 LAND

PHYSIOGRAPHY

The Eastern Himalayan part in Arunachal Pradesh consists of very high relative relief with deep gorges and valleys. The height ranges from 120 m to 7089 m above mean sea level. The Eastern Himalaya is divided into four physiographic divisions i.e. the Himalaya, Mishimi Hills, Purvanchal Hills and Foot hill Plains (Joshi 2006). The study area falls under the Himalayan physiographic division. Himalayan mountains are further divided into four regions i.e. Tethys, Great, Lesser and Outer (Siwalik) Himalaya. The dividing lines in between two divisions are thrusts and mountain specific individual litho-structural characteristics. A brief description of the physiography of eastern Himalaya is given as below:

Outer Himalaya (Siwalik)

In the extreme south, the plain area is separated from the abruptly rising Siwalik Hills (Outer Himalaya) by the Foot Hill Thrust (FHT). Uneven topography, dendritic and parallel to sub parallel structurally controlled drainage pattern, swift-flowing consequent streams and deep valleys of antecedent rivers are the main geomorphic characteristics. In the Western and Central Himalayas, flat bottom structural valleys known as Dun are common. But, in the Eastern Himalaya these are not seen. From the view point of human settlement the Outer Himalayan parts in earlier days were not inhabited in comparison to the Lesser Himalaya. However, nowadays due to the introduction of road communication and other infrastructural facilities people are migrating to this region. The height of Outer Himalaya ranges in between 120m to about 800m above MSL. The important localities in the lower part of this region are Pasighat, Likhabali, Kimin, Itanagar, Balijan, Ramghat and Bhalukpong.

Lesser Himalaya

The Lesser Himalaya is separated from the Outer Himalaya by the Main Boundary Thrust (MBT). This thrust zone is marked by very wide valleys, characterized by fans and cones of landslide debris, recent to sub-recent fault and triangular facets on spurs. The Lesser Himalaya is made of Precambrian and Paleozoic sediments over thrust by vast thick sheets of metamorphic rocks injected by Precambrian - Paleozoic granites. The height ranges in between 900m to 3500m above MSL. The main localities of this region are Seppa, Tenga valley, Bomdila, Kalaktang, Ziro, Raga, Tamin, Daporijo, Mengio, Along, Kaying, Boleng, Jamiri, Thrizino and Buragaon. Throughout the state of Arunachal Pradesh majority of settlement concentration is found in this region.

Great Himalaya

The Great Himalaya is separated by main Central Thrust from the Lesser Himalaya in the South. The height of this range is from 3000 to 6000m above MSL. Taksing, Lemeking and Nacho are the main localities of this region. Because of cold climate and less fertile soil population density is very low. It is made up of high grade metamorphic rocks that are extensively injected and magmatized by mid tertiary granite. It is characterized by extremely rugged and youthful topography, sharp peaks, deep gorges with vertical to convex wall and very steep gradient.

Tethys Himalaya

The Tethys Himalaya is separated by Trans Himadri Thrust from Great Himalaya in the south. The height ranges in between 3000 to 7000m above MSL. Bumla, tefhngla of Tawang district, Migyetung pass. Tung pass of upper Subansiri and Tunga, Lemdo pass of West Siang are situated in this region.

Relief

The study area is covered with forests, mountains, and numerous numbers of streams and rivers. The whole area is characterized by high mountains, deep gorges, waterfalls, passes and valleys. The highest peak of the area is *Dile Phu,* which measures 2,936 m above MSL. The other important peaks of the area are *Vojophu, Liriphu, Jajulaye, Dhrphu, Nischophu,* etc, the height of which ranges in between 2,200 to 2,800 m above MSL. The whole area can be divided into three physiographic divisions i.e. the high mountains of the extreme north, Shimphu hills at the middle part, and the nearly flat plain landscape of Bhalukpong and its peripheral areas towards the south. A natural lake exists in between Khuppi and Ramdagania village which is known by the name *Nearma Husu* (*Husu,* a local term that means a lake or pond) at the height of 1,800 m above MSL. There are two important passes i.e. the Nechiphu pass and the Elephant Flat pass. The Nechiphu pass is situated at the height of 1,708 m while Elephant Flat pass is situated at the height of 334 m above MSL. These passes were significant during the post independence period, because through it people make themselves easy access to the plains of Assam for acquiring some essential commodities like salt, cloth, etc. Most of the higher peaks ranging from 2800 – 3000 m in height are found in the north-western part of the area. However, a narrow mountain belt of such elevation is also evident at the middle part of the area which runs from Sessa in the west through Nechiphu to Palizi – Bana in the east. Generally, the altitude of the area declines from the north-western part towards the south, but suddenly it starts rising at the middle part and again decline towards further south. The southern foothills and the river valleys have low altitudes i.e. less than 200 m above MSL. The altitudinal zones of the area are shown in Figure 2.1.

Geology

The geologic formations so far encountered in the study area may be grouped in the following order if seen from north to south. The geologic features of the area are shown in Figure 2.2.

ALTITUDINAL ZONE OF THE STUDY AREA

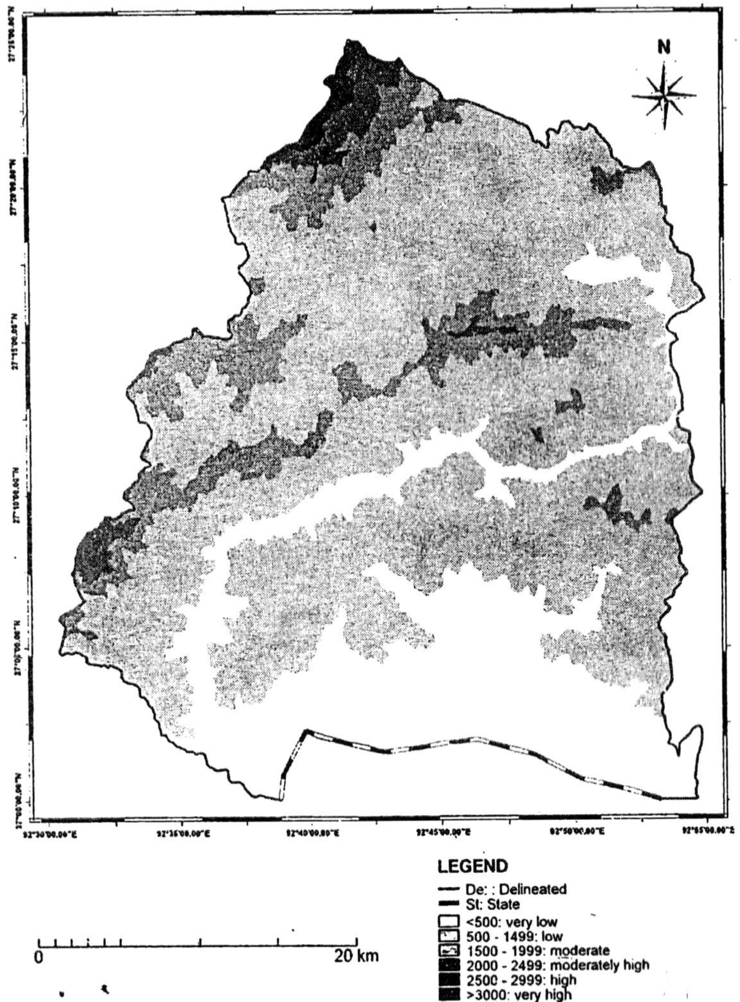

Fig. 2.1 : Altitudinal zone.

Lithology

Bomdila Group

Lesser Himalayan rocks are named as Bomdila Group which is further subdivided as Dirang formation and Bomdila Gneiss. Bomdila group of rocks form the major part of the

GEOLOGY MAP OF THE STUDY AREA

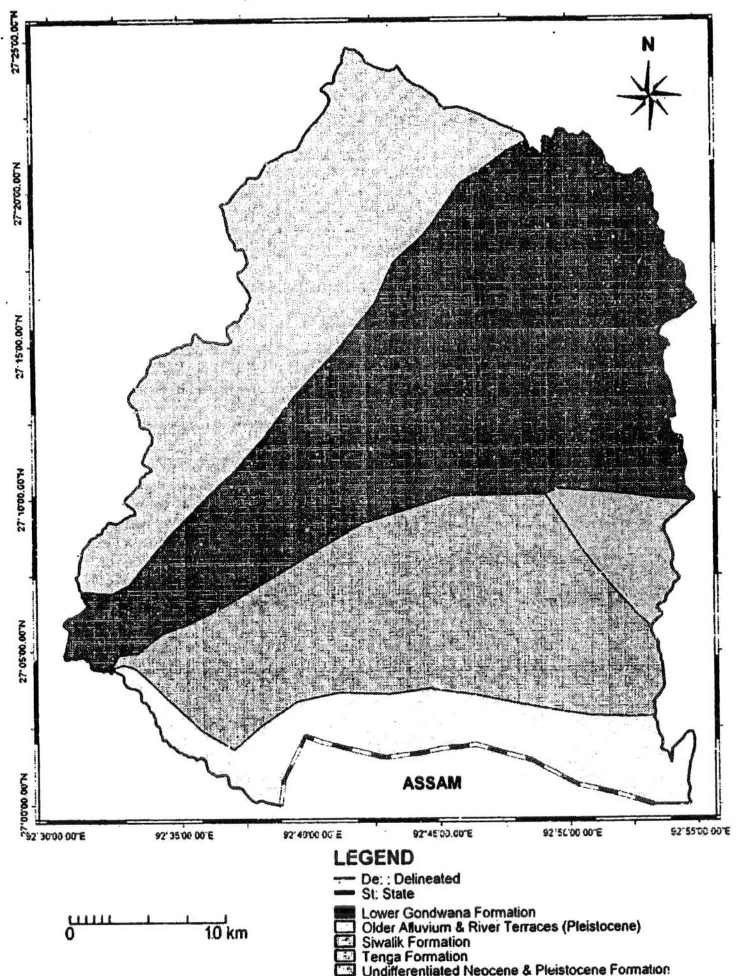

Fig. 2.2 : Geology.

lower Himalaya and show extensive distribution in the Digien valley, Bomdila ridge and far north around Bulu and Pankar localities. Bomdila gneiss and the overlying Dirang formation are well exposed in Tenga area from west of Kalaktang to Dirang and further north-east respectively. Bomdila gneiss consists of augen and streaky gneisses, biotite gneiss with amphibolite and pegmatite. Dirang Formation, not exposed in the study area, is unconformably overlying the Bomdila group in south and truncated in north by the MCT. It includes garnet-muscovite-biotite schist, flaggy and platy garnet-quartzite, intrusive biotite, augen, gneiss, schist and quartzite.

Tenga Group

Tenga group of rocks occur in both East and West Kameng districts. It is divided into Buxa formation and Tenga formation. Buxa formation is well exposed in Rupa – Shergaon area whereas the Tenga formation is occurs in the south-west of Tenga and extends in the north-east direction through Dedza up to west of Pankar, from where it extends in south-east direction up to north of Takachin. Tenga group comprises of Dolomite-quartzite-Phyllite schist sequence, quartzite, and low grade schist. In Jamiri area it includes quartzite with thin bands of phyllites.

Bichom Group

Bichom group is further divided into Bichom/Salari formation and Takachin formation. Takachin formation is not exposed in the area whereas Bichom/Salari formation is well exposed in the lower reaches of the Bichom valley and extend as a narrow strip from Bhutan border in the west to the south of Bana in the Kameng river section through Buragaon and Karangania. This group consists of Quartzite, dark grey phyllite, slates, conglomerate with fossil bryozoa, lamelli branchis and brachiopods.

Gondwana Group

Gondwana rocks are found to be unconformably lying over Bomdila Group along the south. It is divided into Khelong formation and Bhareli formation. These rocks occur as a narrow linear belt along the Himalayan foothills from Bhutan border in the west to the east of Takachin through Khuppi. Gondwana group consists of Diamictite, dark grey feldspathic sandstone and grey to black carbonaceous shales with lenticular coal beds.

Table 2.1
Geological Formations

Unit	*Sub-Unit*	*Lithology*	*Age*
Siwalik Group		Shale, Sandstone, Conglomerate	Lower Miocene to Lower Pleistocene
Kimi Formation		Quartzite and lateritized trap, sandstone, shale and siltstone.	Pre-Tertiary? Triassic?
Gondwana Group	Bhareli Formation	Diamictite, dark grey feldspathic sandstone and grey to black carbonaceous shales with lenticular coal beds.	Permian
Bichom Group	Bichom/Salari Formation	Quartzite, dark grey phyllite, slates, conglomerate with fossil bryozoa, lamelli branchis and brachiopods.	Permo-carboniferous
Tenga Group	Tenga Formation	Quartzite, phyllite and low grade schist.	Lower Palaeozoic
Bomdila Group	Bomdila Gneiss	Augen and streaky gneisses, biotite gneiss with amphibolite and pegmatite, phyllite, schist, quartzite, graphitic phyllite with bands of marble, calc-silicates, conglomerate, quartzite with thin bands of dolomite, black phyllite, dolomite, carbonate with phyllite.	Pre-cambrian

Source: Arunachal Pradesh District Gazetteers East Kameng, West Kameng and Tawang Districts, [illegible]96.

Kimi Formation

Kimi formation occurs in a small area abounding the present location of Kameng Hydel Power Project. It consists of Quartzite and lateritised trap, sandstone, shale and siltstone.

Siwalik Formation

Lithological sequence of the Outer Himalaya in Arunachal Pradesh is grouped into four rock stratigraphic units in the western part which are from bottom to top Kimi, Dafla and Subansiri and Kimin formation roughly corresponding to the Lower, Middle and Upper Siwalik of the Western Himalaya.

Joshi and Rawat (2001) observed that Kimin Formation is mainly made of conglomerate, soft sandstone and clay beds. In the lower horizon the pebbles have an orientation parallel to the bedding whereas in the upper horizon it is random. The classed material is composed of gneisses, quartzite, schist and vein quartzite. Colour varies from grey, blue grey to orange brown. Carbonized wood fragments of the length ranging in between few cm to 2 meter. This formation has a gradational contact with underlying Subansiri Formation and is unconformably overlain by Sub-Recent terraces and flood plain deposits. Subansiri Formation includes soft massive sandstone and commonly known as salt pepper sandstones. The sandstones are bluish grey in colour, medium to coarse grained, and poorly micaceous. On weathering they turn yellow brown in colour. Irregular shaped calcareous concretions, similar to those present in the Middle Siwalik in the Western Himalaya are common. These rocks are current bedded and thickness ranging from a few cm to 3 meter. Occasionally, they have pebbles of purple and grey quartzite. They also contain carbonized and silicified wood fragments. Dafla Formation covers the alternative beddings of indurated sandstone and shale. This sandstone is light grey to brown in colour and poorly micaceous. The clay beds are greenish grey in colour, exhibit spherical weathering and in thickness range from 1 to 5 cm. Greenish grey to dark grey thin shale bands normally forms the base of these shales. The Dafla Formation is always exposed in the northern structural unit between the Tipi and the Main Boundary Thrust. It rests unconformably over the Gondwanas, and is closely folded with the Subansiri Sandstone in some sections.

Structure

Main Boundary Thrust (MBT)

The junction between the Lesser Himalaya and the foot hills is generally represented by a major line of dislocation, designated as Main Boundary Fault (Karunakaran and Ranga Rao, 1976). This thrust is known as Murree thrust in Jammu, Nahan Thrust in Himachal Pradesh Krol in Central Himalaya, Mahabharat Thrust in Nepal and Garu thrust in eastern Arunachal Pradesh. In the study area Gandwana formation and Dafla formation are being divided by Main Boundary Fault. In Pachin and Dikrong river section Permo-carboniferous sequence consisting of sandstone, grey, calcareous shale, pebbly slate, carbonaceous shale with marly limestone nodules and very thin crushed coal occur in the North of the Main Boundary Thrust. A few kilometers west of study area in Papum river (tributary of Dikrong River) section the metamorphics directly come in contact with the Tertiaries over the thrust plane. To the west of Papum River in Paso River section the Lower Gondwana sediments occur between Tertiaries and metamorphics. In satellite imageries this thrust is making prominent linear feature along which some streams are aligning.

Tipi Thrust

Dafla and Subansiri formation is separated by this thrust. It is running parallel to the Main Boundary Thrust. This is first observed near Tipi locality, Bhalukpong - Bomdila road section by earlier worker therefore, known as Tipi Thrust.

Foot Hill Thrust

Abrupt termination of Siwalik Hills towards Assam plain indicates the presence of Foot Hill Thrust. Nakata (1972) demarcated this structure along the foothills and named it as Foot Hill Thrust. In the satellite imageries a broken lineament is seen.

Average Slope

Slope is defined as an angular inclination of terrain between the hill tops and valley bottoms resulting from a combination of many causative factors like structure vegetable cover, drainage texture and frequency, dissection index, relative relief, etc. which are significant geomorphic attributes in the study of landforms of drainage basin (Calef 1959). In Himalayan region generally the slope is controlled by the bedding dips, but the erosionary process is active to deform its inclination dominant in several places, which is subjected to creating environmental hazards of soil erosion, mudflow and landslide. Slope analysis has been done according to the method suggested by C. K. Wentworth (1930) to determine the average slope of the region. The original formula of Wentworth is converted into the metric system which is as:

Average slope: Tan Q = N × CI/636.6

Where, Q = Average angle slope

CI = Contour Interval

N = Average Number of contour crossing of different values in a grid of 1 km^2

636.6 = A constant figure

Table – 2.2
Slope Characteristics of the Study Area

Slope Category (in degree)	*Area (in km^2)*	*Cumulative Area*	*Percentage of Area*	*Slope Class*
Less than 7	234.1225	234.1225	18.79408	Level
7 – 14	164.91	399.0325	13.23807	Gentle
14 – 21	198.3125	597.345	15.91944	Moderate
21 – 28	241.0425	838.3875	19.34958	Mod. Steep
28 – 35	206.8525	1045.24	16.60499	Steep
35 and Above	200.485	1245.725	16.09384	Very Steep
Total	1245.725		100	

The study area is divided into six slope categories viz. Level (less than 7°), gentle (7° - 14°), moderate (14° - 21°), moderate steep (21° - 28°), steep (28° - 35°) and very steep (35° and above). Slope characteristics of the area are shown in Figure 2.3.

Level Slope Zone

This category comprises of the parts of the study area where average slope is below 7°. It covers an area of about 234.1225 km^2 which is 18.79408% of the total area. The settlements of Thrizino, Jamiri Point, Dedza, Balefu, Subu, Sopung, Bana, Kadeya, Bhalukpong and Tipi are situated in this slope zone. Generally, these zones cover the valley floors and foothills area. Most of the areas are devoted to agriculture and human settlement in this zone. The major share of level slope towards the south bordering Assam has no human settlements and remained unused till now.

Gentle Slope Zone

This zone includes 13.23807% of the total area which is about 164.91 km^2. This zone lies just above the valley floors and foothills area. The settlements located in this slope zone are Elephant Flat, Jamiri Village, Morkha, Thissa, Khamsiri, Kararamu, Palatari, Tania, Pichang, Chijang and Yangsey. Majority of the human settlements are situated in this zone and the shifting cultivation is also cover major share of the area in this zone.

Moderate Slope Zone

The area above the foothill zone comes in between the average inclination of 14° - 21° covering an area of about 198.3125 km^2. This zone covers 15.91944% of the total area. Dijungania, Giziri, Husugo, Prizin, Yayong, Sakrin, Buragaon, Khuppi, Husigaon, Nechiphu, Pochong and Kimi are the villages situated in moderate slope zone.

Moderate Steep Slope Zone

This zone includes regions where average slope ranges between 21° - 28°. It covers an area of 241.0425 km^2 that is

SLOPE CATEGORY MAP OF THE STUDY AREA

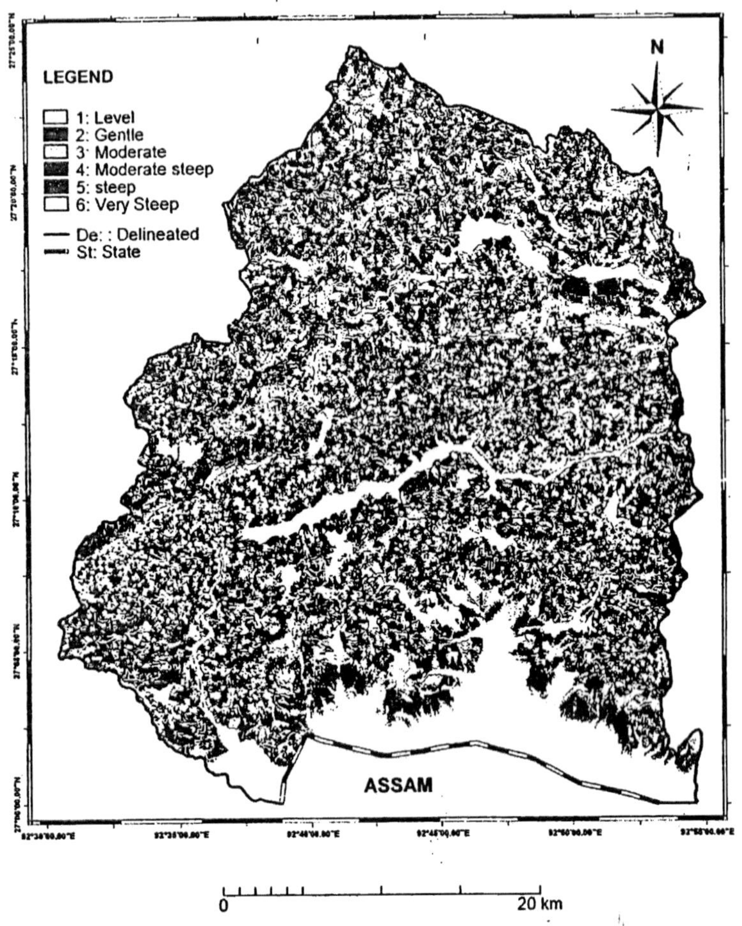

Fig. 2.3 : Average Slope.

19.34985 % of the total area. This category covers the largest portion of the study area. The villages like – Gohaithan, Saljipam, Palizi and Ramdagania are located in moderate steep slopes.

Steep Slope Zone

Those parts of the study area that comes under the average slope of 28° - 35° are included in this slope zone. It covers an area of 206.8525 km^2 accounting for 16.60499 % of the total area. Karangania is the only village that is located in steep slope.

Very Steep Slope Zone

The rest of the area comprising the summit parts and its surroundings with 35° and above average slope covers this slope zone. It has a share of 200.485 km^2 accounting for 16.09384% of the total area. This zone has no human settlements due to high altitude and inaccessibility.

Drainage System

The study area is drained by Kameng river (*Ksum*) and its tributaries. Kameng river is one of the main tributaries of mighty Brahamputra that flows in the western part of the state. The catchment area of this river system is about 9860 sq. km. Tenga and Bichom are the main tributaries. Flowing through the high ranges of Himalaya and the plains of Assam it meets with Brahamputra river. In Assam it is known as Jia Bharaili.

The area is dissected by numerous numbers of small streams and rivers. Majority of the important streams and rivers are perennial in nature and there is continuous supply of water in the streams throughout the year. During summer one can fully enjoy the small streams oozing out from the hills and mountains. The relief features favours for occurrence of waterfalls of varying heights that provides natural advantage for hydro power generation. During the summer months water comes out of the mountains everywhere in the area. The small rivulets turn into stream and the stream turn into river at successive points of journey. The important streams of the area are *lodbha, hudgha, kadbio, lushogo, dhr, hudhi, ghji, kaya or kuvo, kade, kichikini, namiri,* etc. Tenga (*Hudgji*) river originates from the high mountains of the Kalaktang area and enters the study area at Nag Mandir/ New Kaspi. Bichom (*Humtru*) river is another important river that originates in the snow clad high mountains of Nafra and enters the area at Bichom camp. Both the rivers flow in

DRAINAGE NETWORK OF THE STUDY AREA

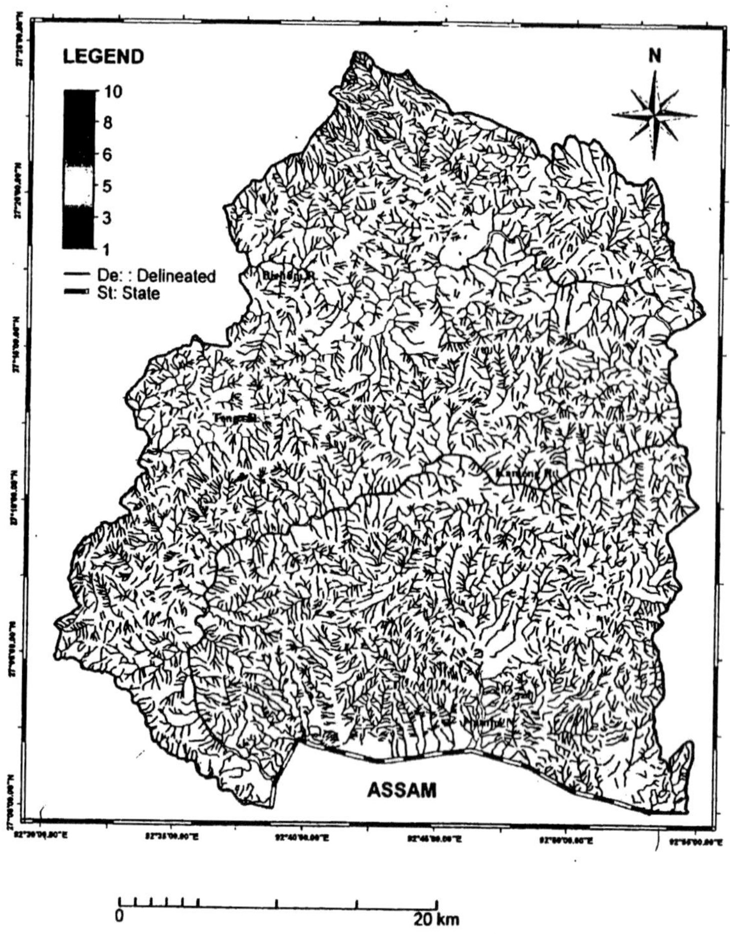

Fig. 2.4 : Drainage Network.

parallel to each other and meets at Ramdagania and flows down the stream under a single name Bichom river. It flows for approximately 73.26 km in the area. Most of the settlements are sited along the valleys and plains of these two rivers. Ultimately, these streams and rivers join the Kameng river, which originates in the high mountains of Lada circle in East Kameng district and enters the study area at

Bana. Bichom joins Kameng river at Bana camp and flows towards the south-west in a zigzag pattern and almost divides the area into two equal halves. Kameng river flows in the area for approximately 112.29 km from Bana camp to Bhalukpong. The drainage network of the study area is shown in Figure 2.4.

CLIMATE

The latitudinal location greatly influences the climate of an area. As the area is located amidst 27° 0′N and 27° 30′N latitudes, summer season is hot during days and moderately cold in night. During winter it is very cold. The summer season starts from the last week of April and continues up to September. After September the temperature starts falling and the green grassland hills dry up and turn yellow in colour due to the action of frost. December and January are the coldest months. The minimum temperature falls to about 1 - 2° C during the winter months, when there use to be snowfall in mountain peaks. The maximum temperature during the summer is 30° C. The rainfalls all the year round, but it is more in the months of June to September. Sometimes it continues to rain in these four months, which leads to cut off of communication and pose many other difficulties to the people.

The monthly distribution of rainfall in the area during 2004, 2005 and 2006 shows an interesting trend. The annual rainfall distribution in the year 2004 was recorded as 2235.09 mm that has declined to 2110.00 mm in 2005 and further it declined to 1970.90 mm in 2006. The area is experiencing declining trend of annual rainfall since 2004, this can be attributed to the large scale deforestation and the practice of shifting cultivation. During the year 2006 the highest rainfall was recorded in the month of June amounting to 502.90 mm and lowest of 4.40 mm in the month of January.

Table 2.3
Distribution of Monthly Rainfall (in mm) 2004 – 2006

Month	*Rainfall (in mm) 2004*	*Rainfall (in mm) 2005*	*Rainfall (in mm) 2006*
January	NA	NA	4.40
February	2.29	NA	36.90
March	71.12	5.00	13.60
April	284.23	73.60	109.40
May	NA	158.70	473.80
June	NA	391.20	502.90
July	939.70	431.40	323.80
August	278.75	527.40	185.90
September	298.60	297.80	289.90
October	360.40	203.10	30.30
November	0.00	21.80	NA
December	NA	0.00	NA
Total	2235.09	2110.00	1970.90

Source: S. & I Unit – 1, BLD-II/NEEPCO. Ltd. Tippi (Arunachal Pradesh).

SOIL

It is an important part of land which supports plant and animal life. Therefore, it has a vital role in economy. Soil formation is influenced by topography, parent material organism, time and climate. In Arunachal Pradesh there is wide spatial variation in the above mentioned factors thus, there is change in soil characteristics from place to place. Keeping in view the altitude, parent material and climate soils of Arunachal Pradesh are divided into four major groups by Srivastava, 2002 as below:

(i) Soils of Warm Per-humid, Eastern Himalaya Ecosystem

(ii) Soils of Warm Per-humid, Siwalik Hill Ecosystem

(iii) Soils of Warm Per-humid, Purvanchal Ecosystem

(iv) Soils of Hot Humid, Plain Ecosystem (Brahmaputra valley)

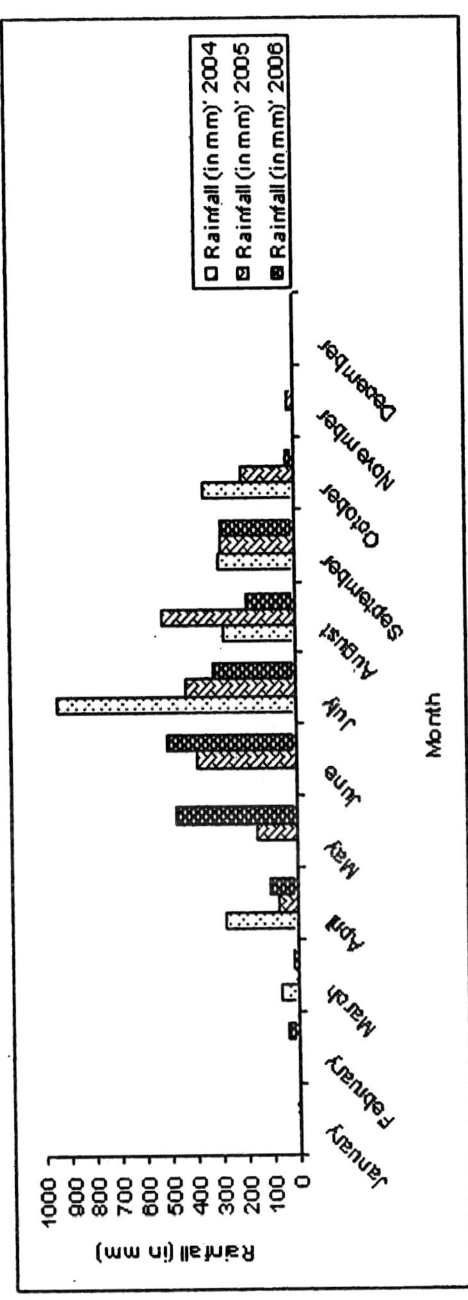

Fig. 2.5 : Distribution of Monthly Rainfall (in mm) 2004 – 2006.

High altitude area which covers Tethys, Great and Lesser Himalaya constitute a specific soil characteristics termed as soils of warm per-humid Eastern Himalaya Ecosystem. Due to high rainfall soil moisture regime is known as 'Udic'. Mean annual soil temperature ranges 18°C to 22°C so, it is termed as Thermic temperature regimes' Soil depth from ridged to valley increased. Soil texture is sandy to loamy. Along river valleys fine particle soils is seen. Most of soil shows no profile development. However, in some places 'b' horizon is found in its initial stage. The range of pH value ranges in between 4.5 to 7.2 which reflect strongly to moderately acidic nature of soils. This group of soils covers 80% of the total area of the state.

Siwalik (Outer Himalaya) group of soils are receiving more temperature and rainfall and qualifies for 'Udic' soil moisture regime and 'hyperthrmic' soil temperature regime. This region is younger than higher Himalaya and rocks are very loose and fragile. Soil depth is relatively high and in some places profile development can also be seen. Soil particles vary from sandy to clayey sand depending on the underlying parent material. The soils are strongly to moderately acidic (pH 4.2 to 5.7).

Till now the classification of soil is not carried out for the area. However, the area is located in a mountainous tract with deep gorges, valleys, hills, etc. So it is obvious that the soils are of mountainous type. The soil is not much fertile, except the small patches of valleys and river terraces.

Natural Vegetation

The state is rich in its abundant species of flora and it varies from open scrub (grass land) to alpine forest in the greater Himalaya. The major forest species and their occurrence may be broadly grouped under the following :

(i) Tropical rain forests and semi-evergreen forest in the plains and sub-Himalayan part are found up to 900m above mean sea level. The main species of this category are *Altingia excelsa, Artocarpus chama, Bischofia javanica, Bombax ceiba, Castanopsis indica, Mesua ferea, Dipterocarpus macrocarpus, Terminalia myriocarpa, Ailanthus indica, A. grandis, Terminalia myrocarpa, Sterospermum chelonoides, Elaeocarpus sp., Canarium strictum, Pterygota alata, Tetrameles nudiflora, Artocarpus lakoocha*, etc.

(ii) Subtropical forests are found in between 800 to 1900m above msl. The forest species found in this group are *Castanopsis indica, Quercus lamellose, Quercus spp. Michelia oblonga, Ficus spp., Acer oblongum, Ulmus lancifolium, Schima wallichi, S. khasiana*, etc.

(iii) Pine forests growth can be seen in between 1000 to 1800m above msl. The species found in this are *Pinus roxburghii, P. wallichiana, P. merkusii, Quercus spp., Prunus spp. Betula alnoides, Alnus nepalensis, Tsuga dimesa*, etc.

(iv) Temperate Broadleaved forests and conifer forests are ranging at the height of 1800 to 2800m and 2800 to 3500m above msl respectively. In this group main species are *Quercus lamellosa, Michelia spp., Acer oblongum, Castanopsis indica, Magnolia spp., Rhododendron spp., Populus ciliate, P. gamblei, Pinus wallichiana, Tsuga dimesa, Rhododendron spp., Abies spectabilis, Cupressus torulosa, Abies delvayai,, Picea spinulosa, larix grifithiana, Juniperus recurva*, etc.

(v) Alpine forests are found in between 4000m to 5500m above msl. These forests are mainly dominated by bushy shrubs and herbs such as *Rhododendron spp., Sedum sp., Festuca sp., Rhodiola sp., Saxifraga sp., Saussaria sp., Rheum sp., Arenaris sp.*, etc.

(vi) Bamboo forests are extending up to 2000m above msl. *Bambusa tulda, B. pallida, Dendrocalamus spp., Pseudostacheum polymorphum, Chimonobambusa spp., Cephalostachyum sp., Arundinaria spp.* are the main forest species of this forest category.

The southern parts of Kameng region receive a heavy rainfall of more than 400 mm per annum both from South-west and North-east monsoons. The terrain is of high hills and deep valleys, all of which are covered by a thick forest of tall trees and impenetrable evergreen shrubs and herbs intertwined by various twiners. It is difficult to split up the area into well defined phytogeographic regions, and fix clear-cut demarcation of vegetation owing to the richness of the components of flora. There is much of overlapping and co-mingling of floristic elements under the influence of elevations, general topography and rainfall. The tropical evergreen forest along the foothills of Bhalukpong is quite dense. The forests are characterized by dense vegetation, chiefly comprising of tall evergreen tree species like *Dipterocarpus, Artocapus, Tetrameles, Altingia, Bombax, Chukrasia, Meusa, Phoebe, Duabanga, Eugenia, Dillenia* mixed with bamboos, *Pandanus*, climbing canes and tree-ferns like Cyathea gigantia, forming impenetrable thickets with an altitudinal range up to 900 metres. The sub-tropical evergreen forests or mixed forest forms an intermediate stage combining both tropical and temperate species and covering an altitudinal range of 900 to 1800 metres. These forests are dominated by species of *Ficus, Castanopsis, Callicarpa*, in the lower ridges and *Sisni* and *Schima, Castanopsis, Englhardtia* in the higher ridges. Most of the trees are very old and usually they attain a height of 30 to 35 metres. *Pinus wallichiana* mixed with *Rhododendron arboretum, Lyonia, Berberis, Quercus* and members of *Rosaceae* is predominant. Three types of forests, namely dense scrub, open scrub and dense mixed jungle, cover the whole region. Dense scrub forests cover the northern part; a small area of western part is covered by open scrub and the southern and eastern parts are completely covered by dense mixed jungle. The area is endowed with variety species of flora and fauna. The forests are thick with dense under growth of climbers, creepers, epiphytes and bamboo. Commercially valuable tree species such as hollock *(Terminalia Myrocarpa)*, jutuli, hingori, amari, dhuna *(Canarium strictum)*, pine, chapa, gomari, bonsum (*Phoebe sp.*), walnut, hokon (*Duabanga grandiflora),* bola *(Marcus Laevigata)* etc. are abundantly found in the area. These timbers are useful for making furniture and construction of houses. There are other important trees with great socio-economic importance abundantly grown in the area such as *Xanthoxyllum alatum, Callicarpa arborea, Myristica fragrance, Picus semichordata, Castanopsis indica, Hodgsonia macrocarpa, Rubus sp., Rubus niveus, Picus hispida.*

Numerous species of orchids flourish in the area, which made the state authority to establish an Orchid Research and Development Centre at Tippi in the year 1972. Another Orchid Sanctuary was established at Sessa in the year 1984 as a branch of the ORDC, Tippi. The area harbours about 200 species of orchids of sub-tropical types belonging to many genera. Genera, such as *Dendrobium, Bulbophyllum, Coelogyne, Calanthe, Eria, Liparis, Cymbidium, Cirrhopetalum* with more than five *spp. Galeola falconeri*, a tall leafless saprophyte, attaining a height of 5 metres are found in abundance. So far five hybrid genus – *Renades "Arunodaya", Arachnocentron "Tippi Jubilee star", Esmeranda "Millennium Dawn", Cymbidium Sessa "Green Beauty", Ascocenda "Tippi Blue Boy"* has been registered in the Royal Horticulture Society, London. Many more orchids of horticultural and commercial value are likely to be discovered in course of intensive and planned explorations. Besides, these trees and orchids, the area has plenty of trees and plants of medicinal value. The forests also abound in a good number of dye and tan yielding species, such as *Berberis aristata, Coriaria nepalensis, Symplocos theaefolia, Geramium nepalensis, Rubia cordifolia, Englhardtia spikata, Taxus baccata, Gallium mullugo, G. triflorum*, etc. Lots of edible vegetables are found in the nearby forest, which isolates the inhabitants away from the market vegetables. Different species of bamboo are also found in the region, Living under such a close proximity with the forests their existing life is very much influenced by their nearby forests.

The area is also rich in different kinds of faunal species. In the group of mammalian – leopard (*Panthera pardus* Linnaeus), jungle cat (*Felis chaus* Guldenstaedt), jackal (*Canis aureus* Linnaeus), tiger (*Panthera tigris* Linnaeus), leopard cat (*Felis bengalensis* Kerr), Indian elephant (*Elephus maximus* Linnaeus), wolf, barking deer (*Muntiacus muntijak* Zimmermann), reindeer (*Axis axis*), wild boar (*Sus scrofa* Linnaeus), black bear (*Sclenarctos thibetanus*), monkey (*Macaca radiata*), etc. are the important ones. Among the primates, the Assamese macaque (*Macaca assamensis*) and the capped langur (*Presbytis pileatus* Blyth) are found in small or large groups. Among the rats, the long tailed tree mouse (*Vandeleuris oleracea* Bennet), the long toothed rat (*Dacnomys millardi* Thomas), the house rat (*Ratus ratus* Linnaeus), the Himalayan rat (*Ratus nitidus* Hodgson) and the white bellied rat (*Ratus niviventer* Hodgson) are the most common varieties. Different types of squirrels namely the Pallas squirrel (*Calloscirus erythraeus* Pallas), the Irrawady squirrel (*Callosciurus pygerythrus* Geoffroy), the giant flying squirrel (*Petaurista petaurita* Pallas), the Malayan giant squirrel (*Ratufa bicolor* Sparrmann), and big size squirrel (*Dremomys lokriah*). Porcupine (*Porcupine hystrix*) and Pangolin / Scaly anteater (*Manis tricupis*) are also found in the region.

Table 2.4
Various Species of Fish

Sl. No.	*Name of Species*	*Family*
1	2	3
1.	*Accrossocheilus hexagonolepis*	
2.	*Tor tor*	
3.	*Tor putitora*	*(Mahaseers) Cyprinidae*
4.	*Labeo dero*	
5.	*Labeo dyocheilus*	
6.	*Labeo spp.*	
7.	*Creinus plagiostomus plagic*	*Schizothoracedae*
8.	*Garra spp.*	*Garridae*

1	2	3
9.	*Noamacheilus spp.*	*Cobitidae*
10.	*Anabas Testudineus*	*Anabantidae*
11.	*Mystus seengala*	
12.	*Mystus Aor*	
13.	*Rita rita*	*Bengridae*
14.	*Mystus tengra*	
15.	*Mystus vittatus*	
16.	*Ophicephalus spp.*	*Ophicepalidae*
17.	*Notopterus spp.*	*Natepteridae*
18.	*Clarias battachus*	*Claridae*
19.	*Heteropneustus fossilis*	
20.	*Belone concila*	*Belonidae*
21.	*Bariltus spp.*	*Cyprinidae* (Sub-family – *Rasboridae*)

Source: Census of India, 1981.

In the group of birds – black-necked crane (migrated), babblers (*Pallorneum sp.*), warblers, chats, jungle fowl (*Gallus gallus*), black-breasted kaleege (*Lophura leucomelana*), hornbill rufous necked (*Aceros nipalensis*), wreated (*Ryticeros undulats*), common grey hornbill / Dhanesh in Hindi (*Tochus birostries*), bulbul (*Molpastes cafer*), parrot (*Psittacula eupatricia*), green pigeon (*Treron sp.*) imperial pigeon (*Ducula enea, D. Badia*), sparrow, owl, crow, eagle, etc. are commonly found in the area. The area also abounds a wide variety of amphibians and reptiles such as frogs, turtles, lizards, snakes, tortoises, etc.

The area is gifted with vast natural resources of various species of fish. Some of the important and high priced fishes are mentioned in Table 2.4. Of all these *Mahaseer*, medium cold water tolerant species, is highly economical and an indigenous game fish. Apart from the known species of fish there are number of other small seasonal fishes, the names of which are locally known but not classified scientifically.

3 PEOPLE

FAMILY

Two or more persons, living in a household, related by blood, marriage or adoption is known as family. For example, a son of the head and the wife of the son living in the household are treated as part of the head's family. The husband-wife example is called a sub-family. Sub-families are not included in the count of families as there can be only one family per household. The definition of family has not changed over the course of the 1970-1990 censuses, but some documentation for 1970 indicates that married couple families living with relatives are counted as families (Not all households include families). Unrelated individuals can live within households with families.

Families are classed by type viz. married couple families (husband-wife family), Male headed family with no spouse or female headed family without husband. A family may comprise "own children" or "related children". Own children are never married persons under age 18 that are son, daughter, stepchild or adopted child of the Head of the family. Related Children are own children plus all other family members under 18 (regardless of marital status) related to the family head.

Classification of census families (a census family is composed of a married couple or a couple living common-law, with or without children, or of a lone parent living with at least one child in the same dwelling) by the number or age group, or both, of children living at home. A couple living common-law may be of opposite or same sex. "Children" in a census family include grandchildren living with their grandparent(s) but with no parents present.

The isolation of the people from their neighouring tribes has helped the Akas to evolve an independent society. The sons stay with the parents till they attain maturity and got married in their turn. However, it is not mandatory for a son to separate from the parents, but usually separation of the sons from the parents took place only after marriage locally called as *Nyetroh Dow*. There is a condition which is followed by the people since the early days that if a son wants to part from their parents due to quarrel or unwillingness to live with, etc. then, he must do the *Trastrii Dow* (sacrificing either a *mithun* or a pig for the parents). The daughters stay with the parents till their marriage because after marriage they go to live with the husbands.

Family Type

In strict sense both joint and individual type of families are perceptible in the society. All the households that have been surveyed had responded that there was only joint family during the post independence period. There is a slight decrease in joint family during the statehood period but still 80% households were practicing joint family system. However, there has been a sharp change in the family type of the society since 2000 onward. About 80% of the households were found to be an individual type of family during field survey i.e. 2006. This change is the result of the exposure to other cultures and society, increase in literacy rate, employment in service

Table 3.1
Type of Family

Period	*Joint*	*Individual*	*Joint and Individual*
Post Independence	862 (100%)	—	—
Statehood Onwards	684 (79.3%)	5 (0.6%)	173 (20.1%)
2000 Onwards	98 (11.4%)	713 (82.7%)	51 (5.9%)

Source : Field Survey, 2006.

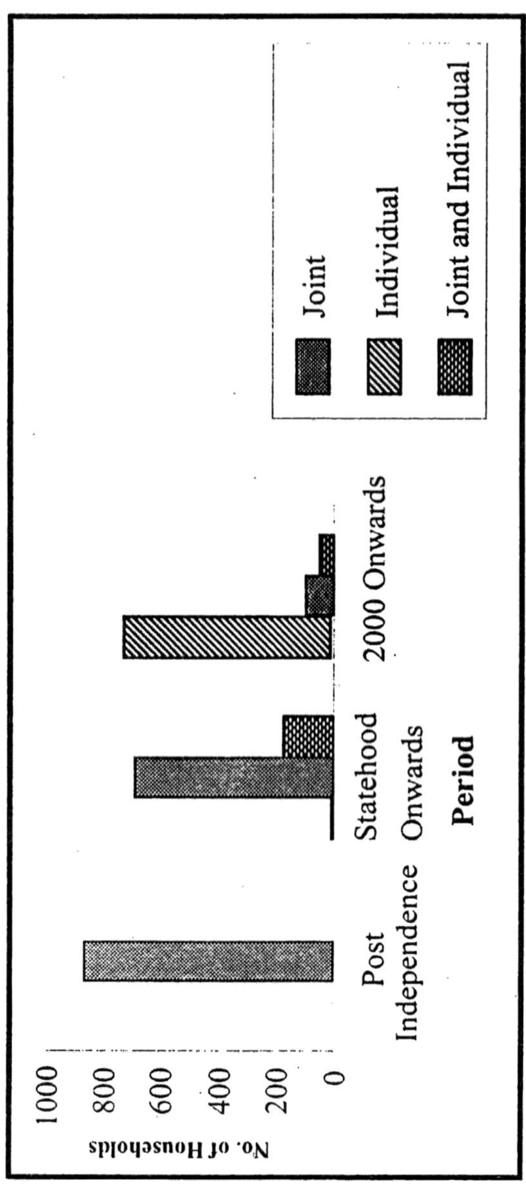

Fig. 3.1 : Family Types.

sectors, etc. In other words, the overall change and development is brought due to access to education, television, radio, roads, etc. which had caused the families to become more individual than joint. The emerging trend of family type as told by the respondents is shown in Table 3.1 and Figure 3.1.

Family Composition

Generally, at present a family in Aka society is comprised of husband, wife(s) and the children. But, traditionally joint family prevailed having more than three generations living together in a house. During the olden days a family consists of grand parents, parents, children and grand children. The main reason to prefer joint family was security and man power for agriculture. However, the constituents of family had changed with the passage of time. Since, the statehood onwards the joint family system starts to be as an individual family. However, still 80% families wee in joint family. The rate of change from joint family to individual becomes faster since the statehood to 2000 onward. Nowadays about 86.1% of the household surveyed felt that families consist of the parents and children only which reveals that individual type of family is predominant in the society. The changes in the family composition are shown in Table 3.2 and Figure 3.2.

Table 3.2
Family Compositions

Periods	*G. Parents, Children G. Children*	*G. Parents, Parents, Children, G. Children*	*Parents and Children*
Post Independence	7 (0.8%)	855 (99.2%)	—
Statehood Onwards	3 (0.3%)	337 (39.1%)	522 (60.5%)
2000 Onwards	3 (0.3%)	117 (13.6%)	742 (86.1%)

Source: Field Survey, 2006.

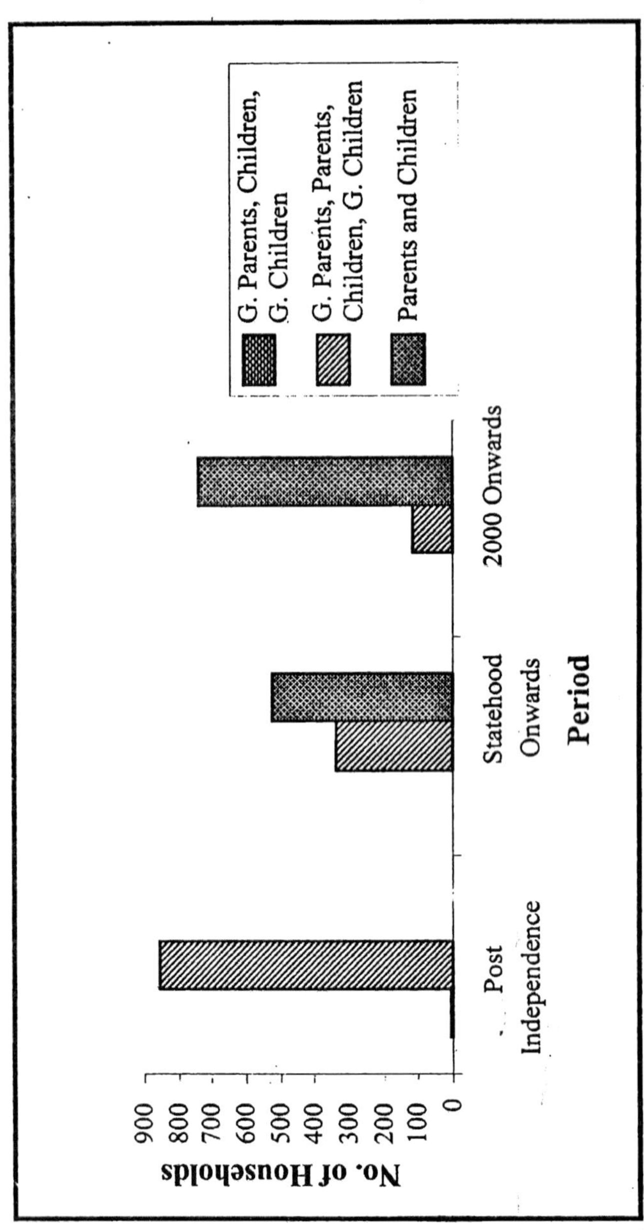

Fig. 3.2 : Family Compositions.

Preference of the Parents to Live with

Generally, the parents either live with the eldest son or the youngest son due to the traditional bond. But, nowadays they prefer to live with any son (in some cases daughter also) keeping in mind the ability, love, care, health and financial assistance during their old age.

Table 3.3
Preference of Parents to Live with

Period	*Eldest Son*	*Youngest Son*	*Eldest and Youngest*	*Any Son*
Post Independence	137(15.9%)	724(84%)	—	1(0.1%)
Statehood Onwards	1(0.1%)	838(97.2%)	22(2.6%)	1(0.1%)
2000 Onwards	137(15.9%)	—	—	725(84.1%)

Source: Field Survey, 2006.

MARRIAGE SYSTEM (*GZEE*)

A marriage is an interpersonal relationship with governmental, social, or religious recognition, usually intimate and sexual, and often created as a contract. The most frequently occurring form of marriage unites a man and a woman as husband and wife. Other forms of marriage also exist; for example, polygamy, in which a person takes more than one spouse, is common in many societies. Beginning in 2001, the legal concept of marriage has been expanded to include same – sex marriage in some jurisdictions. The reasons to marry varies widely but, usually includes legal, social and economic stability, the formation of a family unit, procreation and the education and nurturing of children, legitimizing sexual relations and public declaration of love. A marriage is often declared by a wedding ceremony, which may be performed by a religious officiator, through a similar government - sanctioned secular officiator, or (in weddings that have no church or state affiliation) by a trusted friend of the wedding participants. The act of marriage usually creates obligations between the individuals involved, and in many societies, their extended families.

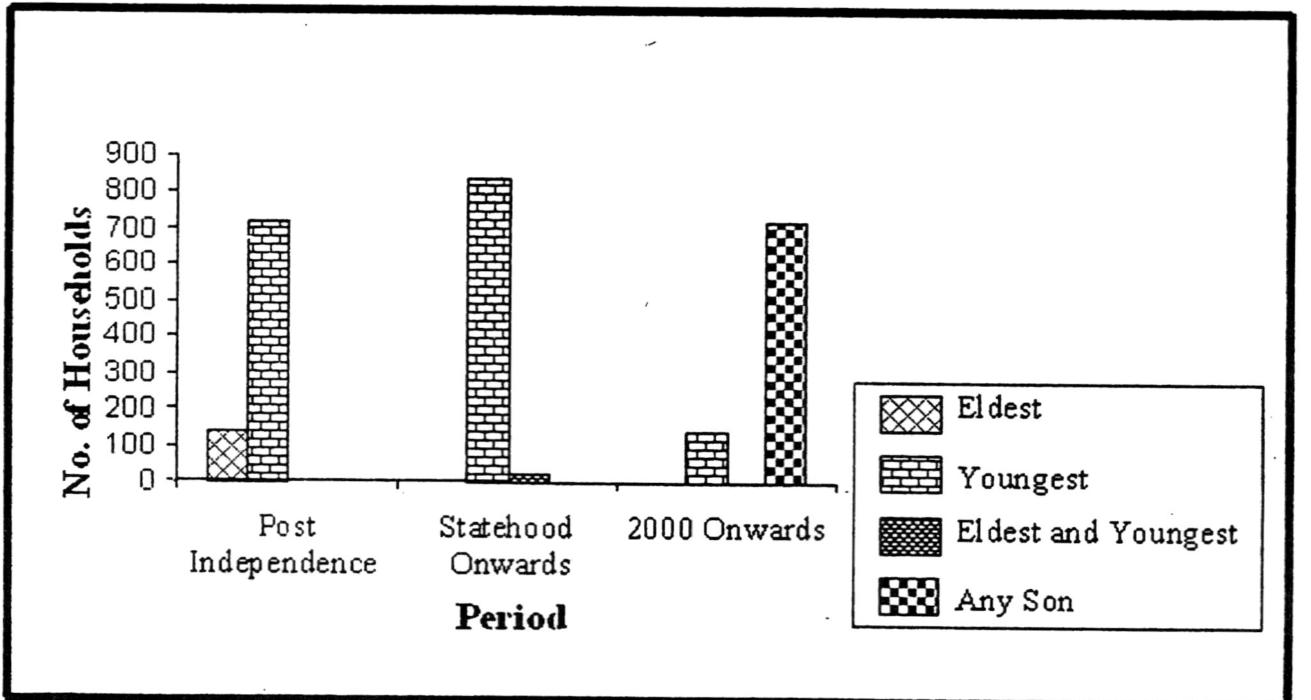

Fig. 3.3 : Preference of Parens to live with.

From time immemorial, marriage in the Aka society has been a part of their life. Unmarried man or woman is looked upon in a different way by the rest of the society. They are called '*mdjeo*' (unmarried male) and '*mdjem* (unmarried female). Though, their presence is welcomed in any social activities, but there remains a different eye for them. Widows are considered and accepted with sympathy but not the unmarried men/women. Even after marriage, if a couple does not have children, they are also called '*mdjeo*'/'*mdjem*' but they are treated/accepted as normal members of the society. In some social rituals some of the *mdjeos*/*mdjems* cannot take part. The children are neither allowed to take the leftover edible items nor allowed to use the cloths used by them. It is believed that by doing so children may also become like them or it may affect to their future generation.

There is no hard and fast rule for selection of mate in the Aka society except in case of rich families. Otherwise they prefer cross cousin marriage (mother's sister's daughter/son). The mother has the main role in such marriages because she prefers a close relation of her own. Moreover, boys and girls in case of cross cousin marriage know each other from their early age. Parallel cousin marriage is strictly avoided as they are considered to be from own blood group.

Generally, other than marriage by elopement, when the boy attains marriageable age i.e. 15 to 18 years of age in early days, the parents start to think for a mate to their children. The selection of a girl is done by performing a ritual known as '*jechi khruw*'. The ritual is performed to determine the indications of yes or no remarks in the liver of sacrificed fowls by '*mugow*' (priest). He sacrifices the fowls after chanting hymns until a good indication is found for the selection of a particular girl. The parents of the boy invite a '*mugow*' and give him the fowl and declare the name of the girl, clan and village. After sacrificing the fowl and taking out the liver, some of the village elders are called to look into the indications shown in the liver. They repeat it in the name of several girls and determine the best among them. When a particular girl is selected, the matter is made known to the girl and her parents so that she takes precautions not to mingle with other boys. After the message is passed a '*mukhow*' (middleman) is sent for negotiation. Once this selection is done any other family cannot try the girl for selection. If someone tries there can be dispute within the village or outside the village, which may lead to feuds. Once a girl is selected the matter of negotiation is left to the '*mukhow*'. The most widely practiced marriages in the society are:

- Marriage by negotiation. *(Mukho Kiinye Gzeeu)*
- Marriage by capture. *(Tsi Low/Tsii Lanye Wullo dow / Gzeeu)*

Marriage by Negotiation

When a girl is selected after studying favourable indications contained in the liver of the fowl, a '*mukhow*' (may be a relative of the boy or any elderly person of the village community who has experience and no enmity with brides village or clan) is called upon to negotiate the marriage proposal on behalf of the parents of the boy. The success of the marriage is largely attributed to the intelligence and tactfulness of the *mukhow*. The *mukhow* should be well versed in the fundamental rules of marriage exchanges and willing to spare time to travel in between two families until the marriage is settled ceremoniously. On the first visit to girl's house he conveys about the selection and obtains views of parents of the girl. If the proposal is agreeable, he also obtains a preliminary estimate of gifts and conveys it to boy's parents on return. There could be several travels to settle the bride gifts as per rule and to negotiate the auspicious season/time for celebration of marriage. The lowest bride gift is 2 *mithuns* in return of which there will be no exchange of gifts except the daily use ornaments from girl's parents. Otherwise the marriages are settled for 5, 10, 15, 20, 25, 30...Nth *mithuns* and accordingly gifts for groom are also counted in terms of beads, silver ornaments, brass plates, utensils and daos (swords). Apart from *mithun* there are also other gifts like - *ukro* (iron-hearth stand), *ge atra / gemso* (endi cloth) and pigs.

The marriage dates are fixed by tying knots on a thread which is called *fomkrii*. The knots are to facilitate counting of days, so that there is no amiss of the date and inconvenience in marriage. Each day one knot has to be cut and burnt. There will be two *fomkrii* and two dates for celebration of marriage-one for false date and another for the final celebration. The *mukhow* brings the first thread tied in knots according to the days fixed which will have to be passed out as a false date. According to their belief there could be malice of devils on the date of marriage fixed on the first date. As such to divert this danger another string of thread is brought by the *mukhow*, which will be the final. The *mukhow* is rewarded with suitable gift in the form of beads, ornaments, brass plates, etc. after the marriage.

As per the dates fixed by the mediator, the marriage party comprising of the groom, his parents and relatives and some members of the village starts procession to the bride's village. The party make loud shouts of *Ho—Ho—Ho* on reaching every hill top (*Jene*). On reaching the entrance of the village they again make loud shout to signal their arrival. The parents of the bride and other villagers come to receive the marriage party and give a small feast to them which is known as *Mipeshra*. The party then march towards the bride's house and again makes a loud shout on which the hosts also shout with their swords (*Vetsiipsii*) in response to that. At last the marriage party enters the house and the function starts in the evening that includes songs and dances by the boys and girls of the village till late night. All the villagers participate in the function. Even after the return of older people to their homes, the youths continue to sing and dance the whole night. Next day the groom's party invites the hosts in a feast by killing a *mithun* brought with them. During the day, competitions of long jump, high jump, shot put, etc. continues in between the boys of both the party. In the meantime, the mediator and villagers of both the party continue to discuss the details of bride price and marriage gifts. The elderly women of the bride's village dress themselves as men and join the groom's party to gossip and joke with them. In the third day the girls of the bride's village crack jokes with the youths in the groom's party. A special blackish paint from wild pine which they call as *Mufo-uhu* is prepared and it is painted in the faces of the boys. The boys return the compliment by black paint the girl's faces.

The dances and songs are regularly arranged in nights during the marriage party's stay in the village. A special dance in such functions is known as *Khchan Chan Pro* in which a girl from any party and a boy from the other dance together to win through different dance steps. The ceremony comes to end in the third day and the marriage party returns to home. The villagers come with the party up to the village gate the place where they received them to see off. Dances, songs and jokes continue before the final parting and then they bid farewell to march towards their own village. However, the bride does not accompany the groom to his home after the ceremony. She has to stay back for about a year more. The husband may visit during her stay with the parents. After the completion of one year or arrival of the fixed date the bride's parents and relatives and some members of the village escort her to her groom's place. The same ceremony is reversed this time because the marriage party is from the bride's party. The same procession, reception, dances, songs, jokes, etc. continues for three days. The only exclusion is the invitation of community feast by killing the *mithun* brought with them. Instead, the feast will be provided by the groom's parents this time also.

Marriage by Capture

In marriages by capture which is a prominent practice during the olden days, the rituals are important because it acts as a restriction for the girl from running away. Girls from any village are captured forcefully and a priest is called for performing the ritual known as *wulo - do* (tying the two souls in a knot). In this ritual all the villagers will be gathered in that particular house of boy who captured the girl and a big pig is sacrificed. The priest will chant mantras stating that from today onwards the root of life of the boy and the girl is tied and they are placed on a same root (*ekri - edro – jumyong*). If any one of them tries to separate from the other then they will not survive in this world. The priest while chanting mantras tie a thread on the right hand of the boy and of the girl. The thread which is known as '*fokki*' is made up of the wool of sheep and contains a piece of valuable bead (*tsum*). In the presence of the villagers the '*fokki*' is tied on the right hand of the girl and the boy is allowed to take her to his room that night. There is always a chance that the girl will try to run away so, the young boys of the village use to remain alert for at least 8 - 10 days. If the girl remains for a week in that house then only the parents of the girl will be informed about the marriage through a mediator (*mukhow*) and the date of marriage ceremony will be fixed. During the olden days there was a strong belief that girls never dare to run away if ritual is performed by the priest against her. In recent days this practice has become very rare due to modernized society. The girls are no more afraid of such rituals but, still it is practiced in one way or the other though in lesser magnitude in the recent days. The changes in the marriage types are shown in Table 3.4 and Figure 3.4.

Table 3.4
Types of Marriages

Period	*Negotiation, Capture*	*Negotiation, Elopement, Capture, Love/Court*	*Negotiation, Capture, Through rituals*	*Negotiation, Elopement, Love/Court*	*Negotiation, Elopement, Capture, Love/Court, Through rituals*
Post Independence	855 (99.2%)	—	7 (0.8%)	—	—
Statehood Onwards	—	856 (99.3%)	—	—	6 (0.7%)
2000 Onwards	—	854 (99.1%)	—	8 (0.9%)	—

Source: Field Survey, 2006.

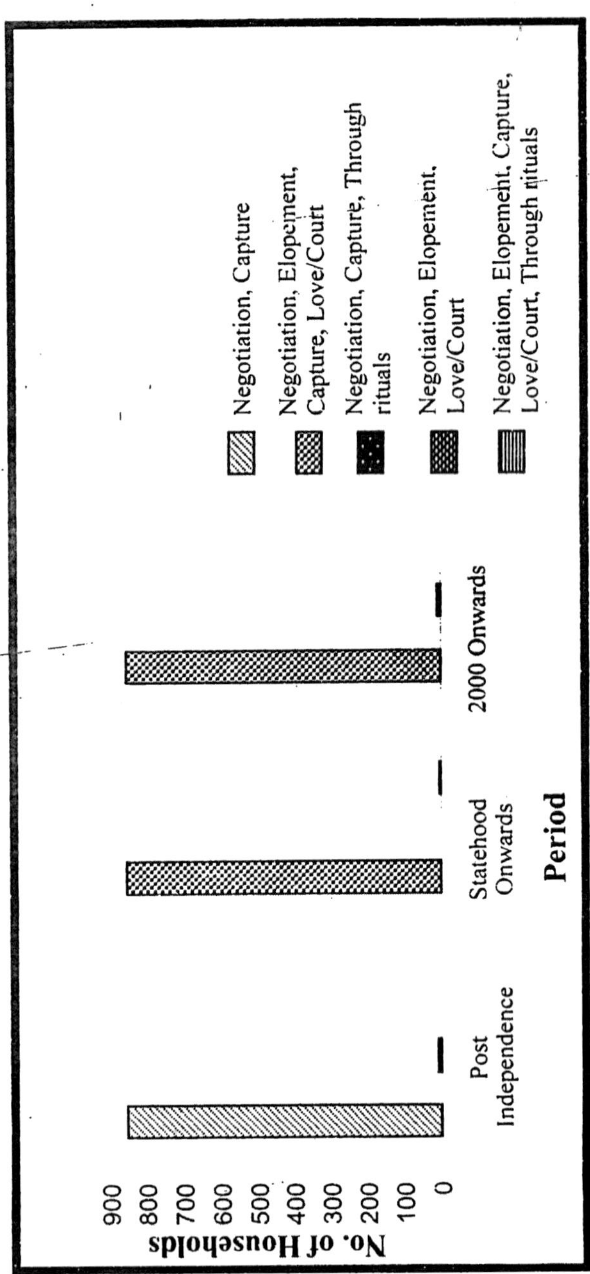

Fig. 3.4 : Types of Marriages

Special Marriages

Polygyny, sororate, levirate are some of the special type of marriages approved in Aka society. Although, in some cases of polygyny, marriage by negotiation take place, where the first wife permits. There will be only a day of marriage ceremony for the couples under sororate and levirate for social recognition.

Polygyny

Polygyny is a marriage practice in which a husband has several wives. The reason of this type of marriage could be as below:

- (i) To enhance one's own status in society and to show off his economic stability by having more than one wife.
- (ii) To have child as the first wife cannot be a mother.
- (iii) Due to the prolonged illness of the first wife.
- (iv) To increase the population of one's own generation or clan.

In these cases the bride-price and exchange of gifts would be lesser than the first wife but where such marriages being allowed by the first wife with an eye on the attractive jewels that are in possession of the parents of second wife to be than, the bride-price can go up as much as their agreed capacity.

Sororate

Sororate marriage is a custom of a man marrying his wife's sister, usually after the death of wife or proven infertile. This type of marriage strengthens the ties between both groups (family or clan of both wife and husband). The Akas also traditionally accept this type of marriage in the form of a man marrying the younger sister of his wife either due to her death or with due permission from the first wife. The causes could be due to the reasons as mentioned in case of polygyny but sometimes the first wife of the husband encourages him to marry her own sister whom she dearly loves and does not want others to marry her. It was highly practiced during the past years up to the statehood period. Though, it is still prevalent in the society but the magnitude has lessened due to the increasing understanding of the kinship relationship.

Levirate

Levirate marriage is a type of marriage in which a woman marries one of her husband's brothers after her husband's death. In other words, the custom or law decreeing a dead man's brother to be the preferred, and in rare cases the mandatory, marriage partner of the widow. The term comes from the Latin *levir*, meaning "husband's brother." In ancient Hebrew society, the levirate served to perpetuate the line of a man who died without offspring. The term was introduced by the British anthropologist Sir James George Frazer. Levirate marriage has been practiced by societies with a strong clan structure in which exogamous marriage i.e. outside the clan, was forbidden. It is or was known in societies including the Punjabis, Jats, Israelites, Huns (Chinese "Xiongnu", "Hsiong-nu", etc.), Mongols, and Tibetans. The strength of levirate is much lesser than that of sororate.

In Aka society if a married man dies leaving his young wife alive, the dead man's younger brother, but not the elder brother, can marry her. The reason behind this type of special marriage is the bride price spent thereon which is considered to be an asset of the family. As per customary law, the women start living with the younger brother where both of them are in favour of the union. If there is no younger brother or they do not agree to the union, she is allowed to re-marry with someone outside the family of her choice among the community members provided the man agrees to repay the bride price incurred on her. If there is any dispute on the re-marriage of the woman, the matter is referred to village council for settlement. There may not be any celebration where the younger brother marries the woman but there will be one-day celebration if she is re-married to someone outside the family. This practice was strictly adhered up to the statehood period but during the last decades very rare cases of such marriages in the society are seen. The influx of modern culture coupled by the education and law has led to the decline of such marriages in the recent days.

Endogamy

Endogamy is the practice of marrying within a social group. Cultures that practice endogamy require marriage between specified social groups, classes, or ethnicities. For example, a Danish endogamist would require marriage only to other Danes. Just about any accepted social grouping may provide a boundary for endogamy. Despite the fact that many people tend to marry members of their own social group. There are some groups that practice endogamy very strictly as an inherent part of their moral values, traditions or religious beliefs. The caste-system of India is based on an order of (mostly) endogamous groups.

Endogamy encourages group affiliation and bonding. Endogamy is a common practice among displanted cultures attempting to make roots in new countries as it encourages group solidarity and ensures greater control over group resources (which may be important to preserve where a group is attempting to establish itself within an alien culture). It helps minorities to survive over a long time in societies with other practices and beliefs. Endogamy occurs in the form of Village endogamy, Lineage endogamy, Caste endogamy and Class endogamy.

Endogamy exists among the Akas in the form of tribe endogamy or in other words marriage within the community. Traditionally, brides from other tribe were not accepted in the society and anyone wedding girl from outside the tribe was looked down in the society. However, marital relations with the Mijis (a tribe in West Kameng District) have been in existence. Endogamy is practiced outside the clan or no marriage takes place within the same clan. The survey results show that traditionally, tribe endogamy is practiced by the people and is still in practice. Due to the influence of the modernization and education, marriages are also taking place outside the tribe.

Exogamy

There may be a drive in humans as well as animals to engage in exogamy (outbreeding); this is because procreating with individuals who are more closely related means any children will be more likely to suffer from genetic defects caused by inbreeding. Individuals who date more exotic partners thereby avoiding incestuous relationships will have healthier offspring due to the benefits of outbreeding. There are many conditions where inbreeding takes place, one example being cystic fibrosis when a couple of primarily European genetics have children, another being sickle-cell anemia when a couple of primarily African genetics have children. Therefore, the drive to date individuals genetically different from oneself may derive from an innate drive to seek the healthiest combination of DNA possible for one's offspring by out breeding (Thornhill 1993).

Exogamy is the custom of marrying outside a specified group of people to which one belongs. In addition to blood relatives, marriage to members of a specific totem or other group may be forbidden. Clan exogamy is strictly adhered by all in the Aka society. The members of same clan are restricted from any kind of marital relationship as per the tradition. This tradition is continuing in the society as it was during the past without any change or transformation that means no member of the same clan is permitted for marital relationships. Apart from clan exogamy, lineage exogamy was also practiced by some clans. But, some of them have discontinued it and marriages are taking place among the clans of same lineage also. For example the Nimasow and Parisow clan of Palizi village do not maintain any kind of marital relationship. Village exogamy is also evident in some villages where the clan members belong to same lineage. For example the Desisow, Regisow and Sasusow clans of Sakrin village always marry a girl from neighbouring villages. But, those villages where the clan members do not belong to the same lineage marry each other within the same village also i.e. the Parisow clan members keep marital relations with the Tisasow and Libasow clans at Palizi village.

Preference of Marriage

The expansion of marriage field of a society largely depends upon the preference of marriage or selection of mates by the people. If the preference of marriage is confined to a small area or selected tribes then the marriage field of the society could not expand. Consequently, there will be less interaction of the people with the other communities. This may decelerate the pace of development due to lesser influx of knowledge from outside world.

The Akas remain isolated from rest of the neighbouring tribes by restricting themselves from any kind of marital relationship with them. The tradition was that anyone who keeps such relationship with the neighbouring tribes i.e. Nyishis, Monpas, Sherdukpens and Buguns was looked down in the society. As the interaction with the other tribes of Arunachal Pradesh (Adis, Galos, Apatanis, Tagins, etc.) was least thus marriage with such tribes was restricted in the society. Apart from this the matrimonial relations were restricted with the non-tribal people also. However, the only tribe traditionally preferred is the Mijis/Sajolangs of Nafra and Lada circles. Marriages had taken place with the Mijis since hundreds and thousands of years back and it is still in practice. The survey results reveals that the people of Aka society started to go beyond the traditional tribe endogamy since the statehood period. Number of marriages had taken place with the neighbouring tribes and even the other tribes of the state. Some of them had even married with the non tribal people (Assamese and Nepalese). Majority of the people still prefer marriages within the community. However, marriages are also taking place with the different tribes of the state as well as the non–tribal people. The liberty of choosing mates from any other community in the society had expanded the marriage field and side by side the level of interaction that has enhanced the pace of development in the area.

Bride Price and Marriage Gifts

Akas have evolved a unique system of bride price and exchanging marriage gifts. The tradition of bride price and exchanging marriage gift was standardized by their forefathers that are mentioned below:

Nowu Pom

This is the most common form of bride price or exchange of marriage gifts. Most of the marriages since the olden days had taken place through this rule of gift exchange. The term '*Pom*' refers to the Aka numerical stands for five (5). *Nowu Pom* involves five main gifts from the groom's parents in the form of *mithun* with an iron hearth (*Shhthwo/Ukro*). On the other hand, the bride's parents return beads, silver ornaments, brass plates, swords, etc. as prescribed. The mediator counts the marriage gifts of both the parents as per the tradition by placing small sticks (*Syobotro*) in the presence of the village elders, who are well versed with the tradition of gifts in all types of marriages.

Nowu Ghii

It is commonly practiced by the middle class people who are in position to afford the more number of gifts involved. The term '*Ghii*' is in Aka numerical system represents ten (10). It means ten marriage gifts in the form of *mithun* and two iron hearths from the groom's parents will be presented as bride price. In return beads, silver ornaments, brass plates, swords, etc. will be given from the bride's parents.

Nowu Ghiitriipom

The rich people who have good possession of *mithuns*, ornaments, beads, brass plates, etc. practice this type of marriage. The term '*Ghiitriipom*' is denotes the Aka numerical of fifteen (15). It means 15 marriage gifts in the form of *mithuns* and iron hearth are to be given as bride price. In return, the bride's parents also present equal number of gifts in the form of ornaments, beads, brass plates, swords, etc. It was more common during the past but, nowadays due to decline in the number of *mithuns* and other marriage gifts it is rarely practiced.

Nowu Biisha

The term '*Biisha*' represents twenty (20) in Aka numerical system. Here at least 20 gifts (*mithuns* + iron hearths) are given as bride price and equal numbers of marriage gifts are returned by the bride's parents.

Nowu Biishatriipom

'*Biishatriipom*' is an Aka numerical that refers to twenty-five (25). At least 25 *mithuns* + iron hearth as bride price and equal number of marriage gifts from the bride's parents are involved in such form of marriages.

Nowu Dziighii

The term '*Dziighii*' stands for thirty (30). *Nowu Dziighii* comprises at least 30 numbers of gifts including *mithuns* and iron hearths (not exceeding four iron hearths) as bride price and equal number of marriage gifts from the bride's parents.

Nowu Dziighiitriipom

This is the last limit of marriage ever known to them. The term denotes thirty-five (35) which mean at least 35 *mithuns* + iron hearth are given as bride price and equal numbers of marriage gifts are given by the bride's parents. This is considered to be the highest ever division of marriage rule. Such marriage has been never reported till now but it is the highest marriage rule as per the tradition.

The above division of marriage rule is well known to the village elders and those who have acted as a mediator in one or more occasions. The second term in all the divisions is local term which is indicative of number with a gap of five in each division. Sometimes, a gap of two is also adopted i.e. *Nowu Shgzii* (8) and *Nowu Ghiitriishgzii* (18). *Tsastrii Dow* is a special form of marriage mostly adopted by the poorer people. This involves only two *mithuns* i.e. one to be sacrificed for community feast and another to be given to the parents of the bride alive. Such kind of marriage happens among the poorer families who are not in a position to afford the gifts as prescribed in the marriage rules. In such marriages the bride's parents only return 10 pieces of brass plates (*Miyan*), which is also not mandatory. The tradition is still in the minds of the people but the decline in the number of *mithuns* and beads has markedly reduced the number of marriages in which more *mithuns* and marriage gifts are involved. Nowadays, people mostly prefer *Nowu Pom* in which only 5 *mithuns* and equal number of marriage gifts are used. Further, the society is opening up more and more towards the other cultures and marriages are taking place with the outside mates in which no *mithuns* and marriage gifts are being exchanged.

Changing Trend in Bride Price

The bride price given to the bride's parents and other relatives during the marriages includes *Fu* (*mithun*), *Shhthwo/Ukro* (iron-hearth stand), *Vo* (pig) and *Gemso Atra* (Endi/markin cloth).

Mithun (Fu)

Mithun (*Bos fontalis*) forms the basis for marriage gifts / bride price not only in the Aka community but also in other tribes such as Mijis, Nyishis, Galos, Adis, Mishmis, etc. in the state. This semi domesticated animal has been used by all right from a poor family to the rich in marriage ceremonies either in the form of community feast or bride price. The tradition of sacrificing and presenting *mithuns* to the bride's parents is still very significant however, the number of *mithuns* used in the marriages since post independence to the present has decreased as shown in the Table – 3.5 and Figure 3.5.

Table 3.5
Marriage Gifts from Groom's Parents (Mithun)

Period	*5 – 10*	*5 – 15*	*5 – 35*	*6 – 40*
1947 – 1987	—	—	138 (16%)	724 (83.9%)
1987 – 2000	—	33 (3.8%)	104 (12.1%)	725 (84%)
2000 Onwards	33 (3.8%)	—	104 (12.1%)	725 (84%)

Source : Field Survey, 2006.

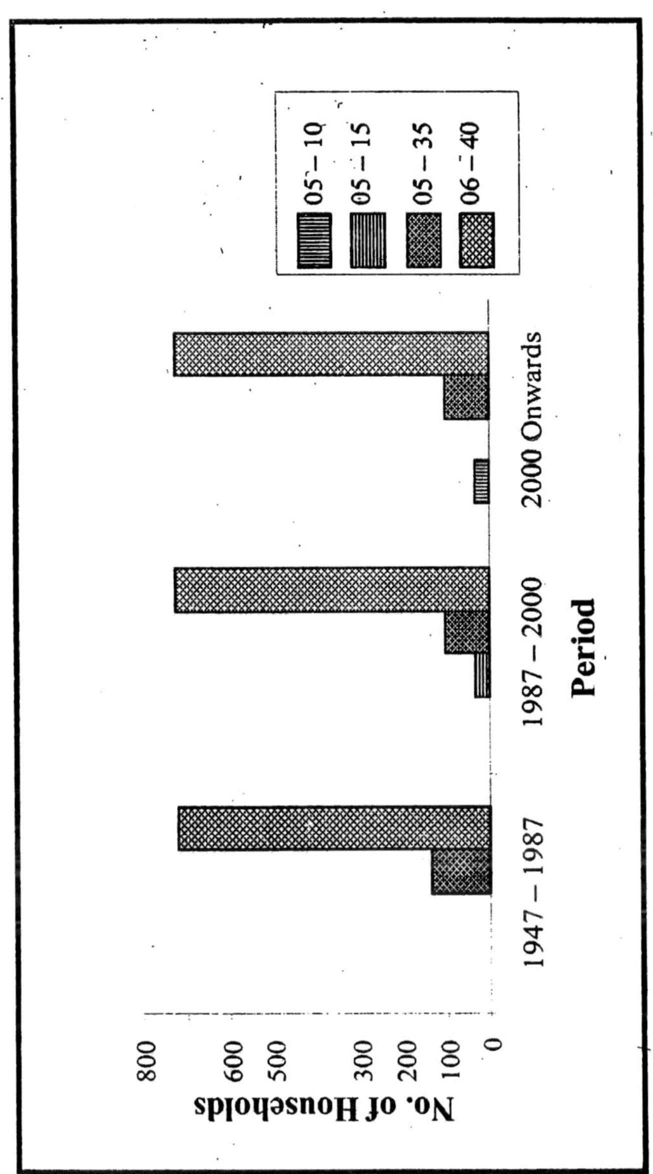

Fig. 3.5 : Marriage Gift from Groom's Parents (Mithun).

The graph shows that during the post independence period *mithuns* used for the purpose were in between 6 (*Nowu Pom*) to 40 (*Nowu Dziighiitriipom*). During the statehood period number of *mithun* used was decreased to 5 to 15. However, nowadays the decline in the number of *mithuns* has gone up to 5 to 10. This decline may be because of decrease in the availability of this semi domesticated animal.

Iron-hearth (Shhthwo/Ukro)

Iron hearth stand is used by the people since the early days in the fire place for cooking and heating purpose. As a matter of fact it has been used by the people for bride price in the Aka society. It is presented to show the obligation to the parents of the daughter as she used to do all the activities of the house (cooking, collection of drinking water, firewood, etc.).

Table 3.6
Marriage Gifts from Groom's Parents (Iron hearth)

Period	*2*	*1 – 3*	*1 – 4*
Post Independence	1 (0.1%)	137 (15.9%)	724 (84%)
Statehood Onwards	1 (0.1%)	137 (15.9%)	724 (84%)
2000 Onwards	1 (0.1%)	137 (15.9%)	724 (84%)

Source: Field Survey, 2006.

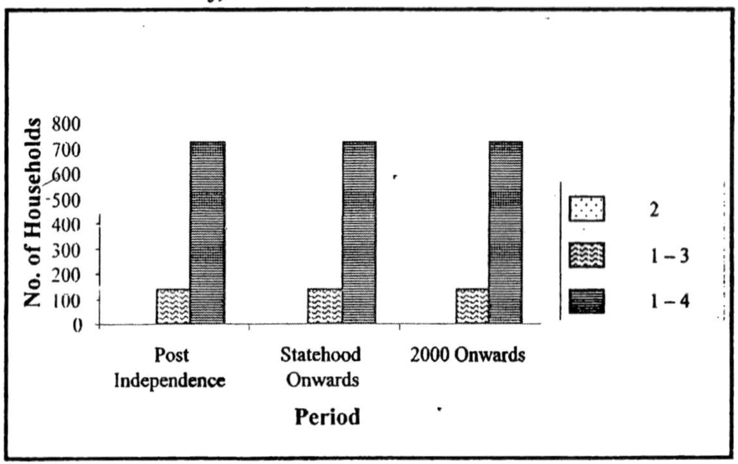

Fig. 3.6 : Marriage Gifts from Groom's Parents (Iron hearth).

The tradition of iron hearths as a marriage gift ranges from 1 (in case of *Nowu Pom* and 4 (in case of *Nowu Dziighiitriipom*). Though, some of the respondents reveal that it ranges from 1 to 3 that might be due to actual practice which they had experienced in reality.

Pigs (Vo)

The pigs are given to the bride's parents known as '*Aao Tsase*' for the father and '*Aanyi Tsase*' for the mother. Pigs form an important part of marriages in the Aka society. The specified pigs are killed and given to the parents for parenting the daughter whom the boy is wedding. Presentation of the pigs to the parents is considered as compensation for the efforts made to bring up the daughter. Besides, pigs are also killed and given to the bride's parents during the other visits of groom.

As per the tradition bride price involves minimum 7 pigs to be given to the bride's parents in any type of marriage. The survey results show no change or variation in the number of pigs used in marriages during the post independence, statehood and 2000 onwards. They have strong belief in the tradition and confess that the system still persists but people prefer the option in which lowest numbers of pigs are involved.

Table – 3.7
Marriage Gi ¿s from Groom's Parents (Pigs)

Period	*7*	*6 – 8*	*6 – 12*
Post Independence	725 (84.1%)	—	137 (15.9%)
Statehood Onwards	725 (84.1%)	33 (3.8%)	104 (12.1%)
2000 Onwards	725 (84.1%)	33 (3.8%)	104 (12.1%)

Source: Field Survey, **2006**.

Endi/Markin Cloth (Atra and Gemso)

Endi cloth is **woven** from the thread made out of cocoon of a worm called **Endi**. The cloths (shawl) are given to the bride's parents and other relatives of the family and it is known as *Basha*. The importance of the clothes (shawl) is evaluated on the basis of the value and size. *Umkhyo* (big

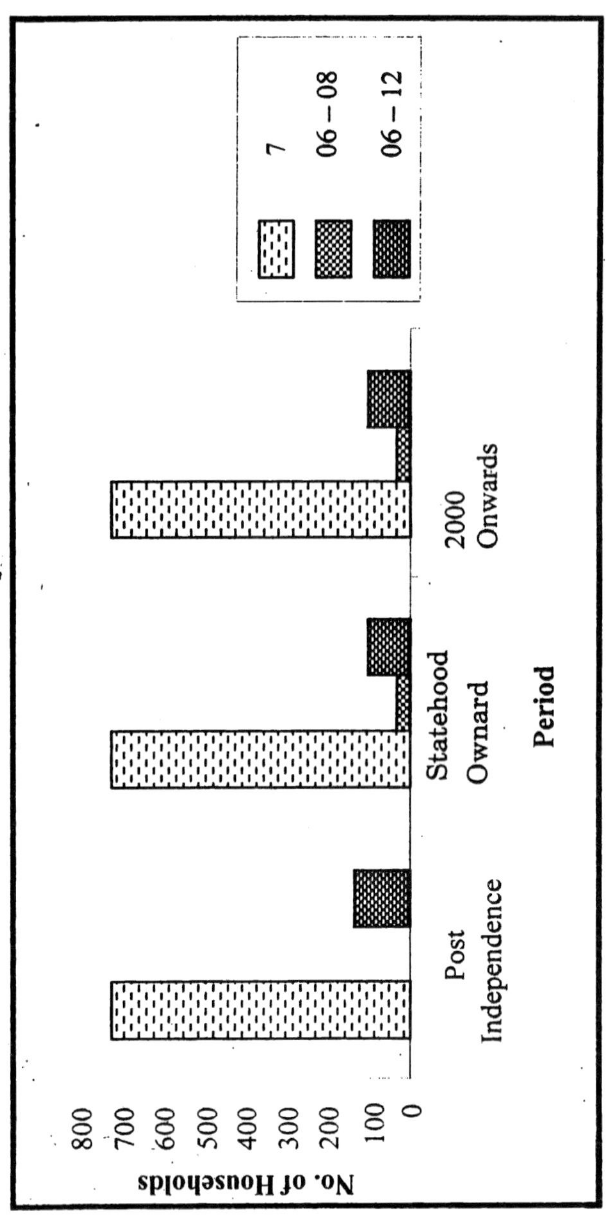

Fig. 3.7 : Marriage Gifts from Groom's Parents (Pig).

size) are presented to the parents and close relatives of the family whereas other relatives of the family are given *Umnyo* (small size). Apart from the marriages the groom as well as his parents presents such clothes during their visits to the bride's parents.

The graph shows majority of households responding for 6 – 12 pieces of such clothes in all type of marriages. There is no change in the number of clothes used for presentation in marriages since the post independence period. Some respondents felt that there is no limit of clothes to be used in marriages because it depends on the number of brothers present in a family.

Table 3.8
Marriage Gifts from Groom's Parents (Endi Cloth)

Period	*7*	*8*	*8 – up to the No. of brothers in the family*	*6 – 12*
Post Independence	1 (0.1%)	4 (0.5%)	133 (15.4%)	724 (84%)
Statehood Onwards	1 (0.1%)	5 (0.6%)	132 (15.3%)	724 (84%)
2000 Onwards	1 (0.1%)	5 (0.6%)	132 (15.3%)	724 (84%)

Source: Field Survey, 2006.

Hence, it varies as per the number of brothers present in a family excluding the two clothes to be presented to the parents as *Aou Aatra* and *Aanyi Aatra*. The same tradition is still followed by the people i.e. two clothes for the parents and one each to all the bothers of the bride. The availability of the cloth in the nearby market of Assam could be the reason behind the unchanging condition of number of clothes used in marriages.

Changing Trend in Marriage Gifts (*Kusu ghiidrii*)

In exchange to the items presented to the bride's parents and relatives the following beads, silver ornaments, brass plates, swords (daos) are presented to the groom's parents.

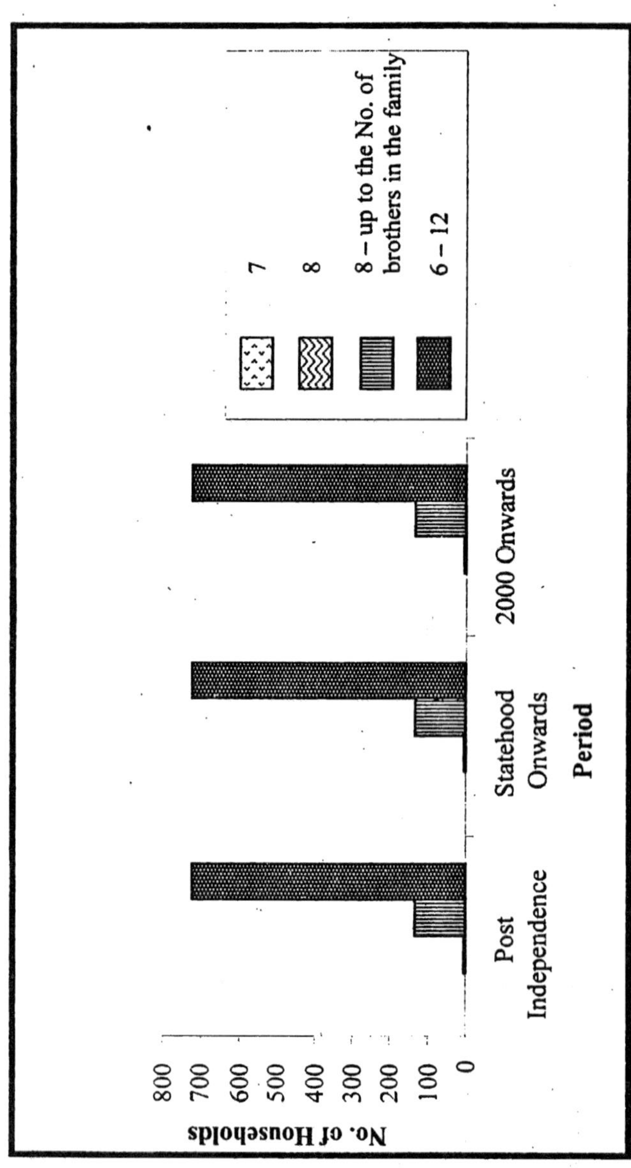

Fig. 3.8 : Marriage Gifts from Groom's Parents (Endi/Markin Cloth).

Beads (Giisen)

Beads form the most important item of marriage gift from the bride's parents. Various types of beads are in use among the Akas since long years back. Most of the beads have close affinity with those of the other tribes of Arunachal Pradesh, but there are some beads that are used by them only. The most important beads used by them include - *Thtrii, Hugeng vojo, Vonyee vojo, Thradzi, Doye, Fupufo, Nuchochifo, Segdrufo, Liimufo, Drangfo, Ajyoyifo, Fugrofo*, etc. Apart from this some single pieces of beads known as *Tsum* is also used for variety of purposes in marriage and other ceremonies.

Table 3.9
Marriage Gifts from Bride's Parents (Beads)

Period	*10 – 70*	*10 – 142*	*10 – 144*
Post Independence	138 (16%)	—	724 (84%)
Statehood Onwards	138 (16%)	—	724 (84%)
2000 Onwards	138 (16%)	24 (3%)	700 (81%)

Source: Field Survey, 2006.

The graph below shows that the tradition of beads as a marriage gift from the bride's parents to the groom's parents ranges from 10 (*Nowu Pom*) to 144 (*Nowu Dzhiighiitriipom*). The tradition is strictly followed by the people at present also, but more and more people are practicing such marriages in which lesser beads are involved. The reason behind such move of the people could be due to decrease in the number of beads and low purchasing capacity. Also, marriages are taking place with the other tribes and outsiders, which had reduced the importance of ancestral beads.

Silver Ornaments (Shii – Liimu)

This category of marriage gifts are known to them as *Shii – Liimu,* that is a combination of two terms *Shii* – meaning Gold and *Liimu* – meaning Silver. People do not use gold ornaments in any form, but it is usually combined with the silver ornaments by them. The important silver ornaments include – *Lyenchi* (head gear for female), *Melu* (ornament worn over chest), *Ghbin* (ear-ring), *Katchbu-Syebu, Keigfanye* (silver sword), *Sapengo, Ghdrii* (wrislets), *Ghaga*

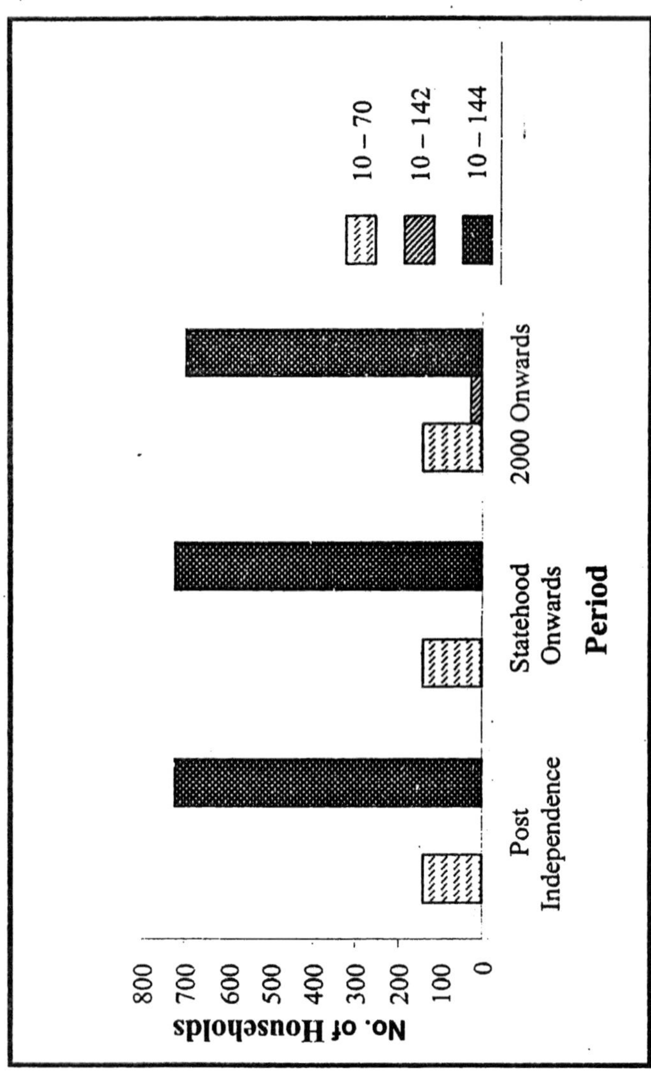

Fig. 3.9 : Marriage Gifts from Bride's Parents (Beads).

(silver cap), etc. The various silver ornaments mentioned above are used as marriage gifts. Its number ranges from 7 (*Nowu Pom*) to 73 (*Nowu Dzhiighiitriipom*). Nowadays, people prefer the lower limit to minimize the number of ornaments. Moreover, most of the groom's parents also prefer the lowest limit of the marriage rules. Therefore, the tradition remains 7 to 73, but people mostly go for 7, the lowest limit.

Table 3.10
Marriage Gifts from Bride's Parents (Silver Ornaments)

Period	*4 – 28*	*7 – 73*	*7 – 73 (Lowest Limit Preferred*
Post Independence	139 (16.14%)	723 (83.8%)	—
Statehood Onwards	139 (16.14%)	723 (83.8%)	—
2000 Onwards	139 (16.14%)	699 (81.1%)	24 (2.8%)

Source: Field Survey, 2006.

Brass Plates (Bela)

Brass plate is an important component of the Aka households that symbolizes the status of a family. A family with higher status usually offers any kind of eatable to the guests in brass plates of various types. Brass plates such as *Gassi* (large brass plate), *Eshyi daw, Bela zem, Bela kuvum* and *Pandow* with varying size are used in marriages and other social visits of the relatives and guests (*Thumona*). Apart from these plates brass cup (*Sinsee*) and brass saucepan (*Dangyi*) are used and counted as marriage gifts to the groom's parents. Such plates are also used in other social occasions, for instance when a sister comes to her brother's house with some meat and local wine then the brother has to give some brass plates to the sister.

Table – 3.11
Marriage Gifts from Bride's Parents (Brass Plates)

Period	*10 (multiplies as per the rules)*	*10 – 70*	*10 – 70 (Lowest Limit Preferred)*
Post Independence	1 (0.1%)	861 (99.9%)	—
Statehood Onwards	1 (0.1%)	861 (99.9%)	—
2000 Onwards	1 (0.1%)	838 (97.2%)	23 (2.7%)

Source: Field Survey, 2006.

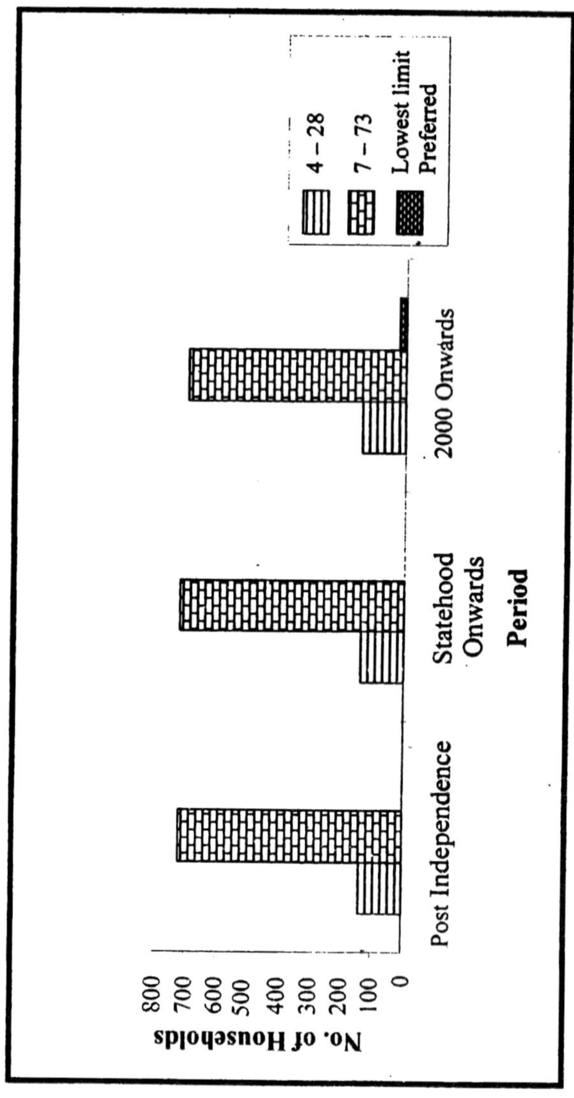

Fig. 3.10 : Marriage Gifts from Bride's Parents (Silver Ornaments).

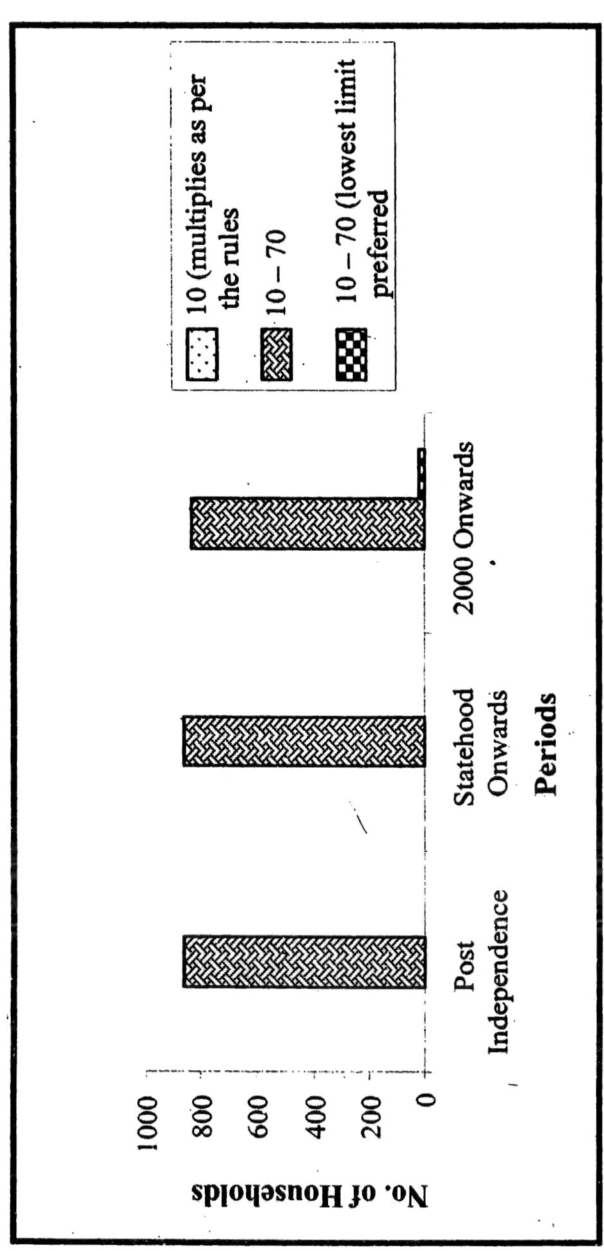

Fig. 3.11 : Gifts from Bride's Parents (Brass Plates).

The graph shows that mostly the number of brass plates used in marriages ranges from 10 to 70, but nowadays people prefer the lower limit due to higher involvement of finance in purchasing those plates. As these plates are not produced by them it is purchased from the nearby markets of Assam and the price is increasing day by day.

Sword (Humo vetsii)

Swords are mainly presented to the groom by the bride's parents to clear the path while returning to home. Hence, it is locally called as *Humo Vetsii, Humo* – son-in-law and *Vetsii* – a sword / dao. Swords are of two types one with silver sheath and another without silver or common sword.

Table 3.12
Marriage Gifts from Bride's Parents (Sword/dao)

Period	*2 – 4*	*2 – 10*	*4 – 28*
Post Independence	25 (3%)	724 (84%)	113 (13%)
Statehood Onwards	25 (3%)	724 (84%)	113 (13%)
2000 Onwards	48 (5.6%)	701 (81.3%)	113 (13%)

Source : Field Survey, 2006.

The number of swords used in marriages ranges from 2 (*Nowu Pom*) to 10 (*Nowu Dzhiighiitriipom*). As swords are easily available in the nearby markets there is no change in the number of swords given in marriage ceremonies, but most of them prefer the lowest rule of marriage in which involvement of all the marriage gifts also became lesser.

TRADITIONAL VILLAGE COUNCIL (*MELE*, EARLIER – *GHAZ*, CORRECTED)

The traditional village council of the Akas has been referred as '*Mele*' by Raghuvir Sinha (1962) who worked as a Research Officer in the Kameng Frontier Division for many years. The village council in a tribal society is the indigenous way of exercising power of authority. However, in the village this term is pronounced as '*Meye*' by the Akas. Village council of the Akas has been governed with the democratic ideas and values by the village community.

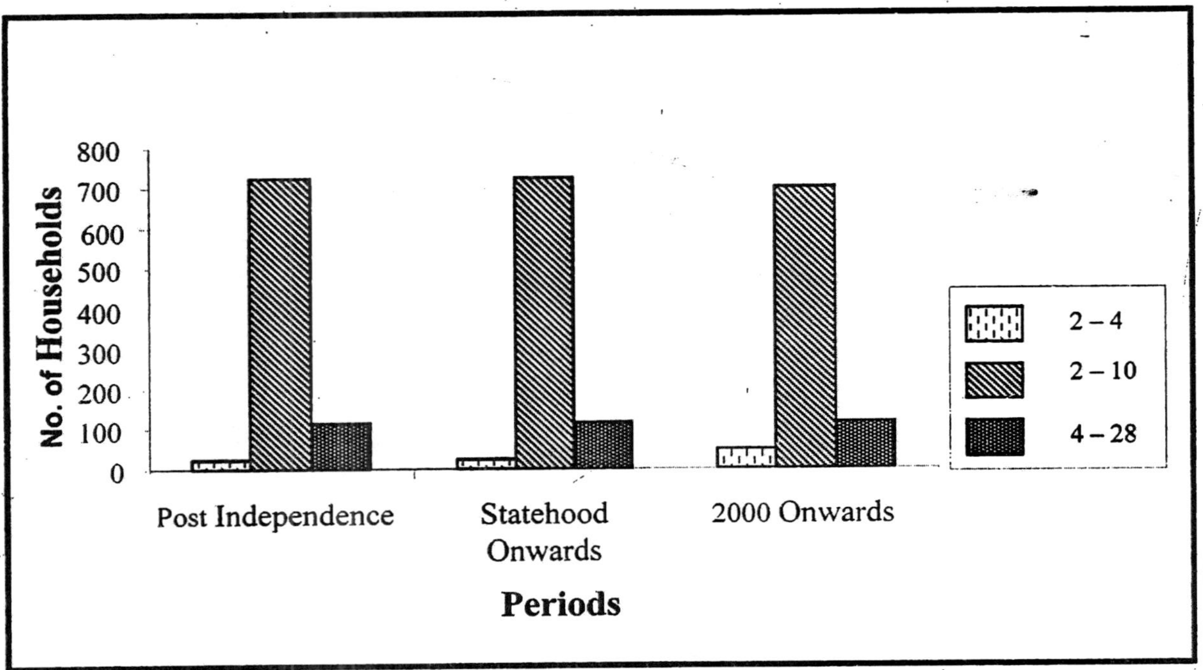

Fig. 3.12 : Marriage Gifts from Bride's Parents (Swor5d/Dao).

Therefore, the literal meaning of *Meye* as designated by the scholars earlier do not fulfil the actual meaning. The term '*Meye*' in Aka dialect means a meeting, in other words it denotes the act of gathering of villagers or council members and discussions over various issues. Hence, in strict sense the term *Ghaz* is more appropriate than *Meye*. Though the term *Ghaz* appears to be evolved from the Assamese word raiz, it is closer to the meaning of tribal village councils. *Ghaz* is an Aka term that denotes the whole village community as a single entity forming a council of members in taking decisions during the meetings and disposing of the cases. The supreme authority rests in the hands of the *Nyetrii Ghaz* (village council) that includes *Nyetrii Kheo/Nugo* (headman), Gaon Bura, *Bagha*, *Giiba* and the village elders (*Nyetrii Kheo-Nyeo*). In all types of offences in the society the judgments of the council are abided by all. It is mandatory for all the members of the village to participate in the meetings of the council, particularly when some important subject has to be discussed. In fact, a representative from each family is supposed to attend the proceedings of the meeting. In most of the meetings the experts who are well-versed with the intricacies of tribal law play their part while others just sit and listen. The age factor is always given respect and the youths are regarded as immature and they are not entertained in handling any case. There is a fixed platform for holding the meetings (*Meye*) of the village council in all Aka villages. The place is locally known as *Nyetrii Psigha*, which is maintained by clearing the weeds and keeping flat stones to serve the purpose of seats for the village members. The platform is considered to be a piece of antiquity and regarded as sacred. People believe that the meetings conducted and decisions taken on important issues by their ancestors are sacred and exemplary to all. The stones are believed to be sacred and any attempt to unearth or displacement would be a bad omen to them. The platform is used for both meetings as well as rituals for festivals. Due to infrastructural development in some villages nowadays the open general grounds has replaced the platforms of meeting. The villages located away from the roads and towns still maintain the traditional platform to conduct the meeting. In the recent years people mostly prefer to go straight to the court and law for easy settlement of disputes and awarding legal punishments to the culprits.

Constituents of Village Council

As stated earlier, the traditional village council constitutes of the *Nyetrii Kheo – Nugo* (village elder – rich man in terms of traditional assets/headman), *Bagha, Giiba* and *Nyetrii Kheo-Nyeo.* The constituents of the village council have not changed since the past, but there has been an addition of Gaon Buras as appointed by the government. After the appointment of Gaon Buras in each village the position of the village elder or the *Nyetrii Kheo* in some villages is being held by them. The other constituents of the council remain undisturbed. The two most important constituents of the council that remained undisturbed with defined functions are the *Bagha* and *Giiba*. The *Bagha* is selected by the villagers through voice vote to a person who possess good knowledge of myths, folklores, proceedings of meetings, marriage rules, and other social and cultural activities. The role of *Bagha* is alike to convener who arranges the meeting and also takes part in the decision making. In some cases in the past the portfolio of *Nyetrii Kheo* and *Bagha* used to hold by the same person. Nowadays '*Bagha*' is appointed a person who does not hold any post as Gaon Bura, ASMs and GPMs. The *Giiba* is a junior of the *Bagha* who assists him in arranging and informing the villagers about the meeting dates. Further, it is the duty of *Giiba* to collect and distribute the eatable items and drinks (*Tsii*) during the meeting to the members present irrespective of both the sexes. The *Giiba* is also assigned the duty to make aware by shouting during the nights in the village from the intrusion of enemies. He draws the attention of the village youths to remain awake and guard from enemies. The introduction of panchayati raj and advancement of the society had many fold impact on the traditional village councils. The elected/selected members of the panchayati raj are mostly young and less educated who are neither perfect in traditional knowledge nor in the desired knowledge of panchayati raj system.

Function of Village Council

The village council or the *Ghaz* (*Meye*) is the supreme administrative agency of the village. Its jurisdiction extends from ordinary house-to-house disputes to inter-village conflicts. All kind of cases of theft, quarrel of fights, elopement, adultery, extra marital relation, murder, sorcery or witchcraft, black magic fall within the province of *Ghaz*. The functions of the village councils are threefold – judicial, administrative and developmental. The Assam Frontier (Administrative of Justice) Regulation of 1945 empowers considerably to the councils to settle disputes within the village boundaries as well as outside the village in case of inter-village meetings. They are abide by the councils decisions so even the serious crimes like murder have been settled in satisfaction to all concerned. The judicial function is the most important and crucial among the three mentioned functions. The councils deal with the maintenance of paths and bridges, water supply, sanitation of the village, fixation of community hunting and fishing dates and related activities of the annual celebration of festival. Similarly, developmental activities sponsored by the state/central government largely depend on the coordination between local officials and the council members.

The laws followed by the village council are largely based on customs and conventions. In all cases, meeting of the council is convened when it is approached to short out the complaint/report from the people. The person alleged of charges is called for explanation by the council. The council members deliberate and examine the issue in light of circumstantial evidences before giving their final verdict. If the person fails to substantiate any sound reason in support of his/her defence, he/she has to pay compensation to the person whom he/she has caused harm or discomfort and a feast to the village council as a fine. If he/she fail to do so, will be left at the mercy of the person to whom he/she stands a culprit. He/she may also be required to take a pledge before the council for not committing the same act in future. Murder is a highly anti-social act which arouses strong sentiment of anger to the murderer and pity to the victims. The principle of justice for such a heinous crime among the Akas is that such person should not go unpunished. The assassin is required to pay some penalty to the victim's family who has sustained a loss by his action. The amount of penalty that may be imposed varies according to the rank and status of the victim. If the victim is a man of prominence in his community and whose loss is a great loss not only to the family but to the whole community the price that may be demanded is not less than 15 to 20 *mithuns*. Apart from this, the culprit has to provide a feast to the whole village community to soothe the antagonism between the two parties in dispute. If the culprit fails to pay the penalty demanded, he may be handed over to the family of the victim as a captive till he agrees to pay the penalty. Such culprits remain as a slave in the house of the person to whom he is a culprit as declared by the village council. Such cases led to the concept of slave system in the Aka area during the old days.

The subsidiary method of administering justice among the Akas is the ordeal which is known as *Trasgha Jiw*. This is the only alternative where other methods of law and justice fail to produce results. The most common ordeal is to ask the suspect to put his/her hands into the boiling water. Such ordeals are done where the suspect decline to accept the crime and pretends to be innocence. When a case reaches such stage the village council calls the priest (*Mugow*) to conduct it. The priest performs rituals and prays to the gods to award full justice to the sufferers and to punish the culprit heavily if he/she have committed the offence. Water is boiled in a bamboo vessel with skin of tiger, snake, excreta of insects and animals in it. The priest offer prayer to the tiger, snake, etc. to punish the culprit if found guilty. The culprit is then asked to cross the puja alters (*Trasgha Nye*) prepared with thorns, leaves, etc. and put his hands into the boiling water. The priest reads the minutest details of the ordeal in presence of all the villagers and declares the results. If the culprit brings out himself without injury to his hands, he proves himself innocent of the crime with which he is charged and is set free. On the other hand, if burns appear on his hand, he is supposed to have succumbed to the ordeal and thus is proved guilty of the charge. He then falls within the province of customary law and has to await his lot there. He has to pay the penalty as fixed by the village council and is required to abide by the decision of the council. Such kinds of ordeals are practiced in variety of ways at present also like putting red hot iron axe in the hands. They have strong belief behind such ordeals and any case which do not yield proper results from the modern judicial courts are bring back by the village council to such ordeals in this age also.

LITERACY RATE

The traditional definition of literacy is considered to be the ability to read and write, or the ability to use language to read, write, listen and speak. In modern contexts, the word refers to reading and writing at a level adequate for communication, or at a level that lets one understand and communicate ideas in a literate society, so as to take part in that society. The United Nations Educational, Scientific and Cultural Organization (UNESCO) has drafted the following definition: "Literacy is the ability to identify, understand, interpret, create, communicate and compute, using printed and written materials associated with varying contexts. Literacy involves a continuum of learning to enable an individual to achieve his or her goals, to develop his or her knowledge and potential, and to participate fully in the wider society." Many policy analysts consider literacy rates a crucial measure of a region's human capital. This claim is made on the grounds that literate people can be trained less expensively than illiterate people, generally have a higher socio-economic status and enjoy better health and employment prospects. Policy makers also argue that literacy increases job opportunities and access to higher education. In Kerala, India, for example, female and child mortality rates declined dramatically in the 1960s, when girls who were educated in the education reforms after 1948 began to raise families. Recent researchers, however, argue that correlations such as the one listed above may have more to do with the effects of schooling rather than literacy in general. Regardless, the focus of educational systems worldwide includes a basic concept around communication through text and print, which is the foundation of most definitions of literacy.

As per the Census of India, a person aged 6 years and above who can both read and write with understanding in any language has been taken as literate. It is not necessary for a person to have received any formal education or passed any minimum educational standard for being treated as literate. People who were blind and could read in Braille are treated to be literates. Whereas, a person, who can only read but cannot write, is treated as illiterate. All children of age 6 years or less, even if going to school and have picked up reading and writing, are treated as illiterate.

The literacy rate of the Aka area is quite interesting because it was very less in the year 1971. The literacy rate was just 12.11% with 18.99 % male and 1% female literacy rates. The highest literacy rate of 54.32% was recorded at Dedza, this village has very less tribal and Aka population and mostly inhabited by Assam rifles and GREF personnel. Some of the villages like Bana, Bihupam, Gijiri, Karangania, Kararamu, Kichang, Linia, Morkha, Prizin, Thesa, Thesari, Tulu and Yayong have zero literacy rates during 1971. These villages are located far from the main road and there was no school that may be the reason why there is zero literacy rates in these villages. The highest male literacy rate of 54.32% was recorded at Dedza and the highest female literacy rate of 11. 54% was recorded at Sessa.

There has been slight increase in the literacy rate during 1981. However, the literacy rates of 1971 and 1981 have been calculated out of the total population due to unavailability of total illiterate population/total population in the age group of 0-6 years in the census. Therefore, it is approximation and the literacy rates may be higher than the figures given above.

The literacy rate increased to 17.80% with 23.79% male and 10.00 % female respectively. Some primary schools have been set up in this year that increased the literacy rate. The highest literacy rate of 65.31% was recorded for Tipi and lowest literacy rates of zero for Sathi (64 km) and 34 km point from Nechiphu. Sathi (64 km) is inhabited by only 2 to 3 households which can be termed as a hamlet in the jhum field, hence there is no school and literacy is zero. The second settlement is a labour camp of GREF and most of them are labourers who are engaged in works daily and in the absence of a school they are unable to send their children to schools located far away. The highest male and female literacy has been found in Tipi with 78.12% and 41.18% respectively.

As per 1991 census the literacy rate was 48.49% with 57.30% male and 36.68% female respectively. The literacy rate has more than doubled in a decade from 1981 to 1991. The increase in number of educational institutions in the area had enhanced the literacy rate remarkably. The highest literacy rate was recorded for Thrizino HQ at 80.99% and the lowest literacy rate of 0% for Dizonganiapam, Khamsiri Hamlet, Sakrin and Sopung villages. The highest male literacy rate was recorded for Nechiphu with 93.18% and the highest female literacy was recorded for Thrizino HQ with 88.94%.

According to 2001 census there was only 4% increase in the literacy rate. The literacy rate was 56.75% and the male and female literacy rate was 66.39% and 45.59% respectively. Thrizino the Sub-divisional headquarter has recorded the highest literacy rate of 80.82% and the lowest literacy rate of 0% has been recorded for Sopung village. The village-wise literacy rates (in %) from 1971 to 2001 is Table 3.13. The total literates (excluding the population belonging to 0 – 4 years group) and illiterates of the Aka population have been collected by conducting survey in 2006 to analyze the current educational scenario. As per the survey the total literacy rate is 63.57% with 71.26% 55.74% male and female respectively. Some villages i.e. Tippi and Nag Mandir recorded a highest of 100% literacy rates because of very less Aka population. The villages with higher concentration of Aka population and

Table 3.13
Village-wise Literacy Rates (in %) from 1971 to 2001

	1971				1981		
Village	Total	M	F	Village	Total	M	F
1	2	3	4	5	6	7	8
Bana	00	00	00	Bana	5.49	10.20	00
Bana Camp	10.98	13.64	00	Bana Camp	37.29	47.30	20.45
Bhalukpong/Thrizino	26.95	34.72	3.08	Bhalukpong (H.Q)	40.80	51.16	23.41
Buragaon	25.43	40.46	3.39	Buragaon	38.00	49.55	23.60
Chizang	00	00	00	Chijang	8.33	5.38	00
Dedza	54.32	54.32	00	Dedza	12.00	18.00	6.00
Dijangania	1.39	2.88	00	Dizangania	14.69	23.44	5.13
Gijiri	00	00	00	Giziri	16.07	36.36	2.94
Gohainthan	1.51	3.03	00	Gohainthan	28.00	42.42	00
Husigaon	4.08	7.69	00	Husigaon	12.31	17.07	14.17
Jamiripoint/Noghupam	7.48	10.38	00	Jamiri Point	15.00	18.29	10.34
Jamiri Village	3.67	7.14	00	Jamiri	6.53	4.66	10.21
Karangania	00	00	00	Karangania	12.41	19.40	6.41
Kararamu	00	00	00	Kararamu	12.90	17.86	8.82
Kichang	00	00	00	Kitchang	2.10	4.11	00

Table 3.13 (Contd. . . .)

1	2	3	4	5	6	7	8
Moracca	00	00	00	Morakha	12.90	20.00	6.25
Palatari	0.67	1.33	00	Palatari	17.32	25.84	8.88
Pharizing	00	00	00	Phrizing	11.11	21.95	00
Pichang	7.75	14.36	0.54	Pitchang	22.29	35.37	10.13
Ramdagania	4.08	7.79	00	Ramdagania	4.35	2.63	6.45
Sakrin	0.49	1.05	00	Sakrin	8.46	14.89	2.11
Sessa	25.64	32.69	11.54	Sessa	7.65	11.02	1.45
Thesa	00	00	00	Thesa	6.66	3.85	8.82
Yayong	00	00	00	Yayong	10.00	14.58	5.77
Tania	1.56	2.50	00	Tania	1.85	3.85	00
				Tuluhu	10.00	00	16.66
				Thrizino HQ	37.54	39.63	34.71
				Elephant Flat	6.59	9.68	00
				Khamsiri	1.96	4.76	00
				Khupi – A	17.14	30.00	00
				Khupi – B	5.41	8.33	00
				Kimi	11.11	21.05	00
..	..	..	..	Palizi	22.50	30.71	13.27

Table 3.13 (Contd. . . .)

1	2	3	4	5	6	7	8
..	..	..	..	Sapung	6.66	13.16	00
..	..	..	..	Tipi	65.31	78.12	41.18
..	..	..	..	Yashey	8.33	14.28	1.75
Bihupam	00	00	00	Bihupam	20.00	33.33	6.66
Tulu	00	00	00	Tulu	10.53	18.60	00
..	..	..	..	Bhorali River Camp	15.79	21.43	00
..	..	..	..	8 Km Point from Khuppi to Tenga River	23.08	32.08	4.00
Huppipam / Dezling	23.32	27.60	3.67	..	..	..	..
Linia	00	00	00	..	..	..	..
..	..	..	..	Mopgramo	17.95	25.00	13.04
Rogupam	3.22	6.66	00	..	..	..	..
Rugugaon	5.55	11.11	00	..	..	..	..
Thesari	00	00	00	..	..	..	..
..	..	..	..	Sathi (64 KM)	00	00	00
..	..	..	..	3 KM Point towards Kimi	36.84	57.14	11.76
..	..	..	..	34 KM Point from Nechiphu	00	00	00
Total	12.11	18.99	1.00	Total	17.80	23.79	10.00

Table (3.13) Contd. . . .

1991				2001			
Village	Total	M	F	Village	Total	M	F
9	10	11	12	13	14	15	16
Bana Village	15.52	32.00	3.03	Bana Village	28.14	38.32	16.30
Bana Camp	42.02	54.84	25	Bana Camp	58.22	72.65	40.62
Lower Bhalukpong	56.91	67.37	41.99	Lower Bhalukpong	65.35	73.79	53.01
Upper Bhalukpong	71.56	78.98	56.92	Upper Bhalukpong	80.41	88.60	71.36
Buragaon	70.00	81.21	57.25	Buragaon	46.34	58.91	32.49
Chijong	15.57	21.87	8.62	Chijang	38.38	57.14	20.00
Dedza	72.53	76.00	68.29	Dedza	68.18	80.43	54.76
Dizangoniapam (Hamlet)	00	00	00	Dizangania	80.00	90.00	70.00
Giziri	45.45	66.66	26.09	Giziri	46.94	58.33	36.00
Gohainthan	25.92	30.77	21.43	Gohainthan	16.22	20.00	13.64
Husigaon	15.69	29.63	00	Husigaon	16.66	22.72	10.00
Jamiri Point	59.64	69.13	39.25	Jamiri Point	56.35	66.66	44.70
Jamiri Village (including labour camp at 3 km)	45.78	58.70	29.73	Jamiri Village	33.33	48.98	25.00

Table (3.13) Contd. . . .

9	10	11	12	13	14	15	16
Karangania	22.35	29.73	16.66	Karangania	50.49	63.41	41.66
Kararamu	17.39	20.00	15.38	Kararamu	42.22	47.37	38.46
Kitchang	20.45	24.53	14.28	Kitchang	42.62	63.64	17.86
Moorakka	26.66	33.33	16.66	Maraka	7.14	12.5	00
Palatary	32.11	41.66	20.41	Palatari	53.15	68.96	35.85
Phirizin	7.84	14.81	00	Pharizin	21.54	28.12	15.15
Pitchang	10.38	17.44	4.12	Pitchang	29.16	30.91	27.69
Ramdagania	8.47	12.5	3.70	Ramdagania	26.09	31.58	19.35
Sakrin	00	00	00	Sakrin	31.63	39.25	22.47
Sessa	37.19	31.74	55.26	Sessa	45.54	63.16	22.73
Thesa	50.20	48.28	51.25	Thesa	35.06	49.31	22.22
Yayung	15.66	28.57	6.25	Yayung	24.61	30.30	18.75
..	..	..	..	Tania	17.50	25.00	10.00
Tuluhui	13.85	22.58	5.88	Tuluhi	31.03	46.15	18.75
Thrizino HQ	80.99	74.51	88.94	Thrizino HQ	80.82	89.86	72.84
Elephant Flat	45.16	56.34	24.00	Elephant Flat	59.43	75.81	36.36
Khamsiri (Hamlet)	00	00	00	Kamsiri	23.53	28.57	20.00
Khupi forest office complex	50.00	70.97	11.76	Khupi forest office complex	25.81	50.00	00

Table (3.13) Contd. . . .

9	10	11	12	13	14	15	16
Khupi model village	21.57	40.74	00	Khupi model village	23.27	31.52	11.94
Khupi Det	23.08	46.15	00				
Kimi Forest office Complex	46.43	52.17	20.00	Kimi Village	18.18	25.00	7.69
Palizi	47.83	58.04	36.84	Palizi	51.38	56.12	44.86
Sapung	00	00	00	Sapong	00	00	00
Tipi	57.20	66.28	37.50	Tipi	68.85	80.65	53.73
Yangse	36.62	46.15	25.00	Yangse	61.73	72.40	51.50
Kaya Valley	19.05	34.15	4.65	Kaya Valley Village	47.30	69.23	22.86
Nechiphu camp (including labour camp at ½ km)	75.18	93.18	66.66	Nechiphu	12.50	12.72	12.12
New Sapung	12.07	20.00	3.57	New Sapong	15.29	24.44	5.00
Pochung	12.50	16.66	7.14	Pochong	16.33	23.08	8.70
Sobu	27.69	34.33	20.63	Sube	27.55	39.13	17.31
				Baliphoo	26.98	42.86	14.29
..	..	..	..	Husago	37.14	51.35	21.21

Table (3.13) Contd. . . .

9	10	11	12	13	14	15	16
..	..	..	..	Humethu (Humethu under Jamiri)	30.00	25.00	34.62
..	..	..	..	Jamiri H.Q.	71.00	75.93	65.22
Labour camp at 2 km from Palizi towards Khupi	22.22	40.00	00	..	..	..	..
Rabang Rugo L camp (Hamlet)	20.00	33.33	00	..	..	..	..
Saljipam (Hamlet)	25.00	50.00	10.00	..	..	..	..
7 km labour camp from Ziro point towards Khupi	31.09	37.66	19.05	..	..	..	..
Tengadam site Labour Camp	100	100	00	..	..	..	..
Total	48.49	57.30	36.68	Total	56.75	66.39	45.59

Source: Census of India 1971, 1981, 1991 and 2001.

Table 3.14
Village-wise Literacy Rate of the Aka Population (in %) 2006

Sl. No.	*Village*	*Total*	*Male*	*Female*	*Gender Gap*
1	2	3	4	5	6
1.	Balefu	55.93	74.07	40.63	33.44
2.	Bana	90.00	100.00	80.00	20.00
3.	Bhalukpong	82.69	91.89	72.16	19.73
4.	Buragaon	65.25	75.61	53.98	21.63
5.	Chijang	43.36	43.10	43.64	-0.54
6.	Dijungania	54.76	70.15	37.29	32.86
7.	Elephant Flat	80.95	90.00	72.72	17.28
8.	Giziri	75.75	81.25	70.59	10.66
9.	Gohainthan	74.07	72.72	75.00	-2.28
10.	Husigaon	69.56	77.27	62.50	14.77
11.	Husugo	58.57	59.46	57.57	1.89
12.	Jamiri	75.37	81.13	69.07	12.06
13.	Janapam	70.04	80.00	58.33	21.67
14.	Kadeya	75.00	84.51	63.93	20.58
15.	Karangania	45.69	50.00	42.19	7.81
16.	Kararamu	59.41	67.39	52.72	14.67
17.	Khamsiri	28.57	33.33	25.00	8.33
18.	Khuppi	66.66	72.72	61.85	10.87
19.	Kichang	61.11	66.66	54.16	12.50
20.	Kimi	40.45	47.50	34.69	12.81
21.	Morkha	48.28	50.00	45.45	4.55
22.	Nag Mandir	100.00	100.00	100.00	0.00
23.	Palatari	57.52	68.75	42.86	25.89
24.	Palizi	77.04	84.21	71.11	13.10
25.	Pichang	45.83	49.06	41.86	7.20
26.	Pochong	50.91	48.28	53.85	-5.57
27.	Prizin	58.75	71.43	44.74	26.69
28.	Ramdagania	47.62	57.57	36.66	20.91
29.	Sakrin	57.99	67.03	47.43	19.60

1	2	3	4	5	6
30.	Saljipam	60.00	83.33	38.46	44.87
31.	Sopung	53.99	61.73	46.34	15.39
32.	Subu	58.73	71.43	46.03	25.40
33.	Tania	55.10	59.09	51.85	7.24
34.	Thissa	42.31	47.94	37.35	10.59
35.	Thrizino	80.05	87.44	72.40	15.04
36.	Thuluhui	62.07	65.52	58.62	6.90
37.	Tipi	100.00	100.00	100.00	0.00
38.	Yangsey	69.09	77.10	61.81	15.29
39.	Yayong	39.05	45.45	32.00	13.45
	Total	**63.57**	**71.26**	**55.74**	**15.52**

Source: Field Survey, 2006.

having higher literacy rates are Bhalukpong (82. 69%), Thrizino (80.05%), Palizi (77.04%), Giziri (75.75%), Jamiri (75.37%), and Kadeya (75.00%). The lowest literacy rate of 28.57 % is found in Khamsiri village while the other villages with lower literacy rates are Yayong (39.05%), Kimi (40.45%), Thissa (42.31%), Chijang (43.36%), Karangania (45.69%), Pitchang (45.83%), Ramdagania (47.62%), and Morkha (48.28%). The remaining villages have average literacy rates ranging from 50% to 70%. The Aka literacy rate has reached the mark of 63.57% in the year 2006, but the composition of literates in various levels of education show significant ups and downs. The level of education has been shown in Figure 3.13. The diagram shows that 56.89% of the literates belong to the category of primary level education. The percentage share goes on declining towards the higher levels of education. Secondary level education shares 39.53%; College and graduates share only 3.42% and Post graduate and other professional courses only 0.15%. The total literacy rate is comparable to the neighbouring tribes but, the composition of level of education requires more share towards the higher level of education.

Table 3.15
Level of Education (in %) as per the Survey 2006

Primary			*Secondary*			*College/Graduate*			*Post Graduate*		
Total	*Male*	*Female*	*Total*	*Male*	*Female*	*Total*	*Male*	*Female*	*Total*	*Male*	*Female*
56.89	53.24	46.76	39.53	59.79	40.21	3.42	74.73	25.27	0.15	50	50

Source: Field Survey, 2006.

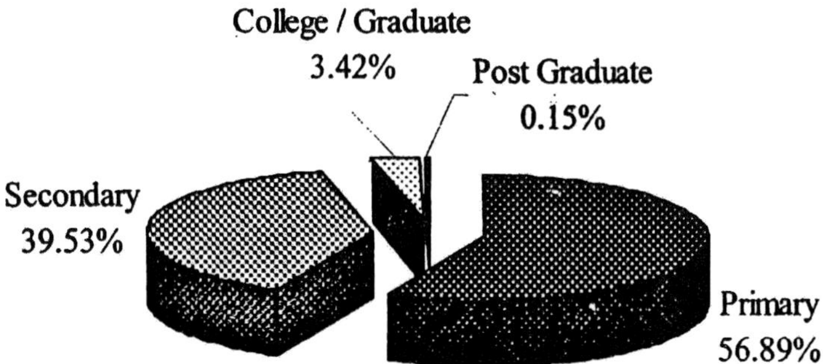

Fig. 3.13 : Level of Education among the Akas.

STATUS OF WOMEN IN THE SOCIETY

The status of women in a society can be assessed by examining the level of literacy rate, sex ratio, development, work participation, etc. The position of women in Aka society is better than many of the women of developed societies. Women take parts is all activities with the husband ranging from social, economic, cultural and political. She shares the social observances like festivals, rituals, social occasions, etc. She works with the husband in economic activities like clearing of forest in the field, sowing, harvesting of crops, food gathering, etc. She also takes parts in the meetings and other political deliberations. However, during the old days the overall status of the women in the society was exploitative but supportive to the husband. Though, the women are very important member of a family and enjoy participation in many activities but, in comparison of modern women they are still deprived of many opportunities. The higher cases of polygyny during those days are evident of the domineering position of the women. Even if a woman resists for polygyny the husband was free to marry another wife during those days. Such cases were also evident up to certain extent during the statehood period and still in one way or the other polygyny is a glaring example in the Aka society. Another aspect of the women's status in the society is the abundance of social taboos applicable to them. They are restricted from the consumption of animal flesh like bear, cow, goat, rat, etc. Even among the non-vegetarian items prepared from a specified animal parts of the flesh is allowed for consumption. These taboos had affected the dietary habits of the women which could be a factor of the diseases and mortality among the women in those days. Another taboo is to separate the women from the hearth of the house during her menstrual cycle. A woman is not allowed to use the fire place and enter the kitchen. A separate plate, cup is given and allowed to either stay in a corner of the room of house or outside the house. Such taboos though have high relevance as a part of their culture but women by staying outside during the midst of the winter cold feel tortured. Apart from these during a fight or a quarrel with the husband, the wife is always the sufferer and bitten up. But, they hardly resists due to lesser muscle power or a respect to the husband. However, women in the society nowadays had come out from all these restrictions up to certain extent to be at par with the women of other advanced societies. The increase in the women literacy rate, inter-tribe and inter-caste marriages have widened the mindset of the Aka women as a result their position has become honourable and supportive to male.

According to the survey conducted for the area the female literacy rate is 55.74% in compare to the male literacy rate of 71.26%. There is a gender gap of 15.52% which is to be reduced to improve the status of women in the area. During the past the gender gap in literacy was more that resulted in lower status of the women in the society, but this gap is narrowing down in all societies with the passage of time. There are some settlements in the area where the gender gap is in negative which shows the higher literacy and better status of women in those villages.

The above Figure 3.14 shows the position of women in the society during the post independence and statehood period as exploitative and supportive to male. It appears to be honourable and supportive to male from 2000 onwards. However, some of the respondents reveal that still the position of women in the society is partly exploitative. Hence, no doubt there is tremendous improvement in the status of women

Table 3.16
Status of Woman in the Society

Period	*Supportive to male, Exploitative*	*Honourable, Supportive to male*	*Honourable, Supportive to male, Exploitative*
Post Independence	862 (100%)	—	—
Statehood Onwards	862 (100%)	—	—
2000 Onwards	—	135 (15.7%)	727 (84 %)

Source: Field Survey, 2006.

but the level of improvement is imbalanced throughout the area. The settlements with lesser access to education, roads, medicals, etc. show a different trend of women's status than a settlement with all those facilities.

Division of Labour

Division of labour is the specialization of cooperative labour in specific, circumscribed tasks and roles, intended to increase efficiency of output. Historically the growth of a more and more complex division of labour is closely associated with the growth of trade, the rise of capitalism, and of the complexity of industrialization processes. Later, the division of labour reached the level of a scientifically-based management practice with the time and motion studies associated with Taylorism (scientific management). The clearest exposition of the principles of sexual division of labour across the full range of human societies can be summarized by a large number of logically complementary implicational constraints of the following form: if women of childbearing ages in a given community tend to do X (e.g., preparing soil for planting) they will also do Y (e.g., the planting) while for men the logical reversal in this example would be that if men plant they will prepare the soil.

The literal meaning of division of labour is different in economics and business administration in the sense that it deals with the specialization of labour in increasing the efficiency of output. Here, in the context of the Akas the term

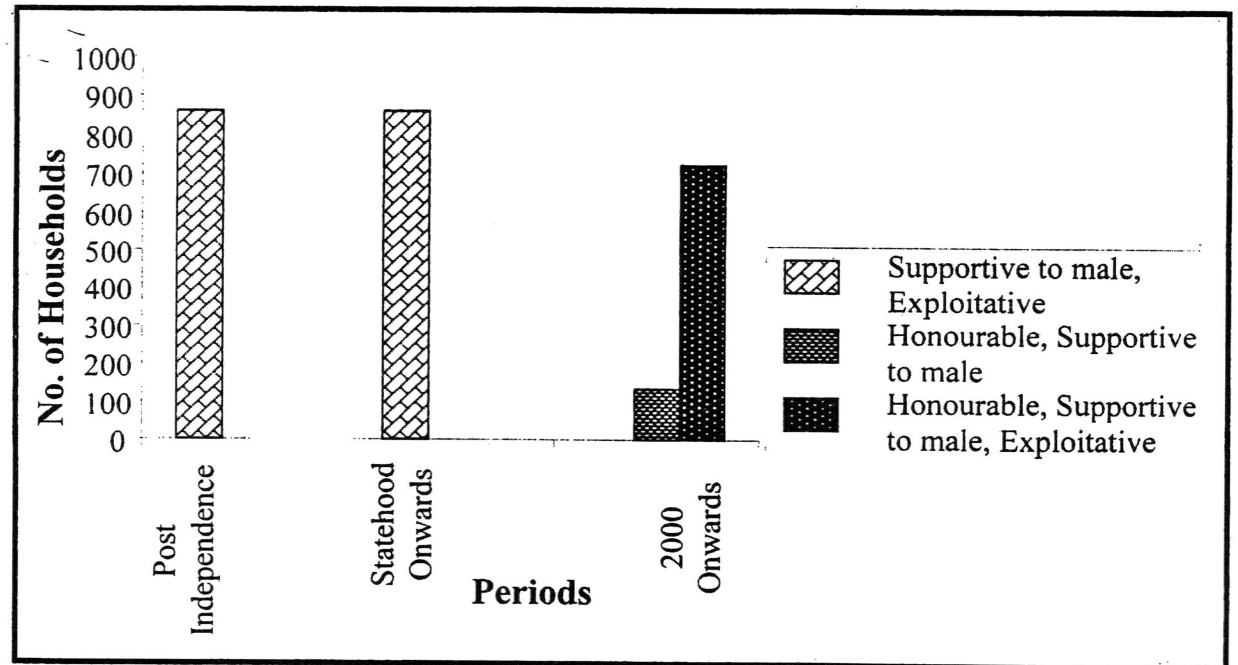

Fig. 3.14 : Status of Woman in the Society.

has been used for the division or distribution of work within the family members in a household. The changes taking place in the distribution of work among the adult male, female and children (both male and female) are due to the introduction of education and other means of developmental activities. In Aka society the men and women share together the economic burden to eke out a living. Usually, women assist the men in a number of occasions and work together throughout the agricultural operations. Hence, a theoretical division of labour is not possible but, a rough division of work for the two sex remains in their minds. The division of labour/distribution of work among the family members in an Aka household are as given below:

Adult Male

The adult male takes the responsibility of such works which requires more hard labour. The common work done by an adult male in a household is construction of house, cutting down the big trees for jhum, collection of firewood, hunting/fishing activities, construction of fence around the fields, collection of food items from the field, guarding the village from enemies, attending meetings, settlement of differences with the guests (*Thumona*), and sowing and harvesting of crops during the olden days. During the statehood period also people continued the same works, but some of the works like guarding the village from enemies has disappeared due to the establishment of the police department. Some works like business, contract, services, etc. had increased in this period mainly due to the introduction of education in the area. More and more people started to acquire education keeping aside the age factor and got services, which had changed the work distribution pattern of the past. Nowadays there is decline in the works like war, hunting, fishing, etc. and increase in the works like educating the children, attending developmental meetings, contracts, business, services, etc. to earn and run the family in modern ways. The most important factor in the changes of work distribution has been the initiation of education system in the area. However, the impact has been varied throughout the area.

Adult Female

The adult females are assigned mainly the lighter activities in comparison to the male. The important works carried out by them are clearing of weeds in the field, cooking food items, collection of firewood, taking care of the children, collection of vegetables, collection of drinking water, grinding food items, preparation of local wine, care of livestock, preparation of food for village community during festivals, taking care of the guests, and sowing and harvesting of food crops. The impact of the education and improved conditions of living some new works i.e. business, services, etc. Nowadays grinding of food items, collection of drinking water has been left out due to access to modern amenities. Adult female are seeking jobs in various departments that has changed the work distribution among them.

Children Male

During the old days there was no school so children used to participate in the works of the family. The important works assigned to the male children were to guard the agricultural fields, look after the smaller children, collection of firewood, hunting/fishing activities and domestic works. There is a remarkable change in the work distribution of the children since the statehood period in the area. Due to the introduction of educational institutions had more and more children started to go school for study. Nowadays no work is assigned to the children as they have to attend school except some help in the domestic works. As stated earlier, the impact is lesser in the remote villages due to the demands of the natural surroundings in comparison to the villages in more accessible places.

Children Female

The works assigned to the female children includes – taking care of the younger children, collection of firewood, collection of drinking water, collection of vegetables, collection of fodder for animals, washing clothes, guarding the agricultural fields, and they also take part in the household activities with the mother. After the statehood period emphasis is given in education so most of them are attending schools. As such the works assigned to them had started to decline but the works relating to the domestic activities like, cooking, washing, etc. are assigned to them in addition to the education. Nowadays there is no distinction in between the boys and girls for education that has declined the works performed by the female children during the past days.

The division of labour within the family in Aka society has changed with the passage of time and due to the influence of various factors like education, developmental activities, accessibility, etc. (Table 3.17). These factors had varied impacts on different environmental settings of the villages. Those areas that had lesser exposure to such factors had resulted in lesser changes in the work distribution whereas those areas with higher exposure to such factors had tremendously changed the division of labour among the adult male, female, children both male and female. Therefore, the geographical location of the settlements has played significant role in the changes in division of labour in the Aka area.

POPULATION GROWTH RATE

The two factors that influence the world's rate of population growth are fertility and mortality. At the scale of individual countries, a third factor – migration – also affects population growth. The population of a country rises because of births and immigrations of people from elsewhere in the world, while the population declines as a result of deaths and emigrations of people (Rubenstein 1992). Migration in context of the Akas is insignificant in the sense that it occurs rarely in the region. The important components involved in demographic studies are natural increase, fertility (crude birth rate), mortality (crude death rate, infant mortality rate), life expectancy, age-sex structure, demographic transition, etc. However, in a tribal inhabited area the proportion of scheduled tribe population to the total population also need full fledged discussion.

Table 3.17
Division of Labour in the Society

Period	*Adult Male*	*Adult Female*	*Children Male*	*Children Female*
Post Independence	1. Construction of house 2. Felling of big trees for jhum 3. Collection of firewood 4. Hunting/fishing activities 5. Construction of fence for fields 6. Carrying food grains to home 7. Guarding the village from enemies 8. Attending meetings 9. Settlement of disputes with the guests 10. Sowing and harvesting of food crops	1. Clearing of weeds in the field 2. Cooking food items 3. Collection of firewood 4. Taking care of the children 5. Collection of vegetables 6. Collection of drinking water 7. Grinding food items 8. Preparation of local wine 9. Care of livestock 10. Preparation of food for village community in festivals. 11. Taking care of the guests 12. Sowing and harvesting of food crops	1. To guard the agricultural fields 2. Look after the smaller children 3. Collection of firewood 4. Hunting/fishing activities 5. Domestic works	1. Taking care of the younger children 2. Collection of firewood 3. Collection of drinking water 4. Collection of vegetables 5. Collection of fodder for animals 6. Washing clothes 7. Guarding the agricultural fields 8. They also take part in the household activities with the mother

Table 3.17 (Contd. . . .)

Period	*Adult Male*	*Adult Female*	*Children Male*	*Children Female*
Statehood Onwards	1. Almost same some works are left out and new works are added such as business and contract. 2. Change in the works due to introduction of education	1. Clearing the weeds 2. Cooking food items 3. Preparation of rice beer 4. Collection of drinking water 5. Maintaining the strength of livestock 6. Taking care of the children 7. Left some activities due to improved conditions of life	1. Due to education and modernization of the society, lesser works are being assigned to the children 2. Children are mostly sent to School	1. Due to education and modernization of the society, lesser works are being assigned to the children 2. Education is given more emphasis
2000 Onwards	1. Business, contract, etc. (added) and guarding of village and some other works (declined) 2. Meetings and educating the children 3. War, hunting, fishing, etc. had declined.	1. Grinding, carrying water, etc. are excluded due to accessibility of modern tools. Besides some of the adult females are in profession so the working pattern had changed in the recent days.	1. Due to introduction of school education children are sent to schools for learning education 2. Works performed earlier had declined further.	1. Education becomes the highest priority for the children in the society 2. Works performed earlier had declined further 3. No distinction between boy and girl for education.

Source : Field Survey, 2006.

The total population of the Aka villages had remarkably increased during the past four decades starting from 1971 to 2001. The total population (including houseless and institutional population) was 4689 with total male population of 2896 and female population of 1793 in the year 1971. The population has increased to 5590 with male population of 3161 and female population of 2429 in the year 1981. The next decade experiences a higher rate of natural increase in the population, it has rose from 5590 to 9357 in 1991 with male population of 5191 and female population of 4166. The past decade from 1991 to 2001 experiences decline in the natural growth rate. The population has increased from 9357 to 11204 in 2001 with 5970 male and 5234 female populations. This trend of increase in population has been shown in Figure 3.15.

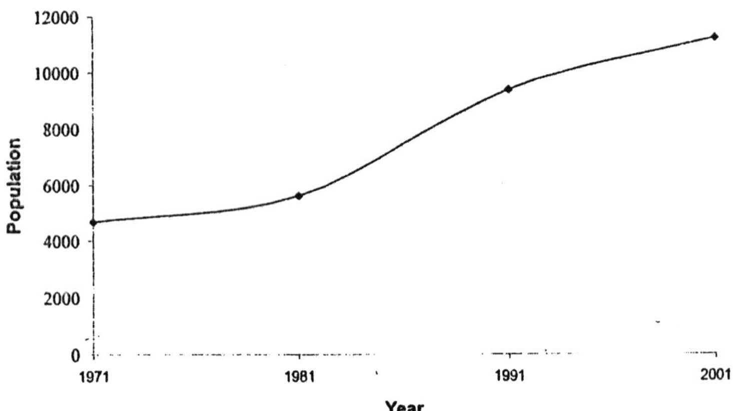

Fig. 3.15 : Total Population of Study Area (1971 to 2001).

Figure 3.15 indicates the increasing trend in population. However, the trend of growth is not maintaining a consistency in the decadal growth. The factors responsible for this may be as below:

- Some of the existing villages during 1971, 1981 and 1991 do not exist at present because those villages were General Reserve Engineering Force (GREF) labour camps and they are liable to move from one place to another. The examples of such villages are Labour camp at 2 km from Palizi towards Khupi (Hamlet), 7 km labour camp from Ziro point towards Khupi, etc.

- Advancement in education and awareness of family planning programmes.
- High Crude Death Rate during the decade due to diseases.
- Possibility of wrong enumeration of data during the census operation.

Population growth is the change in population over time, and can be quantified as the change in the number of individuals in a population per unit time. The term *population growth* can technically refer to any species, but almost always refers to humans, and it is often used informally for the more specific demographic term population growth rate and is often used to refer specifically to the growth of the population of the world. Simple models of population growth include the Malthusian Growth Model (The Malthusian growth model, sometimes called the simple exponential growth model, is essentially exponential growth based on a constant rate of compound interest). In demographics and ecology, Population Growth Rate (PGR) is the fractional rate at which the number of individuals in a population increases. Specifically, PGR ordinarily refers to the change in population over a specific time period expressed as a percentage of the number of individuals in the population at the beginning of that period. This can be written as the formula.

Growth Rate = [(births + immigration) – (deaths + emigration)]/Population

The crude death rate as defined above and applied to a whole population can give a misleading impression. For example, the number of deaths per 1000 people can be higher for developed nations than in less-developed countries, despite standards of health being better in developed countries. It is usually measured in a fraction or per cent in relation to the base population. The rate of population growth is the rate of natural increase combined with the effects of migration. Thus, a high rate of natural increase can be offset by a large net out-migration, and a low rate of natural increase can be countered by a high level of net in-migration. However, these migration effects on population growth rates are far smaller than the effects of changes in fertility and mortality.

The rate of population growth at any instant is given by the equation of exponential growth model :

$$\frac{dN}{dt} = rN$$

Where,

r is the rate of natural increase in

t some stated interval of time, and

N is the number of individuals in the population at a given instant.

The algebraic solution of this differential equation is $N = N_0e^{rt}$

Where,

N_0 is the starting population

N is the population after

a certain time, *t*, has elapsed, and

e is the constant 2.71828... (The base of natural logarithms)

Putting the population of Aka (2006) in the above algebraic exponential equation of growth rate, the population of 2007 is as below:

$$\begin{aligned} N &= N_0e^{rt} \\ &= 5027e^{(0.04018)\,(1)} \\ &= 5027\ (1.0409981) \\ &= 5233.0976 \\ &= 5233.10 \end{aligned}$$

Hence, the population will grow exponentially with a certain time't' has elapsed. The comparison of linear growth rate/natural increase rate and exponential growth rate of

Table 3.18
Comparison of Linear Growth Rate and Exponential Growth Rate

	Start	*Year 1*	*Year 2*	*Year 3*	*Year 4*	*Year 5*	*Year 6*	*Year 7*	*Year 8*	*Year 9*	*Year 10*
Natural Increase Rate	5027	5228.98	5430.97	5632.95	5834.94	6036.92	6238.91	6440.89	6642.88	6844.86	7046.85
Exponential Growth Rate	5027	5233.10	5447.64	5670.99	5903.49	6145.52	6397.47	6659.76	6932.80	7217.03	7512.91

population can be illustrated by the following table in 10 years time interval :

Doubling Times

The doubling time of a given population is calculated by the formula i.e. $N = N_0 \times 2$.

Putting this formula in the exponential growth equation, it is modified as $2N_0 = N_0e^{rt}$

Where,

$e^{rt} = 2$

rt = ln (natural logarithm) of 2 = 0.69

doubling time, $t = 0.69 / r$

So, the Aka population with an r of 4.018% (0.04018) at present has a doubling time

$t = 0.69/0.04018 = 17.17$ years.

Thus, at the prêsent rate of natural increase, the population of the Akas will double in approximately 17 years i.e. 10000 in 2024.

Natural Increase

Natural increase is the difference between the numbers of births and deaths in a population. The rate of natural increase of a given population is calculated by using the formula given below:

The Rate of Natural Increase (r) = Birth rate (b) — death rate (d)

The natural increase rate of the Aka population is calculated by putting the crude birth rate and crude death rate in the above mentioned formula as below:

Birth rate expressed as number of births per 1000 per year (49.73 as per the survey)

Death rate expressed as the number of deaths per 1000 per year (9.55 as per the survey)

So the rate of natural increase is 40.18 per thousand (0.04018 or 4.018%).

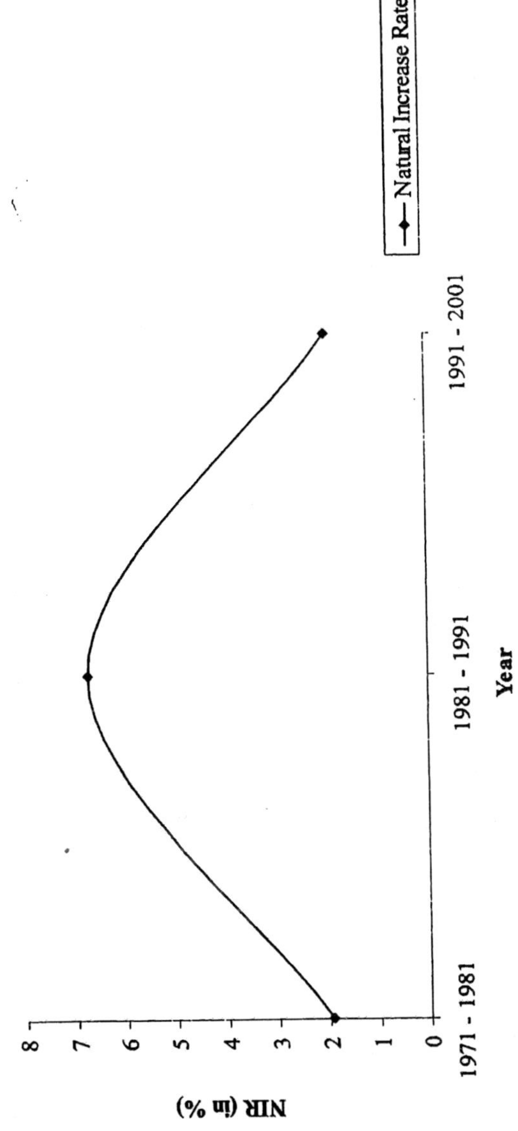

Fig. 3.16 : Natural Increase Rates of Study Area (1971 to 2001).

Although the value of *r* is affected by both birth rate and death rate, the recent history of the human population has been affected more by declines in death rates than by increases in birth rates. The rate of natural increase affects the doubling time, which is the number of years needed to double a population, assuming a constant rate of natural increase.

The natural increase rate for the decade 1971 to 1981 was 1.922% or 0.01922, resulting to an increase of 901 persons. A high rapid natural increase rate of 6.74% or 0.0674 has been achieved in the next decade of 1981 to 1991 that has added a total population of 3767. However, the natural increase rate again touched a lower rate of 1.974% or 0.01974 during the last decade in comparison to the earlier decades.

Proportion of Scheduled Tribe Population

Tribal peoples constitute 8.3% of the nation's total population, which is about 84 million people (2001 census). One concentration lives in a belt along the Himalayas stretching through Jammu and Kashmir, Himachal Pradesh, and Uttarakhand in the west, to Assam, Meghalaya, Tripura, Arunachal Pradesh, Mizoram, Manipur and Nagaland in the northeast. In the northeastern states of Arunachal Pradesh, Meghalaya, Mizoram and Nagaland, 90% of the population is tribal. However, in the remaining northeastern states of Assam, Manipur, Sikkim and Tripura, tribal peoples form between 20 to 30% of the population.

Another concentration lives in the hilly areas of central India (Chattisgarh, Madhya Pradesh, Orissa, and, to a lesser extent, Andhra Pradesh). This belt is bounded by the Narmada River to the north and the Godavari River to the southeast. Other tribals, including the Santals, live in Jharkhand and West Bengal. Central Indian states have the country's largest tribes, and, taken as a whole, roughly 75% of the total tribal population live there, although the tribal population there accounts for only around 10% of the region's total population. There are smaller numbers of tribal people in Karnataka, Tamil Nadu and Kerala in south India; in western India in Gujarat and Rajasthan, and in the union

Table 3.19

Village-wise Total Population (Including Institutional and Houseless Population) 1971 to 2001

	1971				1981		
Village	*Total*	*M*	*F*	*Village*	*Total*	*M*	*F*
1	2	3	4	5	6	7	8
Bana	68	37	31	Bana	91	49	42
Bana Camp	82	66	16	Bana Camp	118	74	44
Bhalukpong/Thrizino	794	599	195	Bhalukpong (H.Q)	549	344	205
Buragaon	291	173	118	Buragaon	200	111	89
Chizang	135	70	65	Chijang	120	65	55
Dedza	81	81	—	Dedza	100	50	50
Dijangania	287	139	148	Dizangania	245	128	117
Gijiri	60	31	29	Giziri	56	22	34
Gohainthan	66	33	33	Gohainthan	50	33	17
Husigaon	98	52	46	Husigaon	65	41	24
Jamiripoint/Noghupam	147	106	41	Jamiri Point	140	82	58
Jamiri Village	109	56	53	Jamiri	842	558	284
Karangania	108	55	53	Karangania	145	67	78
Kararamu	56	30	26	Kararamu	62	28	34

Table 3.19 (Contd. . . .)

1	2	3	4	5	6	7	8
Kichang	132	71	61	Kitchang	143	73	70
Moracca	32	13	19	Morakha	62	30	32
Palatari	149	75	74	Palatari	179	89	90
Pharizing	61	28	33	Phrizing	81	41	40
Pichang	387	202	185	Pitchang	305	147	158
Ramdagania	147	77	70	Ramdagania	69	38	31
Sakrin	205	95	110	Sakrin	189	94	95
Sessa	78	52	26	Sessa	196	127	69
Thesa	156	70	86	Thesa	60	26	34
Yayong	54	26	28	Yayong	100	48	52
Tania	64	40	24	Tania	54	26	28
				Tuluhu	20	8	12
				Thrizino HQ	285	164	121
				Elephant Flat	91	62	29
				Khamsiri	51	21	30
				Khupi – A	35	19	17
				Khupi – B	74	48	26
..	..	..	..	Kimi	36	19	17

Table 3.19 (Contd. . . .)

1	2	3	4	5	6	7	8
..	..	..	..	Palizi	240	127	113
..	..	..	..	Sapung	75	38	37
..	..	..	..	Tipi	49	32	17
..	..	..	..	Yashey	120	63	57
Bihupam	32	18	14	Bihupam	30	15	15
Tulu	94	51	43	Tulu	76	43	33
..	..	..	..	Bhorali River Camp	19	14	5
				8 Km Point from Khuppi to Tenga River	78	53	25
Huppipam / Dezling	609	500	109	..	..	..	..
Linia	30	12	18	..	..	..	..
..	..	..	..	Mopgramo	39	16	23
Rogupam	31	15	16	..	..	..	..
Rugugaon	18	9	9	..	..	..	..
Thesari	28	14	14	..	..	..	..
..	..	..	..	Sathi (64 KM)	8	4	4
..	..	..	..	3 KM Point towards Kimi	38	21	17
				34 KM Point from Nechiphu	5	2	3
Total	4689	2896	1793		5590	3161	2429

Table 3.19 (Contd. . . .)

1971				1981			
Village	*Total*	*M*	*F*	*Village*	*Total*	*M*	*F*
9	10	11	12	13	14	15	16
Bana Village	75	34	41	Bana Village	257	137	120
Bana Camp	441	260	181	Bana Camp	275	154	121
Lower Bhalukpong	1008	580	428	Lower Bhalukpong	2015	1184	831
Upper Bhalukpong	1157	750	407	Upper Bhalukpong	1555	817	738
Buragaon	345	179	166	Buragaon	308	157	151
Chijong	165	85	80	Chijang	128	63	65
Dedza	238	130	108	Dedza	105	56	49
Dizangoniapam (Hamlet)	20	8	12	Dizangania	29	15	14
Giziri	58	26	32	Giziri	67	31	36
Gohainthan	40	17	23	Gohainthan	47	19	28
Hussigaon	77	41	36	Hussigaon	50	26	24
Jamiri Point	418	262	156	Jamiri Point	217	120	97
Jamiri Village (including labour camp at 3 km)	228	117	111	Jamiri Village	141	72	69

Table 3.19 (Contd. . . .)

9	10	11	12	13	14	15	16
Karangonia	100	44	56	Karangania	136	60	76
Kararamu	69	27	42	Kararamu	60	23	37
Kitchang	116	70	46	Kitchang	79	42	37
Moorakka	19	11	8	Maraka	19	10	9
Palatary	135	73	62	Palatari	148	80	68
Phirizin	62	34	28	Pharizin	85	46	39
Pitchang	225	101	124	Pitchang	148	73	75
Ramdagonia	68	37	31	Ramdagania	100	55	45
Sakrin	218	109	109	Sakrin	242	130	112
Sessa	184	137	47	Sessa	124	72	52
Thesa	375	146	229	Thesa	200	99	101
Yayung	102	46	56	Yayung	90	46	44
..	..	..	..	Tania	59	25	34
Tuluhui	77	35	42	Tuluhi	73	28	45
Thrizino HQ	632	331	301	Thrizino HQ	815	386	429
Elephant Flat	257	157	100	Elephant Flat	135	77	58
Khamsiri (Hamlet)	10	4	6	Kamsiri	21	8	13

Table 3.19 (Contd. . . .)

9	10	11	12	13	14	15	16
Khupi forest office complex	66	42	24	Khupi forest office complex	40	22	18
Khupi model village	71	37	34	Khupi model Village	214	123	19
Khupi Det	32	14	18				
Kimi Forest office Complex	34	27	7	Kimi Village	115	72	43
Palizi	368	193	175	Palizi	652	367	285
Sapung	65	31	34	Sapong	70	29	41
Tipi	611	396	215	Tipi	966	529	437
Yangse	379	192	187	Yangse	518	254	264
Kaya Valley	115	58	57	Kaya Valley Village	100	54	46
Nechiphu Camp (Including labour camp at ½ Km)	194	74	120	Nechiphu	103	59	44
New Sapung	75	37	38	New Sapong	122	60	62
Pochung	46	28	18	Pochong	71	39	32
Sobu	181	92	89	Sube	131	65	66

Table 3.19 (Contd. . . .)

9	10	11	12	13	14	15	16
..	..	..	..	Baliphoo	98	45	53
..	..	..	..	Husago	96	48	48
..	..	..	..	Humethu (Humethu under Jamiri)	64	31	33
..	..	..	..	Jamiri H.Q.	116	62	54
Labour camp at 2 km from Palizi towards Khupi (Hamlet)	25	13	12	..	..	..	..
Rabang Rugo L camp (Hamlet)	5	3	2				
Saljipam (Hamlet)	22	8	14				
7 km labour camp from Ziro point towards Khupi	142	88	54				
Tenga dam site Labour Camp	7	7	..				
Total	9357	5191	4166		11204	5970	5234

Source : Census of India, 1971, 1981, 1991 and 2001.

DOT MAP SHOWING VILLAGE-WISE DISTRIBUTION OF POPULATION IN AKA VILLAGES (2001)

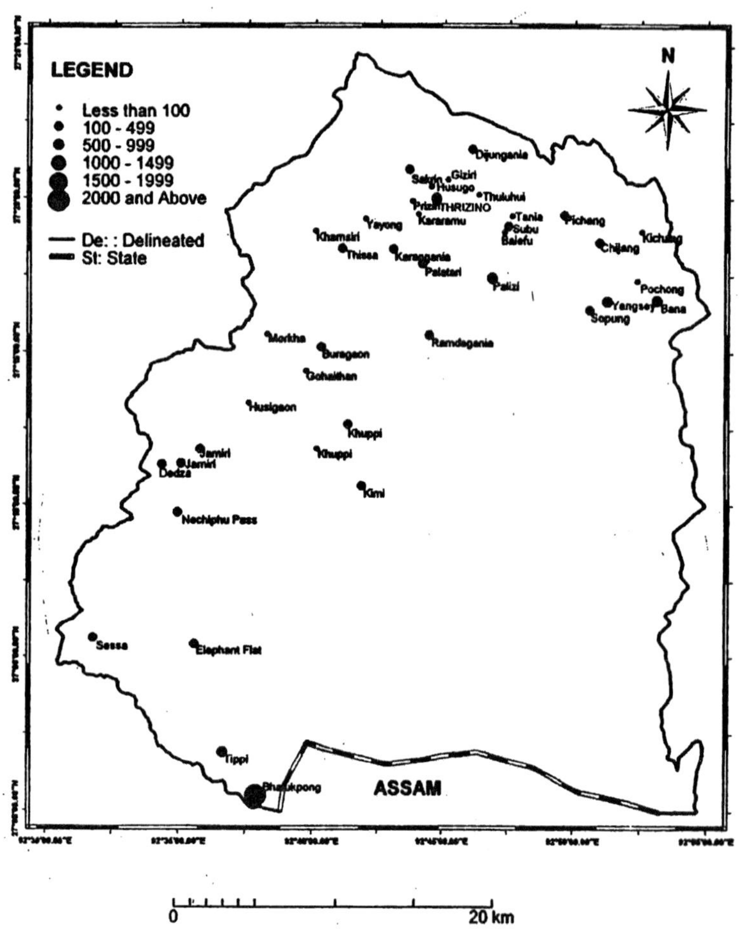

Fig. 3.17 : Distribution of total population in study area (2001).

territories of Lakshadweep and the Andaman Islands and Nicobar Islands. About one per cent of the populations of Kerala and Tamil Nadu are tribal, whereas tribal population is about six per cent in Andhra Pradesh and Karnataka.

Table 3.20

Village-wise Proportion of Scheduled Tribe Population (1971 to 2001)

1971				1981			
Village	*Total*	*M*	*F*	*Village*	*Total*	*M*	*F*
1	2	3	4	5	6	7	8
Bana	68	37	31	Bana	91	49	42
Bana Camp	..	..	..	Bana Camp	36	22	14
Bhalukpong/Thrizino	39	19	20	Bhalukpong (H.Q)	32	13	19
Buragaon	234	130	104	Buragaon	150	75	75
Chizang	135	70	65	Chijang	120	65	55
Dedza	..	..	..	Dedza	4	2	2
Dijangania	282	137	145	Dizangania	231	119	112
Gijiri	60	31	29	Giziri	56	22	34
Gohainthan	66	33	33	Gohainthan	39	22	17
Husigaon	80	36	44	Husigaon	37	20	17
Jamiripoint/Noghupam	32	17	15	Jamiri Point	15	10	5
Jamiri Village	102	52	50	Jamiri	207	103	104
Karangania	108	55	53	Karangania	145	67	78
Kararamu	56	30	26	Kararamu	62	28	34

Table 3.20 (Contd. . . .)

1	2	3	4	5	6	7	8
Kichang	132	71	61	Kitchang	139	72	67
Moracca	32	13	19	Morakha	62	30	32
Palatari	149	75	74	Palatari	178	88	90
Pharizing	61	28	33	Phrizing	81	41	40
Pichang	363	178	185	Pitchang	304	146	158
Ramdagania	143	73	70	Ramdagania	63	34	29
Sakrin	204	94	110	Sakrin	189	94	95
Sessa	..	..	..	Sessa	25	12	13
Thesa	156	70	86	Thesa	60	26	34
Yayong	54	26	28	Yayong	98	46	52
Tania	64	40	24	Tania	54	26	28
			..	Tuluhu	20	8	12
				Thrizino HQ	125	57	68
				Elephant Flat	8	5	3
				Khamsiri	51	21	30
				Khupi – A	5	3	2
				Khupi – B	1	1	..
..	..	..	..	Kimi	36	19	17
..	..	..	..	Palizi	182	88	94

Table 3.20 (Contd. . . .)

1	*2*	*3*	*4*	*5*	*6*	*7*	*8*
..	..	..	..	Sapung	75	38	37
			..	Tipi	6	3	3
..	..	..	..	Yashey	78	32	46
Bihupam	32	18	14	Bihupam	30	15	15
Tulu	94	51	43	Tulu	76	43	33
				Bhorali River Camp			
				8 Km Point from Khuppi to Tenga River	13	5	8
Huppipam/Dezling	89	42	47				
..	..	..	..				
Linia	30	12	18				
				..	..	..	..
..	..	..	..	Mopgramo	39	16	23

Table 3.20 (Contd. . . .)

1	2	3	4	5	6	7	8
Rogupam	31	15	16	..	..	..	..
Rugugaon	18	9	9	..	..	..	..
Thesari	28	14	14	..	..	..	..
		..		Sathi (64 KM)	8	4	4
				3 KM Point towards Kimi	4	2	2
				34 KM Point from Nechiphu	4	1	3
..	..	..	..	..	..	..	..
Total	2942	1476	1466		3239	1593	1646

Table -3.20 (Contd. . . .)

Village	1971 Total	1971 M	1971 F	Village	1981 Total	1981 M	1981 F
9	10	11	12	13	14	15	16
Bana Village	75	34	41	Bana Village	249	134	115
Bana Camp	277	149	128	Bana Camp	221	122	99
Lower Bhalukpong	173	85	88	Lower Bhalukpong	463	244	219
Upper Bhalukpong	145	84	61	Upper Bhalukpong	411	211	200
Buragaon	268	128	140	Buragaon	275	135	140
Chijong	161	83	78	Chijang	123	61	62
Dedza	20	12	8	Dedza	3	3	0
Dizangoniapam (Hamlet)	20	8	12	Dizangania	29	15	14
Giziri	58	26	32	Giziri	67	31	36
Gohaithan	40	17	23	Gohainthan	47	19	28
Hussigaon	59	29	30	Hussigaon	50	26	24
Jamiri Point	65	30	35	Jamiri Point	89	45	44
Jamiri Village (including labour camp at 3 km)	169	82	87	Jamiri Village	125	63	62

Table 3.20 (Contd. . . .)

9	10	11	12	13	14	15	16
Karangonia	97	43	54	Karangania	135	59	76
Kararamu	69	27	42	Kararamu	60	23	37
Kitchang	115	69	46	Kitchang	78	41	37
Moorakka	19	11	8	Maraka	19	10	9
Palatary	132	70	62	Palatari	146	79	67
Phirizin	62	34	28	Pharizin	85	46	39
Pitchang	222	98	124	Pitchang	148	73	75
Ramdagonia	68	37	31	Ramdagania	100	55	45
Sakrin	218	109	109	Sakrin	241	129	112
Sessa	29	19	10	Sessa	62	38	24
Thesa	196	90	106	Thesa	200	99	101
Yayung	101	45	56	Yayung	90	46	44
..	..	..	..	Tania	59	25	34
Tuluhui	77	35	42	Tuluhi	73	28	45
Thrizino HQ	398	174	224	Thrizino HQ	521	226	295
Elephant Flat	40	20	20	Elephant Flat	63	31	36
Khamsiri (Hamlet)	10	4	6	Kamsiri	21	8	13

Table 3.20 (Contd. . . .)

9	10	11	12	13	14	15	16
Khupi forest office complex	12	5	7	Khupi forest office complex	37	19	18
Khupi model village	71	37	34	Khupi model village	146	74	72
Khupi Det	12	6	6				
Kimi Forest office Complex	..	..	..	Kimi Village	74	46	28
Palizi	271	132	139	Palizi	333	164	169
Sapung	65	31	34	Sapong	70	29	41
Tipi	100	57	43	Tipi	359	177	182
Yangse	244	106	138	Yangse	446	206	240
Kaya Valley	112	56	56	Kaya Valley Village	100	54	46
Nechiphu Camp (Including labour camp at ½ Km)	1	1		Nechiphu	14	6	8
New Sapung	45	24	21	New Sapong	95	44	51
Pochung	46	28	18	Pochong	65	33	32
Sobu	172	85	87	Sube	123	60	63
..				Baliphoo	98	45	53
..	..	..	..	Husago	96	48	48

Table 3.20 (Contd. . . .)

9	*10*	*11*	*12*	*13*	*14*	*15*	*16*
..	..	..	..	Humethu (Humethu under Jamiri)	40	18	22
..	..	..	..	Jamiri H.Q.	58	30	28
Labour camp at 2 km from Palizi towards Khupi (Hamlet)	6	3	3	..	..	..	
Rabang Rugo L camp (Hamlet)	5	3	2	..	..		
Saljipam (Hamlet)	22	8	14				..
7 km labour camp from Ziro point towards Khupi						..	
Tengadam site Labour Camp		..	..	..	..	..	..
	4567	2234	2333		6407	3178	3233

Source: Census of India, 1971, 1981, 1991 and 2001.

The proportion of Scheduled tribe population to the total population of the Aka villages shows a slower growth rate during 1971 to 1981. The total ST population in the year 1971 was 2942 which increased to 3239 in 1981 with a natural increase rate of 1.01% or 0.0101. The next decade shows a higher rate of 4.1% or 0.041 and the population increased from 3239 to 4567 in 1991. During the last decade there is a slight decline in the rate leading to 4.03% or 0.0403 and the population has increased from 4567 to 6407 in the year 2001. The village-wise distribution of ST population from 1971 to 2001 is shown in Table 3.20.

The percentage of scheduled tribe population in the Aka area in the past four decades shows ups and downs. During 1971 the ST population was 2942 out of the total population of 4689 that accounts for 62.74%. There is a decline in the percentage of ST population in the year 1981 to 54.55%. It has declined again in 1991 to 50.61%, the lowest in the past four decades. However, the recent decade shows an increase in the percentage of ST population in the area accounting to 57.18% in 2001. The lower percentage of ST population during 1981 and 1991 could be due to the higher rate of influx of labours from the other parts of the country in the area. The timber and other medicinal plants extraction was at its peak during these decades which had led to the lower percentage of ST population in the area. Mostly the wood sawing work is done by Kacharis, Assamese, Adivasis, Nepalese, etc. who had settled in temporary huts for earning their living. As the total population taken by the census includes the institutional and houseless population, it is possible that a good share of population belongs to these groups during those decades. The rise in the percentage of ST population again in 2001 could be due to the ruling of Supreme Court in 1996 to ban timber extraction in the state. After the ban on timber extraction those labourers might had receded back to their own villages or other parts of the state in search of work. The proportion of scheduled tribe population in the Aka inhabited area during the past four decades is shown in Table 3.21.

Table 3.21
Proportion of Scheduled Tribe Population to the Total Population (1971 to 2001)

1971			*1981*			*1991*			*2001*		
Total	*ST*	*%*	*Total*	*ST*	*%*	*Total*	*ST*	*%*	*Total*	*ST*	*%*
4689	2942	62.74	5937	3239	54.55	9023	4567	50.61	11204	6407	57.18

Source: Census of India, 1971, 1981, 1991 and 2001.

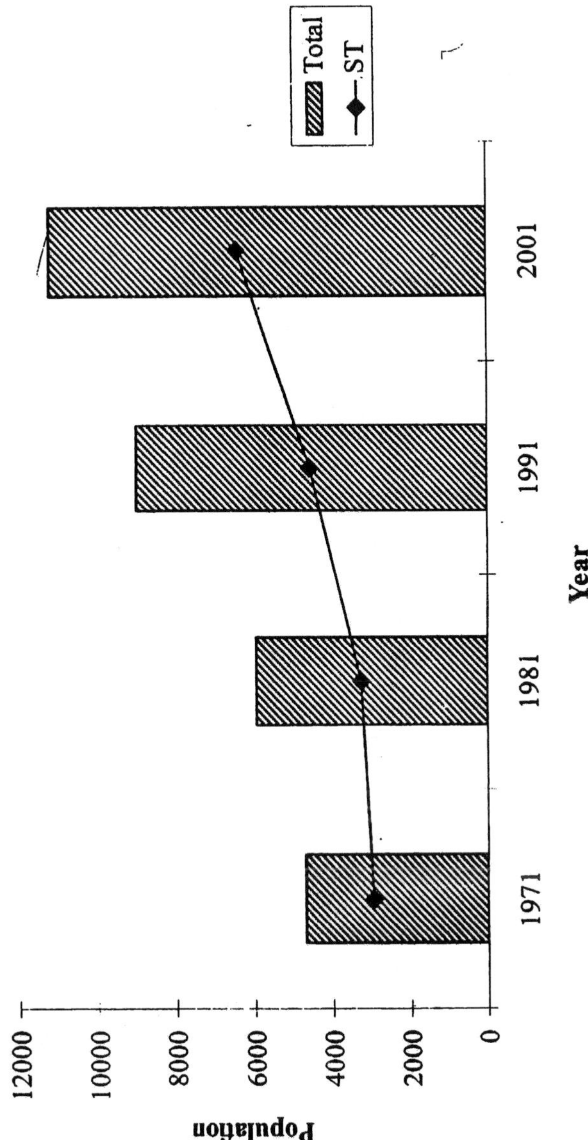

Fig. 3.18 : Proportion of Scheduled Tribe Population to the Total Population (1971 to 2001).

Out of the total population (including institutional and houseless population) of 11204, the proportion of ST population is 6407 which accounts for 57.18% of the total population (2001 census). This shows that the proportion of ST population in the area is much lesser than the state average of 63.7%. This figure clearly indicates the higher rate of influx of outsiders in the area. The villages which are away from the road connectivity like Dijangania, Giziri, Gohaithan, Husigaon, Kararamu, Morkha, Prizin, Pitchang, Thissa, Yayong, Tania, Khamsiri, Sopung, Kaya Valley, Balefu, Janapam, Saljipam and Husugo have 100% ST population and the rest of the villages which are connected with roads and emerging as a small town have lesser ST population. The most important examples of such settlements includes - Bhalukpong (24.48%), Thrizino (63.92%), Jamiri (57.38%), Buragaon (89.28%), Palizi (51.07%), Yangsey (86.10%), Khuppi (69.65%), Tipi (37.16%), Elephant Flat (46.66%), Sessa (50%), Dedza (2.86%), New Sopung (77.87%), Kimi Village (64.35%), Nechiphu (13.59%), Humethu (62.5%), etc. Apart from this some of the villages have more than 90% of ST population i.e. Chijang, Karangania, Kitchang, Palatari, Ramdagania, Sakrin, Pochong, Subu and Kadeya.

Most of the villages are inhabited by the Akas themselves, but there are some villages especially the circle headquarters, towns, and the villages located along the main road have mixed up population of scheduled tribe belonged to other ethnic group. The circle headquarters like – Thrizino, Jamiri and Bhalukpong have more proportion of other ethnic people belonging to Nishis (Bangnis), Dhammai (Mijis), Monpas, Buguns (Khowas), Sherdukpens, etc. The percentage of Aka population in Bhalukpong is lower than the population of other tribes of the state. Some families of Apatanis, Galos, Adis, etc. are also found to be settled down in Bhalukpong. Apart from these circle headquarters, the settlements along the main roads like Tipi, Elephant Flat, Sessa, Nechiphu, Jamiri camp, Nag Mandir, Khuppi, Palizi, Balefu, Subu, Yangsey and Bana have some population belonging to one or the other tribes mentioned above. The commencement of

Kameng Hydro Power Project in the area had also invited lots of other ethnic groups to settle down permanently.

The proportion of Aka population to the total population and ST population is highly remarkable. The total Aka population was 2333 in the year 1971 which increased to 2947 in 1981 with a natural increase rate of 2.632%. There has been slight decline in the natural increase rate falling to 1.98% from 1981 to 1991. The total population increased to 3531 in the year 1991. In the absence of tribe-wise population census in the 2001, the data has been supplemented by the survey data of 2006. As per the survey the population reached 5027 in the year 2006 since 1991 with a natural increase rate of 2.648%. Hence, the Aka population (Plate 3.1) is constantly growing throughout the decades with slight movements in the Natural increase rates. The natural increase rates and proportion of Aka population to the total ST population is shown in Figure 3.19 and 3.20.

The total population of 5027 as per the survey conducted in 2006 has a share of 44.87% to the total population of 11204 (2001 census) and 78.46% to that of total ST population of 6407 (2001 census). The percentage of Aka population in terms of individual settlements is highly uneven, some of the settlements having zero (0) Aka population. Dedza and Nechiphu villages have zero Aka population and Sessa, Nag Mandir, Bana and Tipi has less than 1% of Aka population to the total population and less than 5% to the total ST population. These villages are being inhabited by either labourers of GREF or non-Aka population of Arunachal Pradesh. The percentage of Aka population in Bhalukpong to the total population is 6.50% only and 26.54% to the total ST population. The remaining villages have a good percentage of population to the total population and ST population averaging to 80 – 90%. The village-wise Aka population as per the survey is shown in Table 3.23 and Figure 3.21.

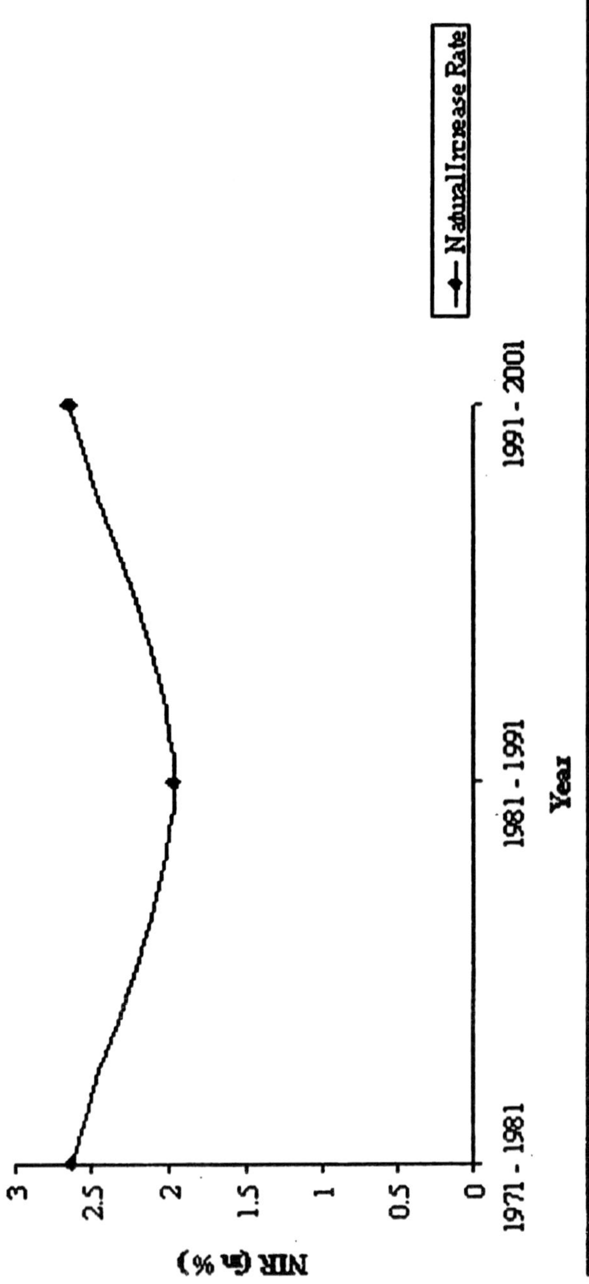

Fig. 3.19 : Natural Increase Rates of the Total Aka Population (1971 to 2006).

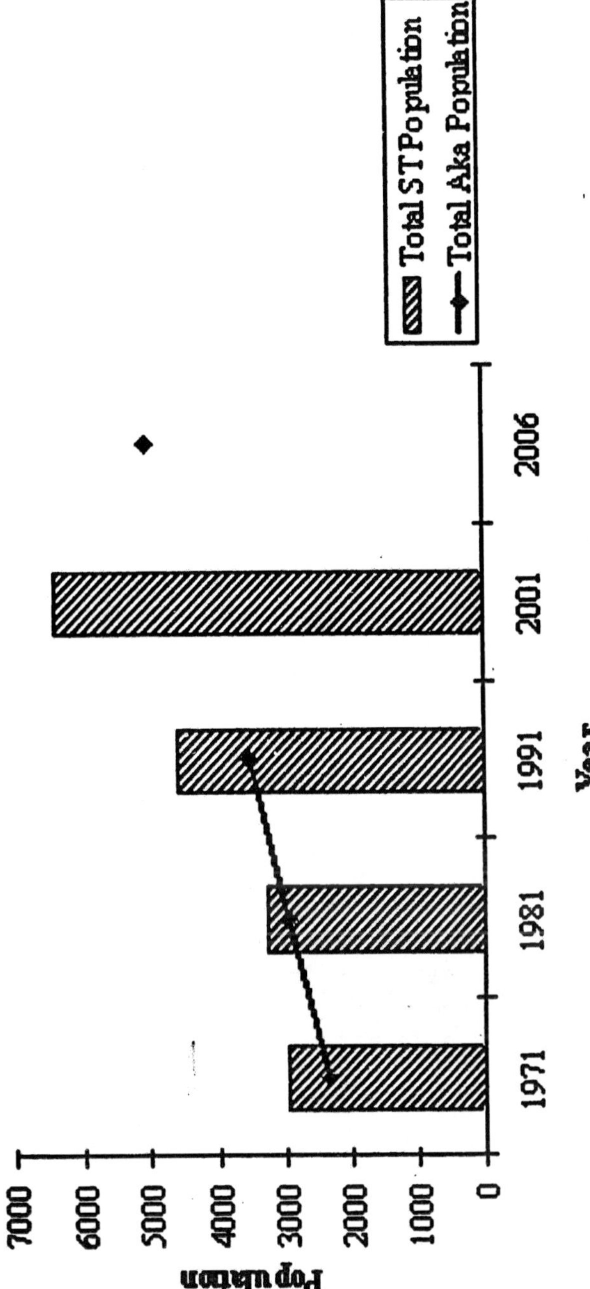

Fig. 3.20 : Proportion of Total Aka Population to the Total ST Population (1971 to 2006).

PLATE NO. 3.1 : DEMOGRAPHIC COMPOSITION

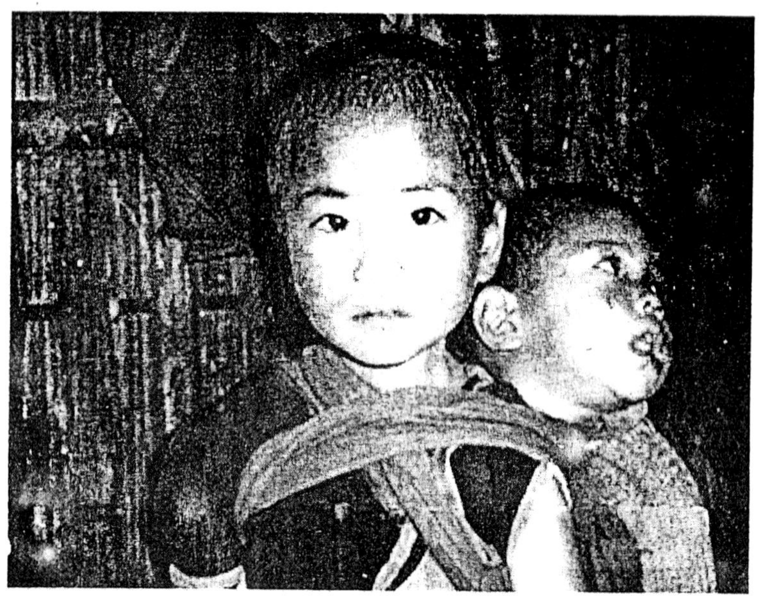

(a)

(b)

(a)

(d)

(e)

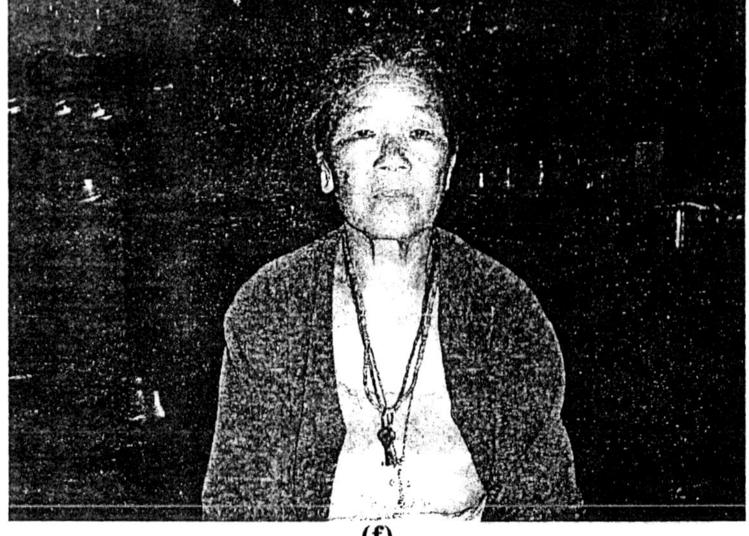

(f)

(g)

(h)

(i)

Photo : (a) A small girl carrying her sister on back, (b) A small boy carrying rice for the family from Thrizino to Yayong (20 kms approx.), (c) Best friends – Aka children roaming on the streets of Thrizino, (d) Oldest woman alive during 2006 survey (Buragaon), (e) Old age pensioner women of Yayong village, (f) An old Christian lady of Palizi village, (g) A retired employee of Yayong Village, (h) Villagers of Kararamu interacting with the investigator, (i) An old man of Buragaon (Ducha Dususow).

Table 3.22
Proportion of Aka Population to the Scheduled Tribe Population (1971 to 2001)

1971			1981			1991			2001	2006	
ST	*Aka*	%	*ST*	*Aka*	%	*ST*	*Aka*	%	*ST*	*Aka*	%
2942	2333	79.29	3239	2947	90.98	4567	3531	77.32	6407	5027	78.46

Source : Census of India, 1971, 1981, 1991, 2001 and 2006.

Table 3.23
Village-wise Distribution of Aka Population (as per the Field Survey, 2006)

Sl. No.	*Village*	*No. of Household*	*Total*	*Male*	*Female*
1	2	3	4	5	6
1.	Balefu	12	70	31	39
2.	Bana	4	12	7	5
3.	Bhalukpong	49	232	124	108
4.	Buragaon	51	282	146	136
5.	Chijang	26	142	68	74
6.	Dijungania	24	150	74	76
7.	Elephant Flat	8	49	22	27
8.	Giziri	14	82	38	44
9.	Gohainthan	4	33	13	20
10.	Husigaon	21	113	52	61
11.	Husugo	19	76	40	36
12.	Jamiri	36	231	113	118
13.	Janapam	4	27	15	12
14.	Kadeya	25	164	85	79
15.	Karangania	17	140	66	74
16.	Kararamu	21	120	54	66
17.	Khamsiri	1	7	3	04
18.	Khuppi	33	216	100	116
19.	Kichang	7	68	36	32
20.	Kimi	23	104	47	57
21.	Morkha	08	34	20	14
22.	Nag Mandir	1	4	2	02
23.	Palatari	17	142	82	60
24.	Palizi	50	323	158	165
25.	Pichang	26	117	68	49
26.	Pochong	13	73	39	34
27.	Prizin	15	90	48	42
28.	Ramdagania	14	74	38	36
29.	Sakrin	35	207	113	94
30.	Saljipam	4	28	13	15
31.	Sopung	30	205	101	104
32.	Subu	26	161	78	83
33.	Tania	11	66	32	34
34.	Thissa	28	186	92	94
35.	Thrizino	81	460	222	238
36.	Thuluhui	13	66	32	34

1	2	3	4	5	6
37.	Tipi	3	9	5	4
38.	Yangsey	66	340	166	174
39.	Yayong	22	127	66	61
	Total	**862**	**5027**	**2506**	**2521**

Source : Field Survey, 2006

DOT MAP SHOWING VILLAGE-WISE DISTRIBUTION OF AKA POPULATION (2006)

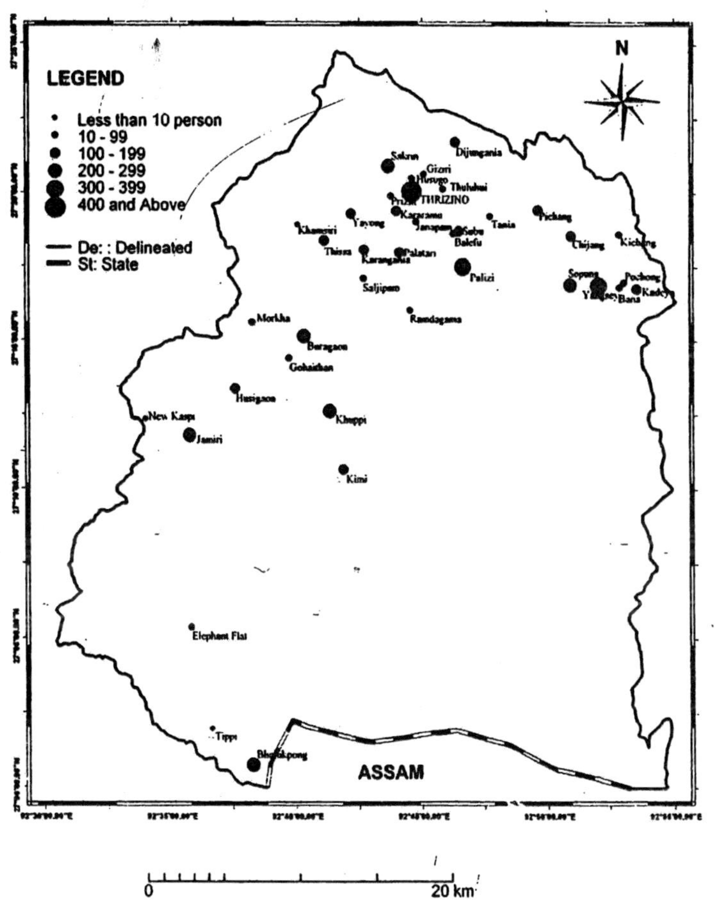

Fig. 3.21 : Distribution of total Aka population (2006).

FERTILITY/CRUDE BIRTH RATE

The crude birth rate is defined as the annual number of live births per thousand people. In demography, the Crude Birth Rate (CBR) of a population is the number of childbirths per 1,000 persons per year. It can be mathematically represented as :

$$CBR = \frac{n}{p}1000$$

Where, n is the number of childbirths in that year and p is the current population. This figure is combined with the crude death rate to produce the rate of natural population growth (do not take into account the net migration).

Another indicator of fertility that is frequently used by geographers is the total fertility rate to measure the number of births in a society. The total fertility rate is the average number of children a woman will have throughout her child-bearing years (roughly fifteen to forty-nine). The crude birth rate provides a picture of a society as a whole in a given year while the total fertility rate attempts to predict the future child-bearing capacity of an individual woman. In general, the total fertility rate is a better indicator of (current) fertility rates because unlike the crude birth rate it is not affected by the age distribution of the population. Fertility rates tend to be higher in less economically developed countries and lower in more economically developed countries.

Other Methods of Measuring Birth Rate

- General Fertility Rate (GFR) - It is the annual number of live births per 1000 women of child-bearing age (often taken to be from 15 to 49 years old, but sometimes from 15 to 44).
- Age-specific fertility rate is the annual number of live births per 1000 women in particular age groups (usually age 15-19, 20-24 etc.).
- Standardized Birth Rate (SBR) - This compares the age-sex structure to a hypothetical standard population.

Factors Affecting Birth Rate

- Pro-natalist policies and Anti-natalist policies from government (Natalism is the belief that human reproduction is the basis for individual existence).

Pro-natalism is an attitude or an ideology promoting child-bearing with emergent sub-replacement fertility and a corresponding demographic transition well underway in Europe and Japan leading towards smaller, older populations, some governments implement interventionist policies, incentivising larger families.

- Abortion rates
- Existing age – sex structure
- Social and religious beliefs – especially in relation to contraception
- Female literacy levels
- Economic prosperity (although in theory when the economy is doing well families can afford to have more children in practice the higher the economic prosperity the lower the birth rate).
- Poverty levels – children can be seen as an economic resource in developing countries as they can earn money. (child labour)
- Infant Mortality Rate – a family may have more children if a country's IMR is high as it is likely some of those children will die.
- Urbanization
- Typical age of marriage
- Pension availability
- Conflict

The crude birth rate of the Aka population is worked out by putting the data in the given formula:

$$CBR = \frac{n}{p} 1000$$

$$CBR = \frac{250}{5027} 1000$$

$$CBR = 49.73$$

The crude birth rate has been found as 49.73 live births per thousand persons for the year 2006-2007 as per the field survey. The birth rate is higher than the national average of 23.8 and that of the state's average of 23.3. The population is growing at a faster rate than the other tribes of the state due to lesser exposure and low literacy rate.

Mortality/Crude Death Rate

The crude death rate is the annual number of deaths per 1000 people. Mortality rate is a measure of the number of deaths (in general, or due to a specific cause) in some population, of an ongoing treatment, or a significant length of time after an acute treatment.

Note that the crude death rate as defined above and applied to a whole population can give a misleading impression. For example, the number of deaths per 1000 people can be higher for developed nations than in less-developed countries, despite standards of health being better in developed countries. This is because developed countries have relatively older people, who are more likely to die in a given year, so that the overall mortality rate can be higher even if the mortality rate at any given age is lower. A more complete picture of mortality is given by a life table which summarizes mortality separately at each age. A life table is necessary to give a good estimate of life expectancy.

Factors Affecting Crude Death Rate

- Age of country's population
- Nutrition levels

- Standards of diet and housing
- Access to clean drinking water
- Hygiene levels
- Levels of violent crime
- Conflicts
- Number of doctors

According to the World Health Organization, the leading causes of death in 2002 were:

- 12.6% Ischaemic heart disease
- 9.7% Cerebrovascular disease
- 6.8% Lower respiratory infections
- 4.9% HIV/AIDS
- 4.8% Chronic obstructive pulmonary disease
- 3.2% Diarrhoeal diseases
- 2.7% Tuberculosis
- 2.2% Trachea/bronchus/lung cancers
- 2.1% Road traffic accidents

However, the causes of death vary greatly between developed and developing countries. Some of the causes that occupy higher percentage for death occur in the developed countries more and lesser in developing countries. The developed countries produce more pollutants due to highly sophisticated machines and chemicals. Some causes like HIV/AIDS, Diarrhoeal diseases, Tuberculosis, etc. mostly occur in the developing countries where illiteracy and poverty are highly perceptible. India is a developing country and the leading causes as mentioned above of death are evident in all the parts of the country. The crude death rate of the Aka people is calculated by putting the data in the following formula:

$$CDR = \frac{n}{p}1000$$

$$CDR = \frac{48}{5027} 1000$$

$$CDR = 9.55$$

where, n is the number of deaths per 1000 person

p is the current population.

By putting the population data in the formula given above the crude death rate of the Akas has been calculated as 9.55 per 1000 persons in a year. This figure is higher in comparison to the national average of 7.6 and that of the states average of 5/1000 persons. The causes for higher death rate are due to inaccessibility to better medicinal facilities, low nutrient intake, alcoholism, epidemics, etc. The villages are located far from the health sub-centers that too without any road connectivity, hence during the emergency cases i.e. outbreak of epidemic diseases like – diarrhoea, viral fever, jaundice, pneumonia, etc. more death cases are reported from such villages. Geographers also compute different death rates for specific age groups or for males and females.

Infant Mortality Rate (IMR)

Another useful measure of mortality is the infant mortality rate, which is the annual number of deaths of children less than 1 year old per 1000 live births. Infant mortality is the death of infants in the first year of life. The most common cause of infant mortality worldwide has traditionally been dehydration from diarrhea. Because of the success of spreading information about Oral Rehydration Solution (a mixture of salts, sugar and water) to mothers around the world, the rate of children dying from dehydration has been decreasing and has become the second most common cause in the late 1990s. Currently the most common cause is pneumonia. Major causes of infant mortality in more developed countries include congenital malformation, infection and SIDS (Sudden Infant Death Syndrome). Infanticide, abuse abandonment and neglect may also contribute to infant mortality.

Statistical Categories of Infant Mortality Rate

- Perinatal mortality includes deaths between the foetal viability (28 weeks gestation) and the end of the 7th day after delivery
- Neonatal mortality includes deaths in the first 27 days of life
- Child mortality includes deaths within the first five years after birth.

Infant Mortality Rate (IMR) is the number of newborns dying under a year of age divided by the number of live births during the year. The infant mortality rate is also called the infant death rate. In past times, infant mortality claimed a considerable percentage of children born, but the rates have significantly declined in the West in modern times, mainly due to improvements in basic health care, though high technology medical advances have also helped. Infant mortality rate is commonly included as a part of standard of living evaluations in economics.

The infant mortality rate is reported as number of live newborns dying under a year of age per 1,000 live births, so that IMRs from different countries can be compared. A good source for the most recent IMRs as well as Under 5 Mortality Rates (U5MR) is the UNICEF publication 'The State of the World's Children' For example; the worst U5MR is 284 in Sierra Leone. (That is, 28% of all children born die before they turn 5 years old.) The 29 countries with the highest U5MRs are in Africa. The U5MR of the United States is 8, and there are 31 countries with lower U5MRs, although many of those use a less stringent definition of mortality than the US. Sweden's is among the lowest at 3. Nearly two orders of magnitude separate countries with the highest and lowest reported infant mortality rates. The top and bottom five countries by this measure (taken from the The World Fact Book's 2007 estimates) are shown below:

Table 3.24
Top and Bottom Five Countries (Infant Mortality Rates)

Rank	*Country*	*IMR (deaths/1000 live births)*
1	Angola	184.44
2	Sierra Leone	158.27
3	Afghanistan	157.43
4	Liberia	149.73
5	Niger	116.83
217	Iceland	3.27
218	Hong Kong	2.94
219	Japan	2.80
220	Sweden	2.76
221	Sigapore	2.30

Source: The World Fact Book's estimates, 2007.

It is usually difficult to estimate the number of person/years lived for children <1 year old (infants). Consequently, the total number of live births is often used as the denominator to calculate the infant mortality rate. The total number of deaths among children <1 year old in a calendar year is divided by the live births in the same year, multiplied by 1000. Calculating the infant mortality rate in this way makes it more appropriately referred to as a ratio. Thus, the infant mortality rate of the Aka population is calculated as:

Total number of deaths among children < 1 year old in 2005-2006 = 23

Total number of live births in 2006 = 25

Therefore, $\text{IMR} = \frac{23}{250} \times 1000$ = 92

The infant mortality rate which is 92 among the Akas is higher in comparison to the national rate i.e. 65 in 2002. The higher rate of mortality in the area is due to inaccessibility, low nutrient content in diet of mother, poor medical facilities, poverty, illiteracy, etc. Mostly, children of this age die due to diseases like diarrhea, typhoid, jaundice, malaria, chicken pox, etc. The far flung location of the villages from the health sub-centers causes death of children before reaching to the hospitals.

DEMOGRAPHIC TRANSITION

The questions like why does Sweden, one of the world's wealthiest nations, have a crude death rate higher than Thailand, one of the poorest? Why does the United States, with its extensive system of hospitals and physicians, have a higher crude death rate than Costa Rica or Panama? The answer is that the population of different countries is at various stages in a process known as demographic transition. Every region whether big or small experiences changes over time in its natural increase rate, fertility rate and mortality rate. The process of change in a society's population is called the demographic transition. It is a process with several stages, and every country is in one of the stages. This process has a beginning, middle and end, and – baring a catastrophe such as a nuclear war – it is irreversible. Once a country moves from one stage of the process to the next it does not revert to an earlier stage.

Stage 1

In stage 1 of the demographic transition the crude birth and death rates are both generally high. These rates may vary considerably from one year to the next but over the long term are roughly comparable. As a result, the rate of natural increase is very low. Survival is unpredictable in a stage 1 society. The population may depend on hunting and gathering for food. When food is easily obtained, the population increases; in times of shortage, the population decreases. People who practice settled farming prosper during abundant harvests and suffer when unfavourable climatic conditions result in low output. Wars and diseases also take their toll on the death rate in a stage 1 society. Most of human history was spent in stage 1 of the demographic transition, but today no such society remains. Every country has moved on to at least stage 2 of the demographic transition.

Stage 2

The crude death rate suddenly plummets, while the crude birth rate remains roughly the same as in stage 1. Because the difference between the crude birth rate and crude death rate is very high, the rate of natural increase is also very high. Some demographers divide this stage into two parts. The first part is the period of accelerating population growth. The second part is when the growth rate begins to slow, though the gap between births and deaths remains high. Some countries in Europe and North America entered this stage during the late eighteenth or nineteenth century. New technology permits increases in the permanent food supply and control of diseases which accounts for the rapid decline in the crude death rate. The countries in Africa, Asia and Latin America reached this stage in the twentieth century only.

Stage 3

In stage 3 the crude birth rate begins to drop sharply. The crude death rate continues to fall but at a much slower rate than in stage 2. The population continues to grow because the crude birth rate is still higher than the crude death rate. The natural increase or the gap between the crude birth and death rates narrows in compare to the stage 2. The European and North American countries moved from stage 2 to stage 3 of the demographic transition during the first half of the twentieth century. In recent years some countries in Africa, Asia and Latin America have also moved to stage 3. The sudden drop in the crude birth rate during the stage 3 is due to changes in social customs unlike the introduction of new technology into the society in stage 2 that led to rapid decline of the crude death rate.

Stage 4

A country reaches stage 4 of the demographic transition when the crude birth rate declines to the point where it equals the crude death rate, and the natural increase rate approaches 0 (zero). Zero Population Growth (ZPG) is a term often used for the stage 4 countries. Such condition may occur when the crude birth rate is still slightly higher than the crude death rate, because some females die before reaching child-bearing years and the number of females in their child-bearing years can vary. To account for these discrepancies, zero population growth is frequently expressed as the total fertility rate that results in a lack of change in the total population over a long-term. At this time, a total fertility rate of approximately 2.1 usually produces ZPG. However, a country experiencing a high level of immigration may need a lower total fertility rate to achieve ZPG. Several countries in Western and Northern Europe have reached stage 4 of the demographic transition, including Sweden, Germany, and the United Kingdom. The diagram (Fig. 3.22) shows the model of demographic transition.

The demographic statistics of the Aka area has entered the stage 2 of demographic transition. As per the survey data of 2006, the area has a high crude birth rate of 49.73/1000 and a low crude death rate of 9.55/1000. Hence, the difference between the crude birth rate and crude death rate is very high i.e. 39.79%. The increase in level of technology had solved many problems of food supply and the advancement in medicines had resulted in decline of crude death rate while the crude birth remains high leading to higher population growth.

Age Sex Distribution

Perhaps the most fundamental of demographic characteristics is the age distribution of a population. Demographers commonly use population pyramids to describe both age and sex distributions of populations. A population pyramid is a bar chart or graph in which the length of each horizontal bar represents the number (or percentage) of persons in an age group; for example, the base of such a chart consists of a bar representing the youngest segment of the population, those persons less than, say, five years old. Each bar is divided into segments corresponding to the numbers (or proportions) of males and females. In most populations

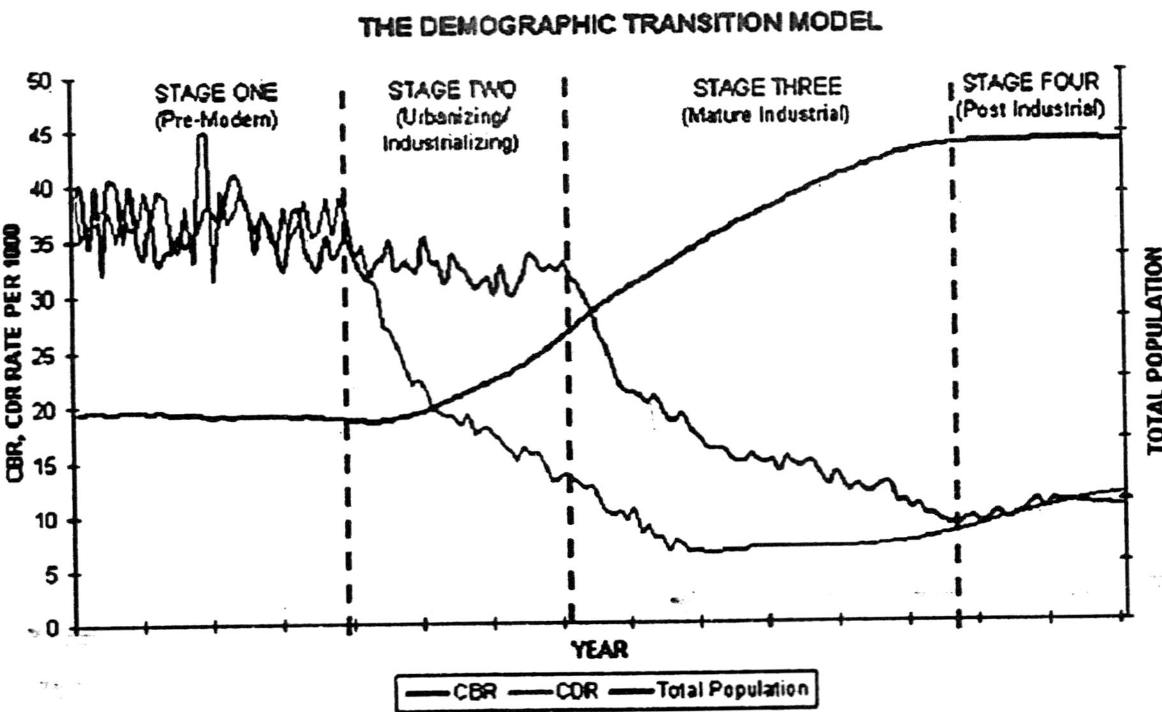

Source : Keith Montgomery, Dept. of Geography and Geology, University of Wisconsin, USA.

Fig. 3.22 : The Demographic Transition Model.

the proportion of older persons is much smaller than that of the younger, so the chart narrows toward the top and is more or less triangular, like the cross section of a pyramid; hence the name. Youthful populations are represented by pyramids with a broad base of young children and a narrow apex of older people, while older populations are characterized by more uniform numbers of people in the age categories. Population pyramids reveal markedly different characteristics for three nations: high fertility and rapid population growth (Mexico), low fertility and slow growth (United States), and very low fertility and negative growth (West Germany).

Contrary to a common belief, the principal factor tending to change the age distribution of a population and, hence, the general shape of the corresponding pyramid is not the death or mortality rates, but rather the rate of fertility. A rise or decline in mortality generally affects all age groups in some measure, and hence has only limited effects on the proportion in each age group. A change in fertility, however, affects the number of people in only a single age group i.e. the group of age zero or the newly born. Hence a decline or increase in fertility has a highly concentrated effect at one end of the age distribution and thereby can have a major influence on the overall age structure. This means that youthful age structures correspond to highly fertile populations, typical of developing countries. The older age structures are those of low fertility populations, such are common in the industrialized world.

The shape of a pyramid is determined primarily by the crude birth rate in any region. A region with a high crude birth rate has a relatively large number of young children. Consequently, the base of the population pyramid is broad. On the other hand, if the region has a relatively large number of older people, the top of the pyramid is wider, and the graph looks more like a rectangle than a pyramid. The population pyramid of the Aka area (figure - 3.23) resembles to the former case i.e. broad base and narrow top. The shape of the pyramid explains that the pyramid is more like a triangle than rectangle which symbolizes high crude birth rate with a large number of young children (2229 or 44.34 % belonging to population below 14 years). Besides, the pyramid shows 2576 (51.24 %) of population belonging to the age group of 15 – 59 years symbolizes the higher fertility rate in the area. This group of population determines the crude birth rate of any region and the higher percentage of population in this category reveals a rapid growth rate of population in a region.

The age structure of the population is extremely important in understanding similarities and differences among different regions in the world. The most important factor is the dependency rate, which is the percentage of people who are either too young or too old to work. The larger percentage of dependents mount more financial burden on those who are working to support. To compare the dependency rates of different regions we can divide the population into three age groups: zero to fourteen (Below – 14 years), fifteen to fifty-nine (15 – 59 years), and sixty and over (Above 60 years). Geographers generally classify people below fourteen and over sixty as dependents. Approximately one-half of all people living in countries in stage 2 of demographic transition are dependents, compared to only one-third in stage 4 countries. Young dependents out-number elderly ones by ten to one in stage 2 countries, but the ratio between young and elderly dependents is roughly equal in stage 4 countries. In most of the African countries and in many Asian and Latin American countries more than 40% of the people are under age fifteen. This high percentage follows from the high crude birth rates in these regions.

The Aka population resembles very much to the stage 2 of demographic transition characterized by high crude birth rate. The classification of Aka population in the above mentioned age groups are as below:

Below – 14	Male	1141	
	Female	1088	
	Total	2229	44.34%
15 – 59	Male	1236	

	Female	1340	
	Total	2576	51.24%
Above – 60	Male	129	
	Female	93	
	Total	222	04.42%

Thus, the percentage of people below the age of 14 years in the Aka area is 44.34 % that symbolizes a region in the stage 2 of demographic transition. The high percentage of population in this age group is a result of high crude birth rate in the area.

Table 3.25
Age Sex Distribution of Aka Population

Male	*Percentage*	*Age Group*	*Female*	*Percentage*
430	17.16	0 – 4	453	17.97
430	17.16	5 – 9	377	14.95
281	11.21	10 – 14	258	10.23
262	10.45	15 – 19	287	11.38
185	7.38	20 – 24	209	8.29
186	7.42	25 – 29	206	8.17
132	5.27	30 – 34	161	6.39
137	5.47	35 – 39	192	7.61
115	4.59	40 – 44	119	4.72
107	4.27	45 – 49	89	3.53
72	2.87	50 – 54	44	1.74
40	1.6	55 – 59	33	1.31
42	1.67	60 – 64	34	1.35
33	1.32	65 – 69	27	1.1
15	0.6	70 – 74	13	0.51
17	0.68	75 – 80	8	0.32
22	0.88	80 +	11	0.43
Total = 2506	100		Total = 2521	100

Source: Field Survey, 2006.

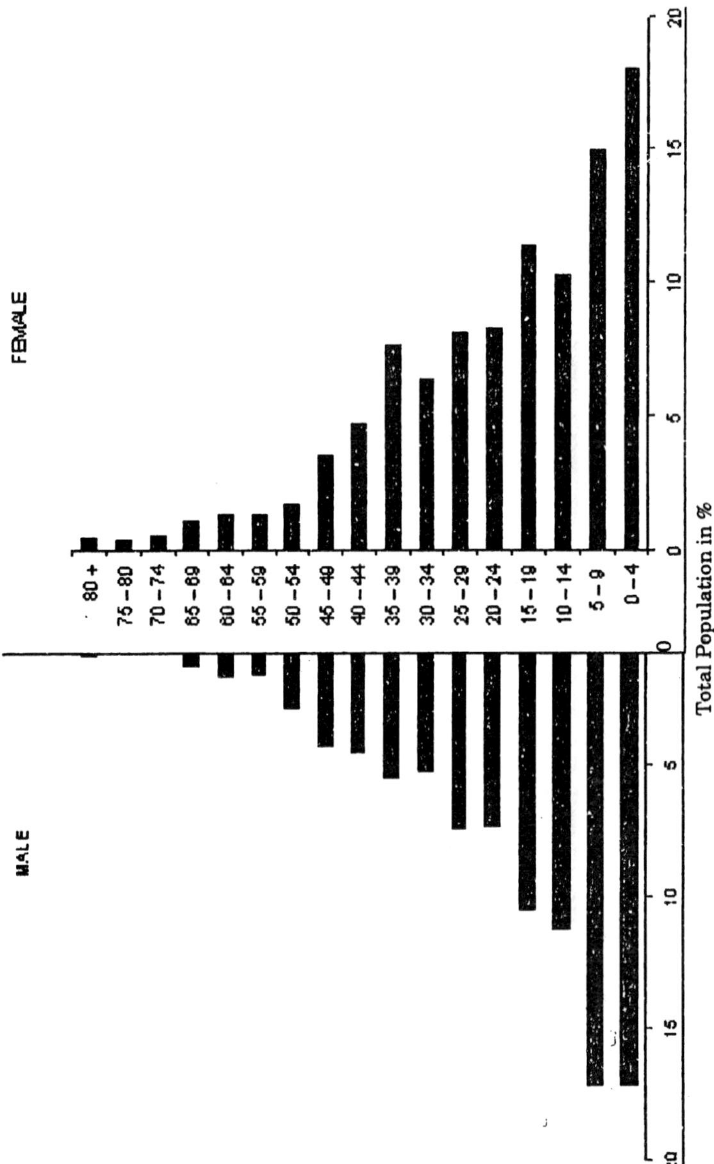

Fig. 3.23 : Age Sex Pyramid of Aka Population, 2006.

Sex Ratio

A second important structural aspect of populations is the relative numbers of males and females who compose it. Generally, slightly more males are born than females (a typical ratio would be 105 or 106 males for every 100 females). On the other hand, it is quite common for males to experience higher mortality at virtually all ages after birth. This difference is apparently of biological origin. Exceptions occur in countries such as India, where the mortality of females may be higher than that of males in childhood and at the ages of childbearing because of unequal allocation of resources within the family and the poor quality of maternal health care.

The general rules that more males are born but that females experience lower mortality mean that during childhood males outnumber females of the same age, the difference decreases as the age increases, at some point in the adult life span the numbers of males and females become equal, and as higher ages are reached the number of females becomes disproportionately large. For example, in Europe and North America, among persons more than 70 years of age in 1985, the number of males for every 100 females was only about 61 to 63. (According to the Population Division of the United Nations, the figure for the Soviet Union was only 40, which may be attributable to high male mortality during World War II as well as to possible increases in male mortality during the 1980s).

The sex ratio within a population has significant implications for marriage patterns. A scarcity of males of a given age depresses the marriage rates of females in the same age group or usually those somewhat younger, and this in turn is likely to reduce their fertility. In many countries, social convention dictates a pattern in which males at marriage are slightly older than their spouses. Thus if there is a dramatic rise in fertility, such as that called the "baby boom" in the period following World War II, a "marriage squeeze" can eventually result; that is, the number of males of the socially correct age for marriage is insufficient for the number of somewhat younger females. This may lead to deferment of marriage of these women, a contraction of the age differential of marrying couples, or both. Similarly, a dramatic fertility decline in such a society is likely to lead eventually to an insufficiency of eligible females for marriage, which may lead to earlier marriage of these women, an expansion of the age gap at marriage, or both. All of these effects are slow to develop; it takes at least 20 to 25 years for even a dramatic fall or rise in fertility to affect marriage patterns in this way.

Table 3.26
Sex Ratio of Total Population and ST Population: 1971 – 2001

Year	*Total Population*		*Sex Ratio*	*ST Population*		*Sex Ratio*
	Male	*Female*		*Male*	*Female*	
1971	2896	1793	619.13	1476	1466	993.22
1981	3328	2609	783.95	1593	1646	1033.27
1991	5034	3989	792.41	2234	2333	1044.31
2001	5970	5234	876.72	3178	3233	1017.30

Source: Census of India 1971, 1981, 1991 and 2001.

The number of males per 1000 females in the total population of Aka villages throughout the four decades was low in comparison to that of the ST population. The sex ratio was only 619 females/1000 males in the year 1971 and it has slightly increased in last three decades to reach 877 in 2001. In contrast to this the sex ratio of the ST population in the area was 993 in the year 1971 that has crossed 1000, though there was slight decline during the last decade i.e. from 1044 in 1991 to 1017 in 2001. The comparison of sex ratio in between the total population and the ST population has been given in the Table 3.26 and Figure 3.24.

Table 3.27
Sex Ratio of the Aka Population (1971 to 2006)

Year	*Total Aka Population*	*Male*	*Female*	*Sex Ratio (Females/ 1000 Male)*
1961	2239	—	—	—
1971	2333	1191	1142	959
1981	2947	1473	1545	1049
1991	3531	—	—	—
2006	5027	2506	2521	1006

Source: Census of India, 1971, 1981, 1991 and 2001.

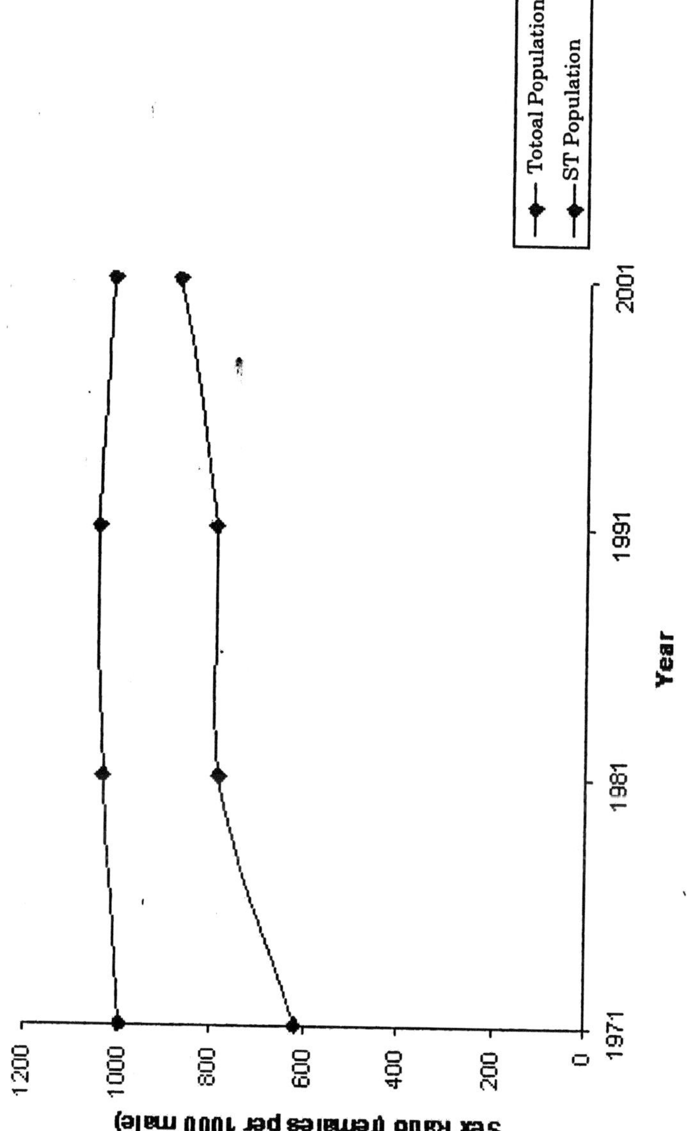

Fig. 3.24 : Comparative Sex Ratio of Total Population and ST Population 1971 – 2001.

4 CULTURE

Cultures, by predisposition, both embrace and resist change, depending on cultural traits. Men and women have complementary roles in this process e.g. one gender might desire changes that affect the other. Thus, there are both dynamic influences that encourage acceptance of new things, and conservative forces that resist change. The following three important aspects to influence both change and resistance are as given below:

- The forces at work within the society
- Contacts between societies
- Changes in the natural environment

Cultural changes take place due to the changing physical environment, inventions (and other internal influences), and contact with other cultures. For example, the end of the last ice age helped to lead the invention of agriculture, which in its turn brought about many cultural innovations. In diffusion, the form of something (though not necessarily its meaning) moves from one culture to another. For example, hamburgers, mundane in the United States, seemed exotic when introduced into Angola. "Stimulus diffusion" refers to an element of one culture leading to an invention in another. Diffusion of innovations theory presents a research-based model of why and when individuals and cultures adopt new ideas, practices and products. "Acculturation" has different meanings, but in this context refers to replacement of the traits of one culture with those of another, such as happened to certain Native American tribes and many indigenous peoples across the globe during the process of colonization. Related processes on an individual level include assimilation (adoption of a different culture by an individual) and acculturation. Cultural invention has come to mean any innovation that is new and found to be useful to a group of people and expressed in their behaviour but which does not exist as a physical object. Humanity is experiencing acceleration in culture change driven by the expansion of international commerce, the mass media, and above all, the human population explosion. The world's population now doubles in less than 40 years. Cultural change is complex and has far-ranging effects. Social geographers and anthropologists believe that a holistic approach to the study of cultures and their environments is needed to understand all of the various aspects of change. Human existence may best be looked at as a multifaceted whole. Only from this vantage one can grasp the realities of cultural change.

Our country India is characterized by diversified cultures with numerous ethnic groups belonging to different castes and tribes. Every culture is in the process of change, transformation and in continuum with the passage of time. They were not spared by the forces of cultural change. The tribal communities inhabiting Arunachal Pradesh were also experiencing changes in cultural aspects in one way or the other. The changes taking place in the culture of Aka tribes has been considered as a basis of assumption that the other tribal groups in the state were also affected in the similar manner though the magnitude of change may differ from society to society. In the present study various cultural aspects viz. house type, festivals, priest, religion, rituals, dress, dialects, ethno-medicine, man-nature relationship, etc. has been considered for assessment of level of changes.

House Type

The oldest reference about the Aka houses is available in the writings of E. T. Dalton, 1872. He wrote that "the Aka houses were more carefully and substantially built. The flooring was of well smoothed and close fitting planks". C. R.

Macgregor, 1884 wrote more elaborately about the houses of the Akas. According to him the houses are substantial erections, the sides of which are planked; they vary in size. An average house was 63 feet long and 15 feet wide; the height of the floor is from the ground and depends on the slope of the ground. It may be 2 feet at one end and 6 feet at the other. One of the house measured 140 feet in length and 22 feet in width. The fireplaces are usually in the middle of the dormitory, and round this all the members of the family, both young and old sleep. The roofs are formed at a good angle for running the rain off by placing mats over the bamboo framework and covering them with cane leave. There is very little attempt in decorating the front of the house; a few horns of the mithun are sometimes put up. Pigs and poultry live under the floor. Sanitary ideas do not exist in the Aka mind (V. Elwin, 1962).

The Aka house varies from short to long in structure, which is raised on a platform, about five to six feet above the ground (Plate 4.1). It is mainly divided into two compartments by a partition wall made of bamboo or wood. The whole house is a work of bamboo and wood, bamboo sheets forming the floor, the wall and the roof, and the wooden logs serving as the main pillars over which the structure of the house is raised. The roof is usually thatched, and tightened by bamboo ropes. The size and materials used in house reveals the status of a family. The high status people usually construct long and wooden house, while poor men always construct short and bamboo house.

The main entrance of the house is from the front, which is locally known as *nyevro*. On the backside there is also an inlet known as *nyeshii*, which is not commonly used as entrance. On the front there used to be a small verandah known as *nyezah*. As the house is raised about the ground for 5 to 6 feet, a ladder known as *molgi* is fixed on the verandah. Just behind the front door, there is a small compartment for guests known as *thumona*. This compartment serves as the lodging for the guests and relatives. Next to this compartment there is a small enclosure known as *nyemkho*, which serves

PLATE NO. 4.1 HOUSE TYPES

(a)

(b)

(c)

(d)

(e)

(f)

(g)

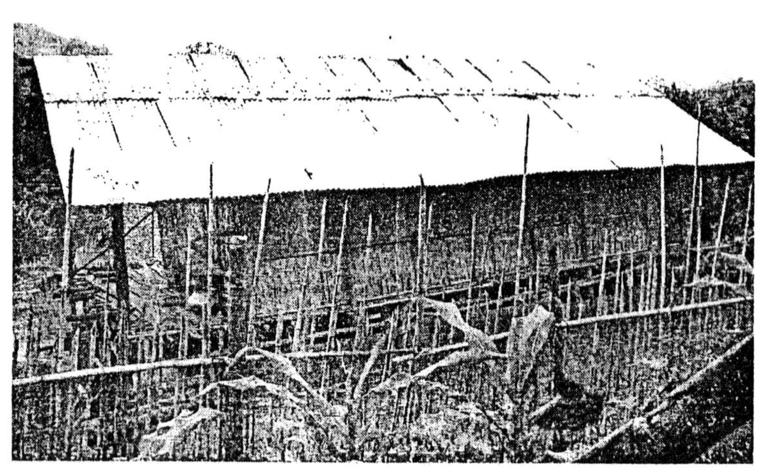

(h)

(i)

Photo : (a) Traditional house thatched by straw (b) Traditional house thatched by wooden planks (c) Traditional house thatched by banana leaf (d) Modern house thatched by banana leaf (e) Traditional house thatched by banana leaf with fencing (f) Traditional house thatched by banana leaf (g) Modern house thatched by banana leaf and tin (h) Modern house thatched by tin, (i) Modern S.P. type building.

as the main entrance to the inner big hall. The main hall, known as *nye-ulung* is a big compartment. It is the compartment for all the purposes by the occupants of a house. In case of a joint family, a separate hearth for each of the families is constructed. All the compartments in the house have at least one hearth with an iron-stand known as *Ushipiyi/ukro*. A small cell is constructed on one side of the house to serve the purpose of storeroom where the articles of the household or any other belongings of the owner is kept. This small cell is known as *nye-giin*. On the other side of the hall, a small enclosure is built to keep firewood, and is known as *syojyo-giin*. A small granary is built usually near the house which is known as *nyechi*. Each house has a separate granary constructed towards the back side of the house. Usually, a small kitchen garden is attached to grow vegetables. The garden is enclosed by bamboo and wooden fencing to protect against wild animals as well as against their own semi-domestic animals like *mithun*.

Construction of House

The construction of house is started after the collection of all the necessary articles of house building. As the house construction is done by mutual co-operation of the community, the house building is simple and completed within a day. For that day all the people engaged in the construction of the house are to be given a feast by the owner of the house. The construction of the house starts with the measurement and erection of wooden logs, serving as the main pillars and ends with the thatching of roof. At the night the house is opened and a party is organized for the new house known as *Nyekiin khayiw*. People ranging from young ones to old came and celebrate by dancing and singing in the newly constructed house.

Figure 4.1 shows that traditionally, the house is built with the joint labour of the members of the village who help one another in building a house for every household of the community. Sometimes, the members of a particular clan form

Table 4.1
Construction of House

Period	*Individual*	*Individual and group*	*Village community*	*Group and village community*	*Individual, group and village community*
Post Independence	—	—	585	277	—
Statehood Onwards	—	3	831	22	06
2000 Onwards	23	839	—	—	—

Source : Field Survey, 2006.

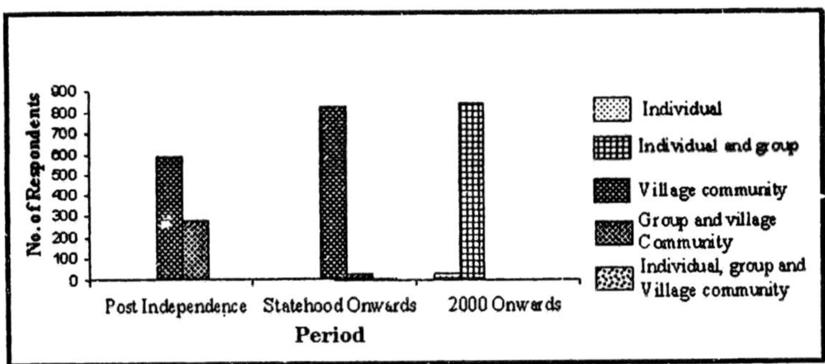

Fig. 4.1 : Construction of House

a group to construct houses of their clan members in such villages where the total population and number of households are more. The tradition has been followed by the people for many decades but at present the figure has shifted towards individual and group of villagers constructing most of the houses. Presently, most of the house types in the villages had changed in all fronts starting from materials, shape, size and structure. Therefore, the joint community effort in the construction of house is losing its significance in the modern era.

Materials Used in Construction of House

Materials used for roofing of a house are determined by the environmental conditions and availability of the thatching materials. The villages located in the lower altitudes usually use banana leaf and cane leaf as a thatching material. The houses thatched by dry banana leaf are locally known as *Wufu Nye* whereas houses thatched by cane leaves are known as *Kiigatso Nye*. The villages located in higher altitudes make use of straw, wooden planks and bamboo mats. The house in which straw is used is known as *Ghiiji Nye* and the house thatched by wooden planks is known as *Syoka Nye*. The various types of wood, bamboo and thatching materials used in house construction are given below:

The materials cited in the Table 4.2 were used during the past for the construction of houses and still those villages located in the heart of the deep forests depends on such materials.

Table 4.2
Materials Used in Construction of House

Sl. No.	*Local Name*	*English Name*	*Scientific Name*	*Purpose of Use*
1.	*Wufu*	Banana leaf	*Musa sp.* (leaf)	Thatching of the roof.
2.	*Ghiiji*	Straw	*Erianthus sp.*	Thatching of the roof.
3.	*Kiigatso*	Cane leaf		Thatching of the roof.
4.	*Kiigiitro*	Bola	*Marcus laevigata-*	Used for the main pillar of the house.
5.	*Syopesan*	—	—	Used for the main pillar of the house.
6.	*Miisanyi*	—	—	Used for supporting pillars.
7.	*Sii*	Bamboo	*Dendocalamus hamiltonni*	This bamboo is used for wall as well as floor of the house. Besides, it is also used for making ropes for binding the poles etc.
8.	*Bje*	Bamboo	*Arundinaria spathiflora*	It is also used for both wall and floor.
9.	*Miisa*	Bamboo	*Arundinaria falcata*	This is the strongest variety of bamboo and used for wall and floor. It is also used as supporting pillar.

Source: Field Survey, 2006.

The changing house types in the form of modified traditional houses, S.P. type and RCC buildings require other than the materials cited above. The materials provided under various schemes of Government (Central and State) i.e. tin have been tremendously used by the people in variety of ways. At present most of the houses are constructed with the sewed wooden planks that form the floor and wall and tins/CGI sheets are used for roofing.

Shape, Size and Structure of House

As per the references available in the books and the narrations of the older people Aka houses are rectangular in shape with an average size of 5 × 12 meters on erected platform from the ground. The shape of the house slowly becomes squarer than rectangle with the passage of time because of the reduction in the size of houses. The size of the houses averages at 5 × 8 meters and even lesser as a result of the families becoming more individual. There is strong correlation between the type of family and shape and size of the house. The structure of the houses has also been affected by the forces of modernization. The structure of the traditional houses is erected on a platform. Nowadays, people construct houses over the ground and also with a modified platform. The shape, size and structure of typical Aka houses are given in the table below:

Table 4.3
Shape, Size and Structure of Aka Houses

Period	*Shape*	*Size*	*Structure*
Post Independence	Rectangular	5 × 12 m	Erected platform
Statehood Period	Rectangular	5 × 10 m	Erected platform
2000 Onwards	Square	5 × 8 m	Modified platform

Source: Field Survey,' 2006.

Major Festivals

The major festival of the Aka (*Hrusso*) is known as *Nyetriidow* which is generally celebrated in the 2nd week of January every year. During the same period a festival celebrated by *Koro*, a sub tribe of Akas is known as *Sarok*. The term '*Nyetriidow*' is a combination of two Aka terms *Nyetrii* – meaning village and *Dow* – meaning do away/drive away/clean out. The mythology behind this post-harvest festival is of the belief that, "*Nyezi*" (Sky) and "*No*" (Earth) and the space between is the abode of all spirits and all the deities (malevolent or benevolent) dwell between these two places. According to their belief, evil spirits and deities very often move around in the village and create trouble for them in the form of diseases and calamities. For their propitiations, they felt some kinds of sacrifices of animals are necessary. So, to keep away from all kinds of suffering, (pain, disease and misfortune) the festival was started by the ancestors. They believe in the existence of evil spirits and the sufferings of the people are caused by the arrival of such spirits in the localities. Diseases like *Ghanye-Psinye, Eghrii-Eghrii, Suposunyu*, etc. are believed to be spread by the evil spirits. Therefore, *Nyetriidow* is conducted which involve a ritual of sacrificing a mithun to drive away such evil spirits from the village. Hence, traditionally, the term is used more as a ritual than a festival because there was no merry making, dances, songs, and competition on games and sports during the old days. The essential materials such as *Duonyo* (plants, creepers, etc.) and *Miithinye* (altars) are mostly collected from the forests.

The festival is celebrated to clean the village from the influence of evil spirits, prosperity, bumper crop production and general betterment of the village community. The god (*Nyezino*) is appeased through the communion of the priest (*Mugow*) to maintain good health of the villagers. Nowadays, they celebrate it by merry making, games and sports and cultural competitions. There is an influence of festivals celebrated by the neighbouring tribes and other festivals of Hindus, Christians, Buddhists, etc. The major additions in the festival celebration are the construction of temple, lighting of lamps, burning of incense sticks, and invitation of musical band groups in place of the traditional music systems.

Method of Festival Celebration

The village elders, after harvest, select a senior priest (*mugow*) to perform '*Huphu – kiiwuw*' (*Hu* – Water, *Phu* – Mountain, *Kiiwuw* – to pray) on an auspicious day around one month ahead of the festival. On the day of *Huphu kiiwuw*, at the end of puja, all the heads of families are invited to hear from the senior priest and other priests present in the meeting to know the fortunes of villagers in the coming year. In the meeting, the priests will decide what performances are to be done to please the God so that no harm is cast to the villagers. The main puja is performed to appease various forms of God viz. '*Thow – Geo*' (*Thow* – who is keeping us alive, *Geo* – who is feeding us); *'Huda – Phuda'* (*Huda* – rivers, *Phuda* – mountains) and *'Nyezi – No'* (*Nyezi* – sky, *No* – earth). The various sub-committees like priest committee, social service committee, contribution/collection committee, hunting and fishing committee and altar preparation committee, etc. are formed in that meeting. The nature of responsibilities of the sub – committees are mentioned below:

Priest (Mugow) *Committee*

The members of this committee gather at the place of *Huphu – kiiwuw* and select a priest to perform *Jechi – kruw* (a ritual through which a priest is selected to perform entire celebration). A ritual *Jechi – kruw* is performed considering the name of all priests available in the entire area and finally the most suitable one selected. It is determined by examining the suitable indications against a particular priest reflected in the liver of the chick. The selected priest has to chant for several days. The initial stage of chanting mantras is allowed at home but he will have to hide in the jungle before 4 to 5 days of the final day with some helpers. Foods and drinks are supplied to them in the jungle secretly. The other priests are to observe how the Gods are reacting to the offerings being prepared. The main priest is rewarded with gifts for performing the puja. Apart from this special foods are supplied to him on free of cost until the puja ends. The priest is responsible for finalizing the number of mithuns, cows, goats, hens, cocks, pigs, chicks and eggs to be sacrificed in the festival.

Social Service Committee

Every household has to send one person to be included in this committee. The responsibility of the committee is to start cleaning the village from one end to the other. Jungles are cleared, paths of village are repaired, all drinking water sources and surroundings are cleaned including the *Huphu kiiwuw* area. The members, while reaching every household start mocking with the house owner which sometimes goes up to the extent of performing cultural function. While cleaning a particular house the owner have to provide food and drinks to the party. Thus, the village is cleaned before the final day of puja.

Contribution Committee

This committee is locally known as *Bagha – Ghba* and each member of the committee is known by the *Ghbow*. They collect rice, maize, arum, ginger, sweet potato, spices, beans, rice beer, maize beer and other edible items from each household and store them for use during the final day of puja. They also supply food and drinks to the main priest and his party. The equitable distribution of food and drinks during the whole celebration lies in the hands of this committee.

Hunting and Fishing Committee

On the evening of *Huphu kiiwuw*, the priest will tell the villagers about the fortune of the villagers in the coming year according to the colour, sex and size of birds or animal that they will kill first. From the very next day, a member from each household will join the hunting and fishing committee. They will start hunting in the jungle in common with younger boys and hunting dogs. Big or small animals that they kill will have to be brought to the *Huphu kiiwuw* place of the village, where village elders will gather to see and compare with the words of priest about their fortune. The process goes on for several days and the flesh is either stored for community use or distributed equally to each household. The main priest also gets separate share of the hunted animals.

Decoration Committee

This committee is closely associated with the priest committee. They collect the medicinal plant (roots and leaves) known as *Duonyo* and tie them in bundles for every household in the village. These bundles are stored with the priest where he chants mantras. They are also responsible for the collection of herbs, leaves, trunks, etc. for the preparation of puja altars separately for *mithuns*, cows, pigs, goats, hens, cocks, chicks, etc. The preparation of instruments for making sound on final day and collection of sands for throwing on the house roofs are also handed over to this committee. Dress for a couple of man (representing both the sexes) to look like ghost is also prepared with tree leaves, barks and mask to dance on the final day. This procession with the two mask men from the upper end to the lower end of the village is termed as *Froh froh – Anh anh.*

*Role of Headman (*Nyetrii – Nuggo*) and the Village Elders (*Kheo – Nyeo*)*

The village headman has an important role in the celebration. He has to bear the maximum contribution of food, domestic animals required for the puja and the gift to be made to the main priest. He gets separate share of hunted animals and the sacrificed animals. The village elders often gather at place preferably the *Nyetrii – Psigha* from time to time and decide how many *mithuns*, goats, hens, pigs, cocks, chicks and eggs will be required for the entire puja and who will bear the costs. They also decide the payment to be made to the main priest after the puja is over as per customary law. If a *mithun* is given by a village elder, the villagers in return ask what he needs. If he wants that his next year cultivation is to be done by the villagers, they have to agree to it and do it in common. If he has some other difficulties, it is looked after by the villagers in common either in cash or kind or by physical labour.

The Celebration

During the festival, different pujas are performed to please different gods. Puja sacrifices are made at the site of drinking water sources. *Mithun* is sacrificed to please the *Thow – Geo*. A different puja is chanted to drive away the fire accident evil. About 4 to 5 days before the final day, the priest and his party hide in the jungle mostly on the upper side of the village. On the final day, leaving only the old men, women and children everybody goes to the place where the main priest is hiding one by one and secretly. It is believed that the evils of the village may come to know what is going to happen to them. All the fire of each household are asked to be put-off by water so that no fire exist in the village. The priest in his traditional dress prepares a fresh wild can with leaves where a lived cock is tied, rigorously chants the puja and orders the gathering to attack the village to drive away all the evils. The young boys carrying the instruments for making sound, *duonyo* and sands attack the houses in the village. They attack house after house and the priest enters each houses from front door and comes out from the back door. He asks every person including children to spit on the lived cock and leaves one bundle *duonyo* for each house. The attack by sand is made to drive away all evil spirits that existed in the village and the spits on cock are collected to drive away the diseases that the people are suffering from. The party goes out of the other end of the village. At a place far away from the village, the priest performs puja by sacrificing some animals and asks the evil spirits not to come to the village again. The boys clean themselves there and seal the roads. The party then comes back to the village and seals all the roads leading to that village from other villages.

They again gather at the place of *Huphu kiiwuw* to perform remaining pujas and some youths make out new fire. To make out new fire dried cotton-like thing collected from the trees is placed below a dried strong wood tied at both end with supports. A dried thin cane is winded around the wood which is pulled from both ends by two energetic young men quickly. The dried cane and wood get heated and fire sparkles out to catch the dry cotton like material placed below. The villagers from each house come to collect new fire for their respective houses. All the villagers gather to eat and to listen to the priest whether the Gods were pleased at the fullest or not. The presentation to the main priest is also done on the spot. The village is closed for entry by outsiders for 2 to 4 days as per the order of the priest. It is believed that anybody enters from other village may bring diseases or any other evils with him. The seals are only opened by the main priest after performing a ritual. Any outsiders entering the village knowingly or unknowingly are fined with cash or kind. The fine ranges from Rs. 2 and above. The outsiders who know it by seeing the seal of the road passes the village through jungle silently.

The festival was traditionally celebrated village-wise but nowadays it is celebrated in a particular village or location and the members from other villages are invited to participate in it. The method of festival celebration has shifted from village-wise to an organized community celebration in the recent years. But, still village-wise celebration may take place in case of a sudden outbreak of dreadful diseases and untoward incidents in the village. The Figure–4.2 below shows method of festival celebration since the post independence to statehood and 2000 onwards. During the post independence period it was celebrated in all the villages but nowadays it is becoming more organized celebration than village wise. Village-wise celebration has taken the shape of optional to organized celebration. The emerging expenses or costs, decline in the number of animals, modernization, technological advancement, etc. are responsible for the present form of the festival.

Table 4.4
Method of Festival Celebration

Period	*Village-wise*	*Group*	*Organized Community Celebration*	*Village-wise and Organized Community Celebration*
Post Independence	862	—	—	—
Statehood Onwards	—	—	281	581
2000 Onwards	—	—	281	581

Source: Field Survey, 2006.

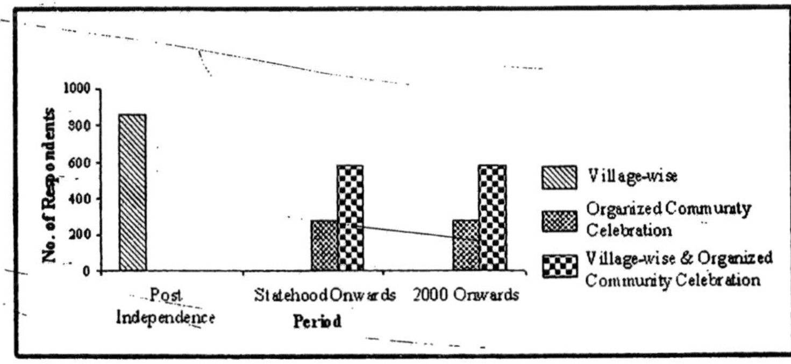

Fig. 4.2 : Method of Festival Celebration.

Animals Sacrificed during the Festivals

Sacrifice of a *mithun* or cow or something else is finalized by the priest during the puja performance. Apart from *mithun* and cow the other important animals sacrificed in the festivals includes chicken, goat and pig. The number of animals for sacrifice varies year to year and depends on the priest who offers prayers to the god. Thus, priest fixes the number, size, colour and sex of the animals to be sacrificed. In some cases cat and dog are also sacrificed to drive away some bad evils present in the village. However, the numbers of animals sacrificed in festivals are declining due to the scarcity and increasing consciousness about the importance of live stocks.

Duration of Celebration

The festival took its present form of organized celebration in the year 1972, when almost all the Aka villagers participated at Buragaon with great zeal and vigour. The festival is celebrated once in a year in the month of January (*liigahu*) w.e.f. 10th to 15th day. Traditionally the chanting of hymns by the priest starts one month before the commencement of the festival and the final celebration lasts for five days. The period of celebration as well as the number of days for chanting hymns has reduced to 15 days (chanting) and 3 days (celebration). This decline in the period of celebration could be the outcome of the more involvement of people in modern life where there is paucity of man power and time. It appears that to reduce money and time people might have reduced the number of days of celebration. Further, the method of celebration adopted by the surrounding tribes had also influenced them to reduce the number of days involved in such celebration. The Akas who are working in and around the capital complex has started a one day celebration of *Nyetriidow* festival in 2007 at Itanagar which may have its far reaching effect on the general celebration among the Aka community.

PRIEST (*MUGOW*)

The role of priest in the society is multifaceted, in other words priest are important in marriages, festivals, day-today rituals, healing from the sufferings, sowing and harvesting of crops, hunting and fishing activities, boosting up of moral or strength, well being of the household and villagers, etc. The belief in priests was so strong during the past that any important event in a society requires the priest. As such the position of priest (*mugow*) in the society is very important (Plate 4.2). The priests become senior as they attain age and sacrifice animals from fowl to *mithun*. The priest who can chant the hymns of sacrificing a *mithun* is the highest rank in his priesthood life. The priests are divided on the basis of seniority or the ability of sacrificing animals. The division is as given below:

(i) *Fucheo mega/miiga kheo* (sacrifices *mithun*)

(ii) *Fulhu cheo miiga* (sacrifices bull)

(iii) *Vo cheo miiga* (sacrifices pig)

(iv) *Jyo cheo miiga* (sacrifices chicken)

(v) *Chi juow/Psiwo cheo miiga* (uses feather of chicken)

(vi) *Tiikrin cheo miiga* (uses only a ginger)

The number of priests is declining due to lack of interest among the younger generation, lack of knowledge regarding the hymns, sense of insecurity of life as well as finance, biasness in chanting proper hymns, quarrel among the priests by chanting hymns of death, lack of knowledge about the myths and legends, etc. In recent days there is a rapid decline in the strength of priests in the Aka area. In some villages it has depleted so fast that even a single priest is not available throughout the village. Lack of interest among the younger generation people is one of the important causes for rapid decline in the number of priests. The scientific knowledge, medicinal development and other related developmental activities had reduced the belief and faith of the people in the priests. However, the conversions of the people towards different organized religions as well as the forces of modernity are responsible for the decrease in the number of priests. The decrease in the number of priests as well as the changing attitude of the localities with the development of the society

PLATE NO. 4.2
PRIEST, RITUALS AND FESTIVALS

(a)

(b)

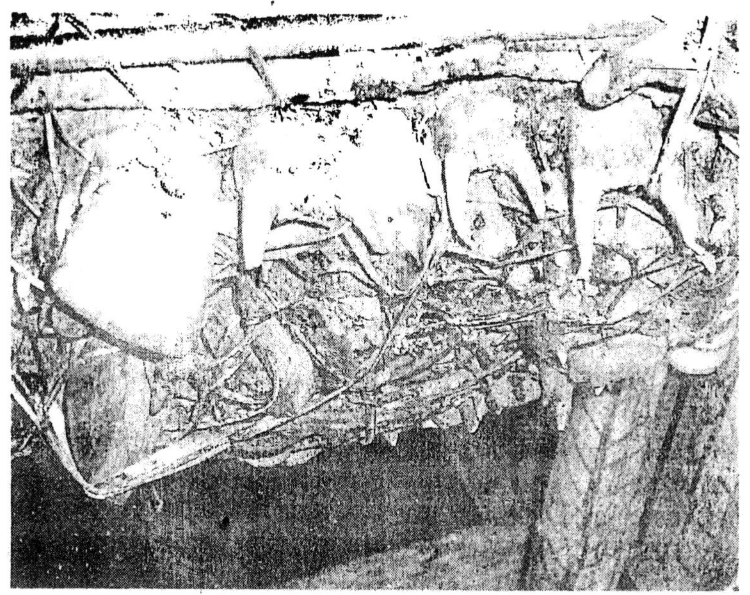

(c)

(d)

(e)

(f)

(g)

(h)

(i)

Photo : (a) A Priest in traditional attire (Palatari village), (b) Essential tools of Priest, (c) Tool of Priest known as *Hütrii-utu,* (d) Altars for *Psiwo* ritual, (e) Decoration of Altars in front of house, (f) Graveyard of a woman with altars, (g) Govardhan Nimasow – the Chief Guest for Nyetriidow festival at Thrizino, (h) Villagers preparing puja altars for festival, (i) The Priest with members performing main ritual of Nyetriidow festival at Thrizino.

has led to decline in the practice of rituals in all the fronts, such as marriage, sufferings, construction of house, hunting, fishing, etc. Besides, the priest in the recent days has lost their importance by leaving their works half done during the performance of rituals. These days the priests are guided by the motives of earning and gaining some good materials as remuneration for the rituals. Such motives of the priests had led to the degradation in the qualitative rituals in the area (The quality of a priest is determined by the people's faith). For preservation of the rituals and their significance, it is necessary to realize by the people regarding the importance of priest. Otherwise, these careers of Aka heritage from one generation to another may vanish.

Religion and Rituals

A religion is a set of common beliefs and practices generally held by a group of people, often codified as prayer, ritual and religious law. Religion also encompasses ancestral or cultural traditions, writings, history, and mythology, as well as personal faith and mystic experience. The term religion refers to both the personal practices related to communal faith and to group rituals and communication stemming from shared conviction. In the frame of (patriarchal) European religious thought, religions present a common quality, the 'hallmark of patriarchal religious thought': the division of the world in two comprehensive domains, one sacred, and the other profane. Religion is often described as a communal system for the coherence of belief focusing on a system of thought, unseen being, person, or object, that is considered to be supernatural, sacred, divine, or of the highest truth. Moral codes, practices, values, institutions, tradition, rituals, and scriptures are often traditionally associated with the core belief, and these may have some overlap with concepts in secular philosophy. Religion is also often described as a way of life.

The development of religion has taken many forms in various cultures. Organized Religion generally refers to an organization of people supporting the exercise of some religion with a prescribed set of beliefs, often taking the form of a legal entity. Other religions believe in personal revelation and responsibility. Religion is sometimes used interchangeably with 'faith' or 'belief system', but is more socially defined than that of personal convictions.

Religion has been defined in a wide variety of ways. Most definitions attempt to find a balance somewhere between overly sharp definition and meaningless generalities. Some sources have tried to use formalistic, doctrinal definitions while others have emphasized experiential, emotive, intuitive, valuational and ethical factors. Definitions mostly include:

- a cultural or behavioural aspect of ritual, liturgy and organized worship, often involving a priesthood, and societal norms of morality (*ethos*) and virtue (*arete*)

- a notion of the transcendent or divine, often, but not always, in the form of theism
- a set of myths or sacred truths held in reverence or believed by adherents

Religion is commonly understood as the belief that mankind has in some unseen controlling powers with a related emotion and a sense of morality (Sinha 1962). Most religious people pray for peace, but religious groups may not share the same vision of how peace will be achieved. Geographers see that the process by which one religion diffuses across the landscape may conflict with the distribution of others. In other words, they are concerned with the regional distribution of different religions and the potential for conflict among them that result from the various distributions. Geographers also observe that religions are derived in part from elements of the physical environment and that religions in turn make a significant contribution to modification of the landscape. Religion, like other cultural characteristics can be a source of pride and a means of identification with a distinct culture. It forms an important characteristic of culture that leaves a deep imprint on the physical environment. Religious beliefs may be derived from elements in the physical environment on the one hand and religious ideas may underlie human transformation of the physical environment on the other. Hence, geographers also look at the relationship between religion and the physical environment. Religions are influenced by both natural events and features of physical environment. Certain features of landscape are incorporated into the philosophy and rituals of a religion and interpreted in a way that is consistent with the religious values. Different religions incorporate environmental features differently; the selection of features is influenced by distinctive physical conditions on the portion of the earth's surface where the religion originated or diffused. The surrounding environment influences the organization of religion in three basic ways. First, natural events are incorporated into the structure of the religion. Second, features of the physical environment are designated as holy. Third, religions organize portions of the earth's surface into administrative units to diffuse religious messages.

The Akas follow traditional religion, which can be grouped under animism. Animists believe that such inanimate objects as plants and stones or such natural events as thunderstorms and earthquakes have discrete spirits and conscious life. Various religious rituals are passed from one generation to the next by word of mouth. In the Aka society there is variety of gods (*Nyezi Aou, No Ain*), deities (*Ape-nyichi nyigyi, Hukeyi*) and spirits (*Chigje, Nyeolo*) who reign over mankind. Akas are strong believers of their religion known as *Nyezino,* which is a combination of two local words i.e. *Nyezi*, meaning the sky and *No* meaning the earth. According to an Aka myth before the creation of the universe the earth and the sky are in the form of circle locally known as *Dzuw-dzjyong, Nouw-nojyong* and out of their interaction the different forms of life came into existence. So, they believe that the earth and the sky are the creators and therefore, they worship them as their god. The forests in Aka society hold the position of a god. The surrounding milieu had made them a strong believer of the nature. The religious life of the Akas is largely determined by the conditions of their habitat. These people are the great admirers and lovers of their surrounding forests. The social customs, beliefs, faith, tradition, culture, etc. reflects the imprint of the surrounding forest ecology. They worship forests as a gift of god to them and refer the forests as *Thow - gew*. This is a combination of two Aka terms, *Thow* meaning rearer and *gew* meaning feeder. They worship forests as it provides food, shelter, agricultural crops, land, fertility, firewood, etc. to them. In the folklores, folk tales, myths and festivities of these people, forest has an important place. The forest resources have tremendous implications on the social, cultural and religious life of the Akas. They are the believers of the nature and unlike the other recognized religions this small tribal group had developed a deep faith on the sky and the earth which they call as the *Nyezi aou* and *No ain* meaning thereby sky the father and earth the mother of all living beings in the universe. Nowadays, due to the introduction of modern infrastructure, education and assimilation of people with different societies changes are taking place in their religious faith and practices. People are getting fascinated with other's culture like Hinduism, Buddhism and Christianity without thinking the fate of their own age old religion. During the field survey, out of total Aka population (5027), 3905 are still continuing their own cultural practices i.e. *Nyezino* and *Mene Alan,* whereas 1117 persons have abandoned their own cultural practices and adopted Christianity. However, 5 persons declared themselves as Hindu (Plate 4.3).

Life Cycle Rituals

They believe in the existence of gods, deities and spirits who reign over mankind. Rituals play an important role in the life cycle of an individual in Aka society. It is an important

PLATE NO. 4.3
TEMPLES AND CHURCHES IN THE AREA

(a)

(b)

(c)

(d)

(e)

(f)

(g)

(h)

Photo : (a) A view of Nag Mandir, (b) Shiv Mandir at Thrizino, (c) Inside view of Shiv Mandir at Jamiri, (d) Local Church at Kararamu Village, (e) Local Church at Karangania Village, (f) Cross used outside a house at Kadeya village, (g) Concrete Church at Yangsey, (h) Concrete Church at Bhalukpong.

aspect of their culture. Their belief on various rites and rituals is distinct in itself that is inherited from the ancestor. Any kind of ritual requires plants, trunks, bamboo, etc. which are extracted from the surrounding forests. Different kinds of altars are made before sacrificing a fowl, pig, *mithun*, etc. for which the forest is the only source of required raw material for the purpose. The propitiations are made by way of rituals, which are performed from time to time. From the conception of a child to the death of an individual the performance of rituals are very much essential in the Aka society. As soon as the women get conceived, some restrictions are imposed on her as well as on the husband also. Both of them are restricted from consumption of dead animals. Moreover, they are not allowed to go to the place where tiger, man, etc. are killed.

Crossing over the dead snakes or insects lying on the way are also tabooed for them.

After two months of conception a ritual is performed known as *chijuow* by sacrificing a fowl and using a small plant known as *mugye* or *musung*. This ritual is performed for the child to be physically well. The chanting of mantra during puja is as given below:

Tsom sivjiew chomutrii toyee

Babro juow lamou no

Tamukho sai no pomenye tsom sivjiew bawonye

Wom sivjiew bawonye no hai kamuso layiew hebey

Buslou huow jiney nowsa druw jyo mugye sivjiew

Heyeow kamuso layiew hebey

(As narrated by shri Govardhan Nimasow)

The meaning of the above puja in English is that I am the priest (*mugow*) as a mediator appeases you (God) by offering this fowl and the plant (*mugye*) on behalf of the parents of the child to be pardoned and cared even if they are not in position to follow the restrictions imposed upon them. And let the child be physically well. After three to four months if the women complaints of pain in stomach then a ritual known as *Tsom-wom-priiw/ekrii-udro juw* is performed by the priest (*mugow*). These people believe that the pain in stomach in this stage is the indication of the delivery of child before the actual time, which may result in the death of the mother as well as the child. So, to overcome this problem the priest performs a ritual known as *jechi-kruw*. By examining the liver of the sacrificed fowl it is finalized that whether a *mithun* or pig is to be sacrificed to appease the god. The priest carry out conversation with God by chanting mantras to know the types and number of animals needed for the sacrifice. The mithun or pig is sacrificed and the earlier soul of the child is exchanged with a new soul, which is locally known as *Ekrii-udro-jugdo*.

In the eve of the delivery of child again a ritual *Chi-juou* is performed to appease the *Nyezi auo, No ain* to allow the delivery of the child without any problem. After the completion of one year of a child, a ritual is performed by inviting a priest (*mugow*) known as *Sise gyeyi pomuow*. This ritual is performed for the child to become a good energetic sportsmen and sports women, singer and dancer and for his /her material well-being. Moreover, in near future the demons, devils, evil spirits may not cause any harm to his or her life. When the child grows up and becomes father/mother, a ritual known as *Baanye-weenye kiiwuw* is performed. For this ritual the priest performs a *Chisa-kunu howu* by sacrificing a foul and examines the liver and decides what is to be sacrificed to appease the *Thabrow-Gebrow* (creator-feeder). Another ritual known as *Syomu sisow – bumu lugjiw duw* is performed to overcome the enemies, jealous persons. After the performance of ritual the priest will tell *Nyee houw* (findings of ritual) to the family members. If the priest tells that the ritual is a success one then no ritual will be performed throughout the life, except a ritual known as *Psiwo* (*pudu punya, sise gyeyi dagow*), which is generally performed every year. These are the rituals mainly performed during the life span of a person.

The Akas believe in the transmigration of soul. It is believed that when a person dies, the soul of the deceased person tries to return in his previous home. The Akas practice burial of dead body. The priest (*mugow*) performs the mortuary rites and rituals on the first as well as the last day of mourning. The ceremonial mourning lasts for ten days in case of men and eight days in case of women. The whole community and relatives of the deceased person get together and make decision where, how and who will burry the dead body. Usually the son is supposed to burry the body. In case the deceased person has no son then the nearest relative is given the task. After selecting the spot, a priest is invited for performing the mortuary rites known as *Chi-juow* or *Simey chi-juow* in the first day and *Wulow-kiw* in the last day of mourning. As the people start the digging of burial ground, the priest starts chanting mantra by holding a fowl and *Mugye*. The *Nyee-wujiow* (person supposed to burry the body) with two helpers would do the *Nyibo-biou* meaning placing the dead body in a birth position. The fire is extinguished and the hearth (*chulla*) is neatly swept away. A basket known as *Pusey* is placed over the hearth. This process is done for examining some symbols after burying of the dead body. The symbols will develop on the hearth, which will be interpreted and explained by the priest after the completion of ritual.

After digging the ground, the *Nyee-wujiow* hold on the head portion and the other persons help him in carrying the body to the ground. As soon as the body is carried out the house is left completely vacant. The hair of *Nyee-wujiow* is tied by a *Musung* (rope) and hold by some person from outside while he puts dead body into burial ground. This is done for the security of the soul of *Nyee-wujiow*, so that his soul may not go with the departed soul. The persons will put down the body on the ground and the belongings, which are very much attached to him/her, on the head of the deceased person. *Syobotro-pom* (five pieces of sticks either bamboo or a plant known as *Tukson* (*Callicarpa arborea*) is put on the right hand of the deceased person. This is done for the deceased person for making arguments with the evil spirits responsible for his/her death. A piece of cane known as *Seji* is touched to the dead body and kept on one side. After this the soil and stones are put on the ground and the outside part is decorated by erecting a stone structure of five-six feet above the surface. Four pieces of *Callicarpa arborea* are erected on the four directions *i.e.* north, south, east and west, which are known as *Baayi-tikheo*. Four pieces of *Syotro* (piece of wood) are also erected on all the sides. A long piece of white cloth is put over the ground by constructing a structure of hut known as *Getuwow/Genya*, a bamboo altar with small pieces of white clothes, numbering six were erected on the burial ground. The priest now puts out the piece of cane, which was put to touch to the dead body. This is considered to be the process of making free the soul of the deceased person and allow it to travel in the heaven. Thereafter, all the persons involved in the burial process have to go on a water source and clean their hands, legs and the implements used for digging ground.

A piece of ginger (*Tiikrin*) is bite and sprayed on the water source, so that evil spirits may not follow them. The priest holds a *Musung* and everyone have to spite on the *Musung* and enter the house. The priest and old persons examine the liver of the fowl and the *Pusey* put over the hearth is removed and examine the symbols (*Esigye*). If there is some symbol towards *Druguw* (west) or *Druyiew* (east) then a person may die immediately and if it is towards the *Chisey* (north) or *Mjey* (south) then no one will die. If any symbol of wild animal is shown then the villagers will go for hunting and hunt the animal.

The people who are involved in the burial process are provided local beer and arum, etc. The *Nyee-wujiow* is tabooed from touching the things of the house for ten days. The family members have to serve food or drink to the soul of the deceased person first of all and consume thereafter. After 5 days a ritual known as *Khunu-aa-nujew* is performed. During these 10 days period relatives such as son-in-law, niece, etc. are tabooed from consumption of chilly, onion, etc. After 10 days in case of men and 8 days in case of women a ritual known as *Dagdraw* or *Wullow-kiw* is performed by the same priest by sacrificing a *mithun* (rich) and a pig (poor). In this ritual the *Nyee-wujiow* has to cut a piece of hair and nail at the water source. A piece of flesh from every part of the animal sacrificed is to be given to the soul of the deceased person. The boys and girls from every house gathered at the house of the deceased person to entertain the family members and also the sound of the assemblage groups are believe to frighten away the soul of the deceased person. Thus, the soul is prevented from entering the house as well as forcing the soul to leave the house as early as possible to the heavenly abode.

Besides, the life cycle rituals the other important rituals performed by the Akas in their day-to-day life **are** ***Mim-miigha, Fupo-nyigyikeo kiyikru, Duw-gyunew*** ***Wagra-gom***, etc. As such the priest (*Mugow*) in Aka society **holds** an important place.

Traditional Dress and Ornaments

Aka traditional dress for both men and women is simple. The traditional dress, which they use to wear, is partly weaved by them and partly they collect it from the plains of Assam. They have been purchasing cloth and other commodities like salt and utensils for a pretty long time from Assam. Men invariably wear a small garment hanging below the shoulders to the knees. A long piece of cloth is used to tie on the waist, which is known as *shashi chupeo*. This garment is made to fit the body and is known as *shashi-ge* or *wuso-ge* (Plate 4.4). Men also wear a kind of coat, which hangs from shoulders to the waist and is known as *shashi-polu*, which is usually made from rough cotton cloth (*markin*). A small white cloth is used as underwear known as *Wopu*. Women wear a long garment over the body, which hangs from the shoulders up to the

PLATE NO. 4.4
TRADITIONAL DRESS AND ORNAMENTS

(a)

(b)

(c)

(d)

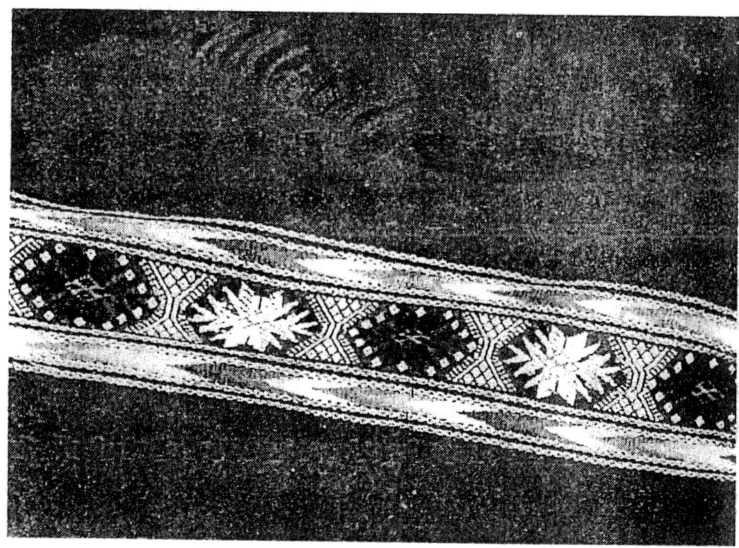

(e)

(f)

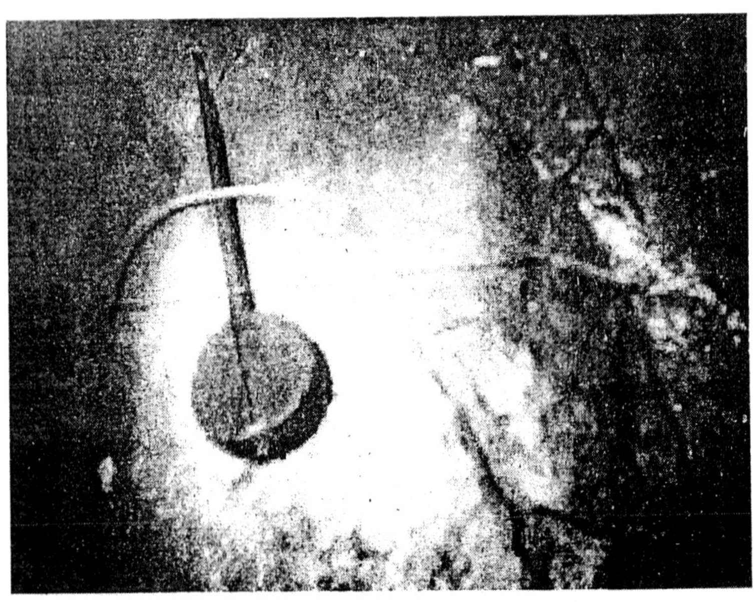

(g)

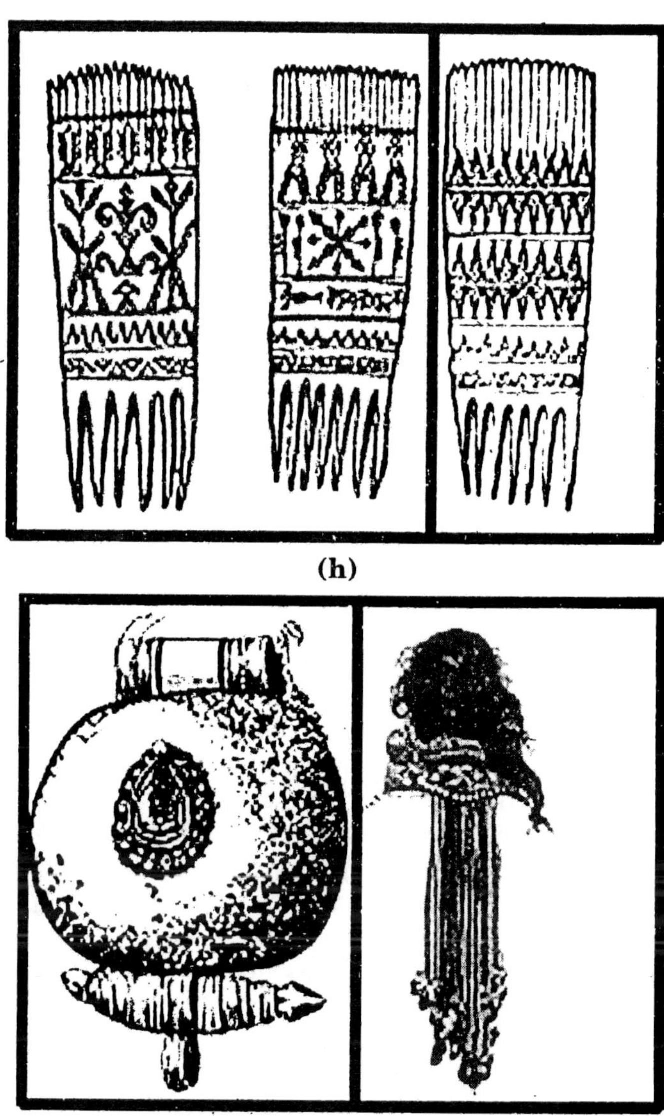

(h)

(i)

Photo : (a) Aka couple in traditional dress, (b) Village elder in traditional attire (Palatari), (c) Anchal Samiti Member of Buragaon in traditional attire, (d) Designs of *Shasi polu* (Traditional jacket), (e) Typical Aka designs applied in modern *Gales*, (f) Aka Cloth designs resembling to insects, (g), (h) Aka comb designs, (i) *Melu* and *Katsibu-syeabu* (Aka silver ornaments worn by women).

ankles. In this case also a long piece of cloth *shashi chupeo* is used to tie on the waist. A coat locally known as *shashi-polu* of red colour is used by the women folk. Both men and women cover the legs with a piece of cloth known as *gudu*, sewn into cylindrical shape which leaves only the feet uncovered. These are worn as a protection against the *dam-dum* flies, which is locally known as *sujum*. These clothes are used regularly, but for some occasions and festivities, every individual is keeping a new piece of cloth. During normal days they use to wear old piece of clothes. Men wear two types of headdress namely *miisanga* and *ghaga*. These headdresses are worn on some rituals, festivals and occasions only. The *miisanga* is a kind of ring-cap of bamboo whereas the *ghaga* is also a kind of ring-cap but it is made of silver. A kind of ring-cap of bamboo, known as *miisanga,* is worn by the men folk as a part of their traditional dress. This cap is mainly wear during some rituals as well as festivals. It is prepared by the inner portion of a common bamboo (*siiva*). On the front part a V-shaped structure is made and some leaves are decorated, which is known as *siigjen*. *Ghaga* is a silver cap which is not prepared by them but collected from either the plains or the northern tribes like Sherdukpen and Monpa. People wear two types of silver caps (*ghaga*) a cap without decoration in the front and another with a decoration in the front known as *Tapuyi*. Men wear a *dao* (*Vetsii*) sometimes with a silver case (*kefanye*) across the waist, particularly when going out to other villages. The women adorn themselves profusely with ornaments around the neck, and the forehead. Men usually tie their hair in the middle of the head in a knot while women wear it at the back.

During the olden days the Akas use to weave some clothes, which were known as *pasa*. The elderly persons of the surveyed village had explained that a small plant known as *mumdra* is used for making yarns. The process of weaving is known as *pasa-triiw* or *ge-triiw*. Another plant known as *wuma* is also used for weaving clothes by following the above-mentioned process. The fruit of a tall tree known as *brovj-je* is used as hair oil as well as oil for relieving body pain. The fruits of this tree are gathered and break-up into small pieces, then the oil is squeezed-out from the fruits and used as traditional hair oil. Another small plant known as *migyim-jyoksu*, which also bears oily fruits is used for hair oil by adopting the same process during the early days of the Akas. Besides, *muksung* (tobacco pipe) made out of a variety of bamboo known as *bje* and *truka* (comb) made out of the same species of bamboo were used by them as a part of their dress. The Aka combs are of two types – (i) *Druba* and (ii) *Trukamso*. These combs are used for combing hair as well as removing head louse. These combs and tobacco pipes are beautifully decorated with poker designs.

The Akas wear a number of ornaments of silver as well as necklaces of beads. The common silver ornaments adorn by them are *melu* (a flat-shaped ornament worn over the chest), *sapengo* (another cone shaped ornament worn over the chest), *lyenchi* (a fillet of silver chain-work), *ghbin* (the big ear bulbs), *fubaliim* (the big ear rings), *ghiidrii* (the wristlets), *liimufo, ajyoyifo,* etc. Along with these silver ornaments they also put around the neck a number of coloured bead necklaces. The Aka men generally and in occasions put only yellow coloured beads around the neck locally call as *tradji* and *dolye*. The women are fond of these beads and put any number of them during occasions as well as in normal times. The common beads are locally known as *thtrii, hugeng vojo, vonyee vojo, doye, fupufo, nuschochifo, segdrufo, drangfo, fugrofo,* etc.

They also wore some ornaments, which are made out of wood, cane, bamboo, etc. An earring usually worn by both men and women is known as *fusva*. This is prepared by a variety of bamboo known as *bje*. A hand bangle known as *musung-pango* is used by the women folk. This is made by a plant known as *musung*, which is also useful for ritual performances. An ornament known as *siiyeagu* is made by a snail shell known as *siiye*. This is usually worn by men folk in a cross-section from shoulder to waist. The small pieces of snail shell are stitched over a small piece of cloth beautifully and worn as an ornament. Another ornament prepared by the same technique is known as *katsiibu-siiyebu* – a tassel is worn by the women on the back side rounding on the neck and running down to the waist. The small pieces of snail are stitched over the corners of the tassel.

FOOD HABITS

Food is the prime necessity of life. Life without food is practically inconceivable. Human beings can get food either through the plants or through the animals. There are large edible plants from which leaves, stems, roots, fruits, etc. are taken as food. Such plants are available in the natural surrounding of the human settlement. It is generally agreed upon that before the knowledge of the art of plant cultivation, man use to gather food from the surrounding forests. Similarly animal food was taken either in the form of meat or milk or through other forms (Singh, et al. 1992). The food habits of the people are largely determined by the conditions in which they live. As such the majority of Indian tribes, living in the isolated hills and mountains are still largely dependent on their natural surrounding forests in order to procure food items.

The main crops of the area figure principally in their staple food. While it is enriched with various types of hunted and collected materials from the surrounding forests. The Akas primarily depends upon the jhum cultivation for their sustenance, thus the staple food mainly consists of maize, which is often supplemented by millet and paddy. Rice was not grown much, hence it was not a staple food. The husks of the paddy are removed by local made mortar and pestles known as *Wulu-miyi*. Maize and millet are grinded by a local made grinder known as *Ghato*. These cereals are taken in boiled form along with vegetables either collected from the jhum fields or gathered in the form of plants and tubers from the forest. The important products of jhum fields like *tro* (Arum), *drubzi* (Pumpkin), *nyeksi* (Yams) served as an important supplementary of food during the past days. These items are boiled or burnt and consumed for either breakfast or one time meal. Some local pulses such as *shapiu* and *labionsu* (*urad* and a pulse similar to it), are also added to the food as vegetable. Spices such as *adii* (Chili), *tiikriin* (Ginger), *mufu, miisi,* etc. are also consumed and used in meetings and social occasions. On important socio-religious occasions the main diet is substantiated by meat of *mithun*, pork, beef, and chicken, though none of these form their daily diet, except for a few persons who can afford it. Beef is less commonly taken since most of the women are tabooed from its consumption. Fowls are more frequently taken by the people during normal times as well as socio-religious ceremonies. They are fond of smoking and chewing of tobacco. Both men and women chew tobacco leaves and smokes with a tobacco pipe either prepared indigenously or procured from the plains of Assam. Wild betel *Tukson (Callicarpa arborea)* is also taken by both men and women. Betel nut is also procured from the plains since the olden days that form an important commodity of barter trade with the Assam people. The alcoholic drink of the Akas is termed as *Tsii/Tsiimso* (Rice beer). It forms a part of their diet and a meal is supposed to be complete only with the addition of a drink. It is prepared either by rice (*Olghii*), maize (*Sibe*), millet (*Kiitse*) or a combination of all. This can be consumed at any time from the morning till evening. It is taken without any reservation by all, men, women as well as children. They prepare the drink for their own use and to serve the guests as well as the visitors from the village. The drink is prepared by a simple method that is better termed as fermentation. The rice, corn or millet is first boiled in adequate quantity of water and is then allowed to cool. After it is sufficiently cooled, a fungus (prepared by fermented rice) locally known as *Pa*, is added completely with the rice, corn or millet and either kept by folding with leaves (*Womsey*) or a jar known as *Khstru*. It is kept for two or more days for fermentation and water is added by transferring it in a big jar if it is kept in leaves. The water after being mixed up completely can be taken out for consumption by all. Sometimes Tapioca is also used for the preparation of local wine by the people. Nowadays, mostly rice and maize are largely used for the preparation of local wine.

The food habits of the people are largely determined by the conditions in which they live. As such the majority of Indian tribes, living in the isolated hills and mountains are still largely dependent on their natural surroundings in order to manage food items. The area abounds numerous variety of edible plants for them. Food gathering is an important part of their occupation and a supplementary source of livelihood. The various edible vegetables collected from the forests are Bamboo shoot (*Dendocalamus hamiltonni*), banana flower/ Spadix inflorescence (*Musa paradisiaca*), *Pouzolzia viminea, Piper pedicellatum, Piplazium esculantum, Clerodendrom colebrookianum, Alocasia sp.*, Mushrooms (*Termitomyces sp., Cantherallus sp., Schizophyllum sp., Pleurotus pulmonarius, Auricularia sp.*) and many more plants, the scientific name of which are still not known. They collect number of fruits from the forest. Some of the important fruits are Bansum (*Phoebe sp.*), wild lichi (*Myristica fragrance*), *Picus semichordata, Castanopsis indica, Hodgsonia macrocarpa, Rubus sp., Rubus niveus, Picus hispida, Musa sp.*, etc. The practice of fishing and hunting are also done to a large extent. The dense mixed jungle of the area provides wide range of animals of different species. Some of the animals, such as tiger and elephant are not killed and consumed. These animals are killed only when they cause damages to the human beings. The different species of animals eaten by them include – Deer (*Cervulus mutijac*), bear (*Sclenarctos thibetanus*), wild boar (*Sus scrofa*), reindeer (*Axis axis*), antelopes, monkey (*Macaca radiata*), wild *mithun* (*Bos fontalis*), porcupine (*Porcupine hystrix*), Pangolin/Scaly anteater (*Manis tricupis*), squirrel big size (*Dremomys lokriah*), squirrel (*Funambulus*), wild rat (*Ratus ratus*), etc. Among the animals hunted beer, monkey, squirrel, rat are not eaten by the girls or women because they believe that if a woman dares to consume it she may have sores all over her face, and soon get tired of her life. Deer and monkey are hunted frequently in the area that threatens the very existence of these animals. Various birds eaten by them are wild chicken, bulbul (*Molpastes cafer*), parrot (*Psittacula eupatricia*), wild pigeon, hornbill rufous necked (*Aceros nipalensis*), wreated (*Ryticeros undulats*), common grey hornbill/Dhanesh in Hindi (*Tochus birostries*), etc. Birds like *gudru* (hornbill), *salvo*, etc. are restricted for consumption to the women folk. The Akas adopt a variety of indigenous techniques of fishing i.e. netting, angling, damming of the rivers, poisoning of rivers by using herbal poisons (roots, stems and leaves), use of bamboo traps, etc. Different species of fishes eaten are Rohu (*Rohita sp.*), *Labeo pangsu, Labeo sp., Glyptothrox sp., Garra sp., Abriricthes sp., Psyudochenies sp., Psilorhynchoides sp.*, eel (*Anguilla japonica*), prawn (*Panoles sp.*), crab (*Cancer sp.*), etc. The surrounding forest provides various species of insects for consumption. During winter season people use to collect *Nyepsio* (stinkbug) *Poisus maculiventris* from the banks of rivers. The old women for the betterment of health and eyesight usually consume insects like *miinye, tronii, bobiow*, etc. More than five varieties of Bee (*Apisdorsata*) are collected and eaten. Insects form a part of their diet, as they believe that insects contain rich proteins and vitamins. Insects are mainly consumed in raw form and through steaming process.

Food Taboos

The Akas restrict themselves from taking the flesh of some animals, birds, fishes and insects. In general the men enjoys little bit of freedom of consumption during feasts and festivities. Some parts of the domestic animals like head, legs, stomach, etc. were restricted from consumption to all during the olden days. Nowadays, they enjoy more freedom and take almost all parts of the domestic animals and chicken. The restriction is much more for the women in comparison to the men. They are permitted to take only a few of the non-vegetarian dishes. Beef, mutton, bear, rat, etc. are tabooed for the women, even some parts of the pork and fowls are also restricted from consumption. The food taboos on women are rigid for which they use to be abided without any lapses.

People believe that any one who violates these taboos would be punished by the supernatural agencies. If a woman dares to violate then the supernatural would disfigure her face with sores all over her face and mouth and may lose her life also. The belief was so strong during the past that a woman would not only avoid the tabooed dishes, but also take special care even not to take food prepared in such pot which might have sometime contained them. Milk in any form or any preparations made from it are also tabooed for women. It is for this reason milk and milk products do not hold much importance in the society. These taboos are still in vogue among the older people however, it has taken backseat for the younger generation. Nowadays, women also enjoy enough freedom in taking non–vegetarian dishes and milk.

Food Preservation

The Akas use to construct granaries (*nyechi*) for preserving food grains such as paddy, maize, millet, arum, etc. The granaries (*nyechi*) were usually constructed at the backside of the house. Such a preservation of food grains is practiced for the need during the crisis period. Two types of bamboo shoot locally known as *suhu* and *siipsi* were made and preserved on some utensils or bamboo tube (*wubji*). The former is preserved by drying in the sunlight, while the later is preserved by cutting into small pieces and kept on a bamboo tube for long period of time. Every household commonly practices smoking of meat. Meat is usually smoked either by keeping over the *chulla* or on the *chulla*. Meat is also preserved by drying it on the sunlight. Meat is also cut into smaller and longer pieces and hanged on a rope tight on the ceiling (*suto*). On the same way fish is also smoked on the *chulla* either by keeping on a net of iron or by using a small stick (*chigdri*). For the preparation of local liquor (*tsimso-tsi*) either banana leaves or another plant known, as *womsey* is important and extensively used. These leaves are used for keeping the local liquor and also covering it. These leaves are very much necessary in the fermentation process of local liquor. Gourd (*kutcho*) is also collected for pouring of water on the liquor and extraction of wine from the utensil. Other items such as *giije* (strainer), *sunu* (strainer), etc. were also made from the raw materials collected from the forests. Seeds of vegetables and other food grains are usually kept in a big variety of gourd, known as *hutum* for the next year's cultivation.

DIALECT/LANGUAGE

Language is one of the basic elements of a society's culture. Geographers look at the similarities and differences among languages to understand the diffusion and interaction of people around the world. Language is like a piece of luggage; people carry it with them when they move from place to place. They add new words to their own language when they reach new places and contribute words brought with them to the existing stock of language at the new location. It is a major characteristic of a region and a source of pride to people, a symbol of cultural unity. It is both the cause and the consequence of the development of a unique culture. Studying the distribution of languages across the earth's surface helps geographers identify the regions that various cultural groups occupy.

Language is a system of communication through the use of speech, a collection of sounds that are understood by a group of people to have the same meaning. Many languages also have a literary tradition, or a system of communication through writing, though hundreds of spoken languages do not have a literary tradition. A language family is a collection of individual languages related to each other by virtue of having a common ancestor. Though several thousand languages are spoken around the world, they can be grouped into a small number of language families.

A dialect (from the Greek word *dialektos*) is a variety of a language characteristic of a particular group of the language's speakers. The term is applied most often to regional speech patterns, but a dialect may also be defined by other factors, such as social class. In popular usage, the word "dialect" is sometimes used to refer to a lesser-known language (most commonly a regional language), especially one that is unwritten or not standardized. This use of the word dialect is often taken as pejorative/derogatory by the speakers of the languages referred to in that way since it is often accompanied by the erroneous belief that the minority language is lacking in vocabulary, grammar, or importance. The number of speakers, and the geographical area covered by them, can be of arbitrary size, and a dialect might contain several sub-dialects. A dialect is a complete system of verbal communication (oral or signed, but not necessarily written) with its own vocabulary and grammar. Just as languages evolve from a common ancestor, so can several dialects derive from one language. A dialect is a form of a language spoken in a local area. One dialect of a language is normally recognized as the standard language, which is the form used for official government business, education and mass communication.

An account of the languages of Kameng District has been given by I. M. Simon, the then Deputy Director, Research Department, Arunachal Pradesh as below:

> Linguistically, the district shows three marked divisions. The entire western area from the northern border to the south is inhabited by Buddhist tribes speaking languages grouped by linguists under the Tibeto-Himalayan branch. These are Monpa and Sherdukpen with related dialects. In the central strip, almost co-extensively, are the Mijis and the Akas who are culturally and socially akin but speak distinct dialects and the western Daflas or Bangnis in the entire eastern area of the district. These are the principal language groups, though there are pockets here and there with distinct speech forms and there are yet to be studied and properly grouped. In a small are hemmed in by the areas occupied by the Sherdukpens, Mijis and

Akas are the Khowas or Buguns. Then between the Akas and the Bangnis there is a small group of people living in Pichang and adjacent villages Chijang and Kitchang, who though they are grouped with Aka speak a dialect that bears little resemblance with Aka. The terrain, the lay of the land and the course of the mountain ranges in West Kameng would appear to have been very powerful factors in the development of the languages spoken in the area.

The next group which can be called the western group of the North Assam Branch consists of Aka and Miji. Although these two tribes have cultural and social ties, the respective dialects show wide divergences. Aka, as spoken have variable cadences, almost of a sing-song character, and a wealth of fricatives and gutturals reminiscent of Sema Naga (Census of India, 1971). This seems to be so much a characteristic of the language that in certain dialect areas, *r* sometimes gives way to *gh*. The intonation in Miji does not have the same striking variations as Aka has. The exact place of Aka in the language complex of the area is problematic at the moment. Miji in some respects seems to provide a link, albeit a tenuous one, between Aka and the neighbouring group to the East i.e. the Central group. One indicator that may safely be seized upon is the numerical system. Table 4.5.1 shows the comparison of Aka, Miji, Hill Miri, Pichang (Koro) and Khowa numerals.

When the Aka and Miji numerals are compared, a curious fact is to be noted that the numbers up to five in Miji are similar to those of the Central group whereas those from six to nine are close to Aka. The Aka numeral 'ten' itself may be compared to Hill Miri írí, the Aka phoneme 'gh' being a variant of 'r'. In Aka and Miji, again, numbers like thirty and forty, etc. are stated in terms of 'ten-three' or 'ten-four' unlike in the languages of the central group or in the Pichang (Koro) dialect where the terms 'three-ten' or 'four-ten', etc. are used. It may be noted that the later system is common to the languages of Tirap.

Table 4.5.1
Comparison of Aka Dialect with the Surrounding Tribes

English	*Aka*	*Miji*	*Pichang (Koro)*	*Khowa*	*Hill Miri*
One	a	ung	eche	Ja	aken
Two	ksi	gni	kene	nyi	enyi
Three	zí	gíthín	kala	um	oum
Four	piyi	bli	kopre	vi	epi
Five	pom	bungu	phre	gua	angngo
Six	ghye	reh	shifi	rek	ake
Seven	mro	myah	re	mulai	kenne
Eight	sígzí	sígín	rala	milau	pi:ne
Nine	sthí	síthín	gíye	digwe	kona
Ten	ghí	lin	fala	soa	írí
Thirty	zí-ghí	gíthín-lin	fala-yal-kala	sa-l-um	
Forty	piyi-ghí	bli-lin	fala-yal-kopre	sa-l-vi	
Hundred	fuwa	bílong	nye-phra	vyung	

Source: Census of India, 1971.

The comparison of Hrusso, Koro, Apatani, Bangni (Nyishi) and Boro numerals is shown in Table 4.5.2. There is no affinity in the numerals of these tribes. However, there appears some similarity in the way of making numbers like thirty as 'ten-three' (zí-ghí in Hrusso, hinge-aliyahe in Apatani, tham dzii in Boro) among the Aka (Hrusso), Apatani and Boro. The Aka (Koro) numerals are closer to the Bangni (Nyishi) in stating the numbers of thirty, forty, etc. (stated in terms of 'ten-three' or ten-four').

Table 4.5.2
Comparison of Aka Dialect with the surrounding tribes

English	*Aka (Hrusso)*	*Pichang (Koro)*	*Apatani*	*Bangni*	*Boro*
(1)	*(2)*	*(3)*	*(4)*	*(5)*	*(6)*
One	a	eche	Kone	akeng	se
Two	ksii	kene	Anye	anyi	nai
Three	zí	kala	Hinge	aam	tham
Four	piyi	kopre	Piilye	api	brai

(1)	*(2)*	*(3)*	*(4)*	*(5)*	*(6)*
Five	pom	phre	Yangohe	ango	phas
Six	ghye	shifi	Khiye	akhe	dho
Seven	mro	re	Kanuhe	kanii	sinii
Eight	sígzí	rala	Pyinye	piinii	dayin
Nine	sthí	gíye	Koahe	kayon	gu
Ten	ghí	fala	Aliyahe	cham	dzii
Thirty	zí-ghí	fala-yal-kala	Hingkhahe	chaam	tham dzii
Forty	piyi-ghí	fala-yal-kopre	aliyang piilyehe	champi	brai dzii
Hundred	fuwa	nye-phra	Langche	lang	dzow se

Source : Census of India, 1971 and Interview.

TATTOOING (*SYATRO PIW*)

Tattooing is an important aspect of the tribe in the sense that the nomenclature of the community itself has its root in relation to this practice. Though, the tattoo tradition is confined to the women only, it has played a significant role in the identification and distinctiveness of the tribe from the neighbouring tribes. The tradition of tattooing is found in two other tribes of the state namely Mijis and the Apatanis but, it is not possible to say with certainty that the tradition has been borrowed from either of the mentioned tribe. The Mijis being a neighbouring tribe the resemblance in culture and tradition can be make out at any point of reference. Tattooing is done generally in the early years of childhood i.e. around ten years but always before attaining of puberty. The faces of the girls is tattooed in a pattern of a straight line running from below the forehead to the chin where it bifurcates into three directions resembling to a bird foot. The tattoo is done with the help of a thorn and resin which is obtained from a green plant. A scratch is made on the face with an idea of the design in which the tattooing is desired and the resin is poured into the wound. When it is completely dried it leaves a permanent blue-black mark on the face. There are no special tattooists in the society, usually women of the house or neighbourhood help each other in tattooing their girls. Besides, the girls also decorate their faces and lips by some artificial black colour prepared by the essence of wild pine, locally known as *Mufo*. Tattooing has declined completely in some villages and very few remained in some villages restricting to the older women. It seems that after 5 to 6 years from now this tradition may totally vanish from the society. It is now felt as a matter of disfigurement of the face and the younger generations do not prefer this tradition. The same tradition is also dying out in the other tribes like Apatanis and Mijis, thus there is a consensus within the tribe to end the tattoo culture as handed over by the ancestors.

5 LINKAGES WITH THE FOREST RESOURCES

FOREST AND ECONOMIC LIFE

The tribal economy without the forest resources is quite unthinkable. The economic organization of the Akas revolves round *jhum*/shifting cultivation. *Jhum* cultivation is locally known as *vee*. Other subsidiary means like collection of forest products, fishing and hunting also form part of their economy. Shifting cultivation is an integral part of tribal culture. *Jhuming* grows out of a particular mental outlook of the tribal people and affects all the other spheres of their cultural life. They deliberately choose hilly and forested areas as their habitats. They venerate the spirits of mountains, rocks, rivers, lakes and trees. They pay special veneration to the fertile soil, the Mother Earth, with offerings of domestic animals like chicken, goats, pigs, *mithuns*, etc. The undulating terrain with higher slope characteristics in the hilly areas naturally demands the *jhum* or shifting type of cultivation where little plain areas are available. Agriculture is the main source of livelihood for the people. They largely depend on shifting cultivation, which has a strong utilization linkage with the natural resources.

Food gathering is a supplementary source of livelihood for the people. They depend on the forests for the requirements of vegetables, fruits, barks, edible plants and leaves, etc. Some of the forest products are collected throughout the year while some others are collected for six months only. An important edible wild plant locally known as *sim-nekchi* (*Dioscorea sp.*) serves the supplementary source of food during the period of shortage. Besides, there are other edible plants locally known as *sawo, saje* (Yams), *gudrolu, lumo*, etc. which are consumed during the period of food shortages. Thus, there is a symbiotic relationship between the forest ecology and the livelihood of the people. The forest provides variety of necessities to the people and in turn people spare the small plants and animals for posterity, keeping in view their future needs and requirements. Further, extraction of forest products in certain months is restricted, which brought a break in the continuous utilization of resources and contribute towards regeneration and growth of vegetation. Such a relationship with the nature had helped in evolving a sustained way of living even in this fast changing technological world.

The thick forest around the settlements compel them to pass through deep jungle and the urge for self defence mechanism against the wild life had made them to become good archers. As such hunting became part of their life and through which they supplement to their shortage of food supply. Hunting is an integral part of tribal way of life. The equipments/weapons used for hunting are the common bows and poisoned arrows (*kiyi, moodra, moo* and *moochi*), spear (*kiju*), gun (*mubyo*) and *dao* (*wetsi*). Deer, wild-pig, monkey, bear, etc. are the important animals hunted. In order to hunt specific animal required for certain rituals in the festival (*Nyechidow*) the community hunting is undertaken. It is also done on the predictions of priest (*mugouw*) who tells that if a particular animal is killed then the sufferings of the people will be cured. Animals such as tiger, wildcat, etc. are neither killed nor eaten by them. Hunting of these animals involves substantial risk to their life as well as observes stringent discipline in their life and expensive rituals. Birds such as crow, eagle, etc. are not killed and consumed because they are believed to be associated with the evil spirits and ghosts. Further, these birds have specific significance as scavenger in cleansing the human/organic waste that eliminate/reduce the danger of certain diseases. Hunting is done throughout the year, except June (*Chiyiw*) and July (*Wuju*), as these months are considered to be *hubey-suyuw* (bad month). It is believed that hunting during these months may cause accidents and loss of life. Therefore, a balanced (symbiotic) relationship has been created by these forest dwellers and loss to bio–resources are not very significant in this part of the country.

They have evolved variety of indigenous techniques of fishing. Fishing in any form has been restricted in the flooded streams probably due to anticipated risk of getting drowned in the river and loss of life. Indigenous techniques of fishing such as *tromo-mo* (netting), *akhgi-jyo* (angling), *hu-view* (damming of the rivers), *gyi-guw,* (herbal poisons i.e. root, stem and leaves) *tuvo-peo* (use of bamboo traps), *huju-dow* (Community fishing – diversion of big river course), etc. are extensively adopted for catching fish. The uses of indigenous techniques of fishing burdened with imperfection have proved significant in meeting their needs and requirements as well as checking the depletion of fish species. Use of blasting and chemical poisons is not allowed in the area. Anyone practicing this mode of fishing is punished up to 6 months jail imprisonment and an amount of Rs. 5,000 payable to the village council as fine. Thus, methods of fishing that are adopted in the area are eco-friendly. They spare the small fishes and some fish species are not consumed due to social beliefs attached to them. However, the modern technology has provided lots of fishing options to the people. In addition to blasting and chemical poison, recently a new technique of fishing has penetrated in the area i.e. use of electric current in the river. This new method is frequently practiced by the local people, which led to faster depletion of important fish species as well as the other organisms present in the river.

Forest and Material Culture

The climatic and edaphic conditions of the area facilitated luxuriant growth of different species of bamboo, cane and reed which provide raw materials for construction of their houses as well as other essential articles of daily uses. Various items of wood, bamboo, cane, leaves or thatches are collected from the adjacent forests. The whole house is a work of bamboo and wood, bamboo sheets forming the floor, the wall and the roof, and wooden logs serving as the main pillars over which the structure of the house is raised. The roof is usually thatched, and tied/tight by bamboo ropes. The various types of thatching materials are Banana leaf (*Musa sp.*), Straw (*Erianthus sp.*), Cane leaf (*Calamus sp.*), etc. The hard woods for the main and supporting pillars are extracted from Bola (*Morus laevigata* Wall.), and others locally known as *Syopesan, Msanyi* (*Macaranga sp.*), etc. Some of the varieties of bamboos viz. *Dendocalamus hamiltonii, Arundinaria sp., Bambusa tulda,* and *B. pallida* are used for wall, floor and ropes for binding the poles. House is decorated with skulls of *Mithuns*, jaws of Pigs and wild boars on the front wall.

Various important agricultural implements are made of either wood or bamboo. A small loop shaped implement locally known as *kiyi* is made out of a variety of bamboo known as *bje* (*Phyllostachys bambusoides*). This implement is used for clearing the small weeds in the *jhum* field. Another implement is made out of a hard wood and locally known as *pallo*, which is used for digging the ground, sowing the seeds and clearing the weeds. The handles (*etrii*) of axe, dao, spade, etc. are also made out of either bamboo or hard wood. The forest is the only source for the equipments of hunting and fishing. The bow and arrows are made out of a hard species of bamboo and the rope for bow and arrow are collected from a bark of small tree known as *mumdra*. The arrows are kept in a quiver, made of bamboo and locally known as *thuvou*. The arrows are poisoned (aconite) on the front part, which is known as *mukhu*. This poison plant (aconite) is not available in the Aka area; hence it is collected from far places locally known to be *lasa-sigyeng* (Somewhere near Tibet area). They also prepare numerous types of traps for hunting. A trap known as *che* hunts bigger animals such as bear, wild pig, deer, monkey, etc. A second type of trap is known as *yetu*, which is prepared with the help of a hard rope. A hard rope is tight on the top of a hardwood pole, and then it is stretched and fixed on the ground by some technique. It hangs the animal on the pole as the animals pass through it. A third type of trap is known as *mudru*. It is prepared with the help of a rope made of a plant known as *mumdra* for hunting birds and rats. Another type of trap is known as *muju*, which is prepared with the help of a stone, two sticks, a bamboo rope and a piece of insect. When the bird attempts to eat the insect, the bird is trapped inside the stone. The local rubber is also used for killing birds. Some 50-100 pieces of small sticks of bamboo are prepared and the rubber is poured on the sticks in a bamboo tube and mixed-up completely. These sticks are placed on the branches of the wild fruits early in the morning. As the bird's tries to eat fruits, they are trapped on the rubber and fall down on the ground. This practice is known as *sejyen-kseo*.

Fishing is done in a variety of ways. The angling stick is extracted from the forest i.e. from a bamboo species known as *bje* (*Phyllostachys bambusoides*). During *hu-vyiew* (damming of the rivers) lots of hard wood and leaves of plants are collected for damming the river. After damming the river if the river is not completely dried-up, herbal poisons known as *Gyi* (*Derris scandens*), *Fuhuliitrii* (*Amphineuron extensus*), *Wukupa* (*Acasia sp.*), etc. are used for killing the fish. Another way of fishing known as *tuvo peo* (bamboo trap) is the work of a bamboo and cane. A community fishing i.e. diversion of the river course by damming is locally known as *huju dow*, which involves large number of hard wood, leaves and stone for damming the river. However, the modern guns, blasting, chemical poisons, electric currents are replacing the traditional equipments of hunting and fishing. It is worth mentioning here that the traditional way of hunting and fishing has great implications in the sustainable management of the resources. But the greater adoption of newer fishing techniques has posed a serious threat on the important fish and organisms of the area.

During the olden days, they use to weave some clothes known as *pasa*. A small plant known as *mumdra* is used for making yarns. The bark of the plant is taken out in the form of ropes and dried in the sunlight for several days for preparing yarns. The process of weaving is known as *pasa-triew* or *ge-triew*. The clothes prepared by this process are very simple and used for the protection of body only. Another plant known as *wuma* is also used for weaving clothes by following the aforesaid process. As the clothes are essential to protect human beings from erratic weather fluctuations it is obvious that weaving assumes importance for them. Earlier weaving was important for them and people use to weave clothes for their daily uses but after assimilating with the plain people they have left their traditional way of weaving. The fruit of a tall tree known as *brovji-je* is used for hair oil as well as oil for body pain reliever. Another small plant known as *migyim-jyoksu* (*Ricinus cumunis*) is also used for deriving hair oil. A ring-cap of bamboo, known as *miisanga*, is worn by the male folk, as an important part of their traditional attire. It is prepared from the inner portion of a common bamboo *siiva* (*Dendocalamus hamiltonni*). Besides, tobacco pipe (*muksung*) made of variety of bamboo known as *bje* (*Phyllostachys bambusoides*) and *truka* (comb) made of the same species were used as a part of their dress.

Some of their ornaments are made of wood, cane, bamboo, etc. An earring usually worn by both men and women is known as *fusva* and it is prepared by a variety of bamboo known as *bje*. A hand bangle known as *musung-pango* is put on by the women folk that are made from a plant known as *musung*. The domestic utensils of the Akas, which form essential articles/items of the household, are purely indigenous ones.

Different kinds of musical instruments of social, cultural and religious importance are carved-out from bamboo, wood, cane, etc. The musical instruments are used on different occasions like rituals and festivals that form part of their material culture. Most commonly used instruments are *bjiva*, which is a work of bamboo or gourd, *silili* (flute) made of bamboo, *dho*, made of bamboo and *sedii* (drum) made of wood and animal skin. Familiarization with these instruments becomes necessary on the part of every individual in the society.

Forest, Food Habits and Ethno Medicines

Food is the prime necessity of life. Life without food is practically inconceivable. Human beings can get food either through the plants or through the animals. Nature provides plenty of edible plants from which leaves, stems, roots, fruits, etc. are taken as food. It is generally agreed upon that before the knowledge of (the art of) plant cultivation, man use to gather food from the surrounding forests. Similarly animal food was taken either in the form of meat or milk or through other forms (Singh, et al. 1992). The food habits of the people are largely determined by the conditions in which they live. As such the majority of Indian tribes, living in the isolated hills and mountains are still largely dependent on their natural surroundings in order to procure food items. The area abounds numerous variety of edible plants for them. The various edible vegetables collected from the forests are Bamboo shoot (*Dendocalamus hamiltonni*), banana flower/ Spadix inflorescence (*Musa paradisiaca*), *Pouzolzia viminea, Piper pedicellatum, Piplazium esculantum, Clerodendrom colebrookianum, Alocasia sp.*, Mushrooms (*Termitomyces sp., Cantherallus sp., Schizophyllum sp., Pleurotus pulmonarius, Auricularia sp.*) and many more plants, the scientific name of which are still not known. They collect number of fruits from the forest (Plate 5.1). Some of the important fruits are Bansum (*Phoebe spp.*), wild lichi (*Myristica fragrance*), *Picus semichordata, Castanopsis indica, Hodgsonia macrocarpa, Rubus sp., Rubus niveus, Picus hispida, Musa sp.*, etc.

The dense mixed jungle of the area provides wide range of animals of different species. Some of the animals, such as tiger and elephant are not killed and consumed. These animals are killed only when they cause damages to the human beings. The different species of animals eaten by them include – Deer (*Cervulus mutijac*), bear (*Sclenarctos thibetanus*), wild boar (*Sus scrofa*), reindeer (*Axis axis*), antelopes, monkey (*Macaca radiata*), wild mithun (*Bos fontalis*), porcupine (*Porcupine hystrix*), Pangolin/Scaly anteater (*Manis tricupis*), squirrel big size (*Dremomys lokriah*), squirrel (*Funambulus*), wild rat

PLATE NO. 5.1
FOOD HABITS AND RELATED MATTERS

(a)

(b)

(c)

(d)

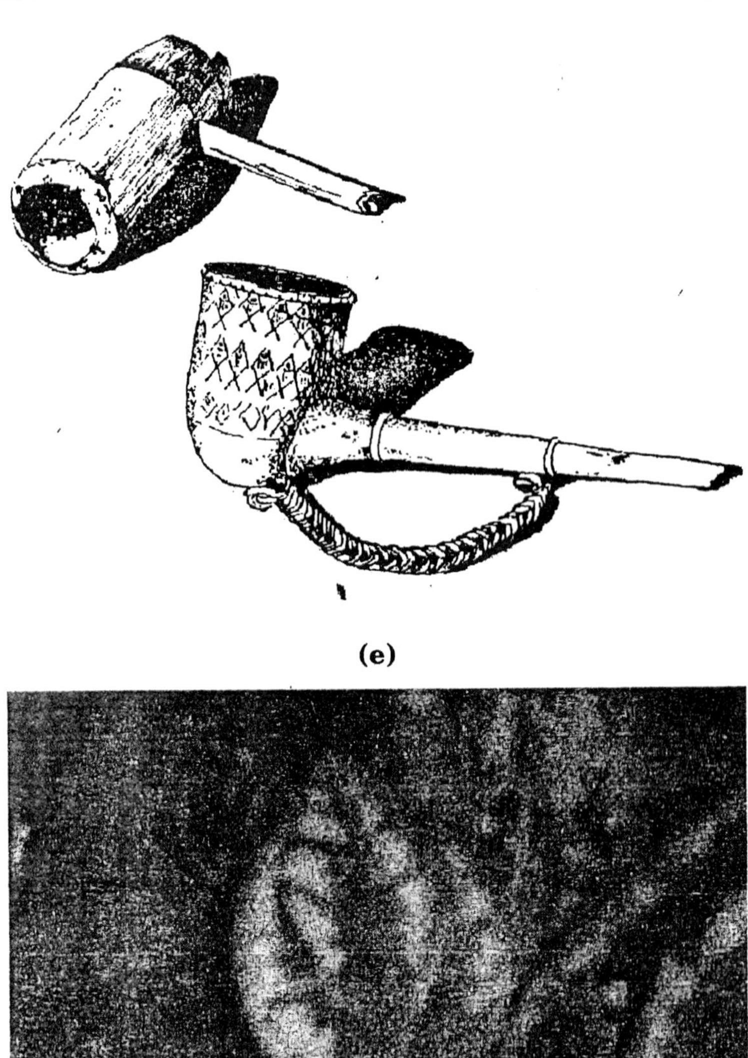

(e)

(f)

(g)

(h)

(i)

Photo : (a) *Nyechi* – Aka granaries, (b) *Tronye* – a small granary constructed especially for storing Arum, (c) *Ukro* – an Iron-hearth used for cooking purposes, (d) *Ghato* – indigenous mortars for both maize and millet made of stone, (e) *Muksung* – Traditional tobacco pipes made of bamboo, (f) Wild Pan chewed with betel nut, (g) *Kusuwun* (*Rubus sp.*)–a species of strawberry, (h) *Kumu* (*Rubus ellipticus*)–another species of strawberry smaller in size, (i) *Kusukabro* (*Rubus niveus*) – a variety of strawberry.

(*Ratus ratus*), etc. Among the animals hunted beer, monkey, squirrel, rat are not eaten by the girls or women because they believe that if a woman dares to consume it she may have sores all over her face, and soon get tired of her life. Deer and monkey are hunted frequently in the area that threatens the very existence of these animals.

Various birds eaten by them are wild chicken, bulbul (*Molpastes cafer*), parrot (*Psittacula eupatricia*), wild pigeon, hornbill rufous necked (*Aceros nipalensis*), wreated (*Ryticeros undulats*), common grey hornbill/Dhanesh in Hindi (*Tochus birostries*), etc. Birds like *gudru* (hornbill), *salvo*, etc. are restricted for consumption to the women folk. Different species of fishes eaten are Rohu (*Rohita sp.*), *Labeo pangsu, Labeo sp., Glyptothrox sp., Garra sp., Abriricthes sp., Psyudochenies sp., Psilorhynchoides sp. nob,* eel (*Anguilla japonica*), prawn (*Panoles sp.*), crab (*Cancer sp.*), etc. The surrounding forest provides various species of insects for consumption. During winter season people use to collect *Nyepsio* (stinkbug) *Poisus maculiventris* from the banks of rivers. The old women for the betterment of health and eyesight usually consume insects like *menye, tronii, bobiow,* etc. More than five varieties of Bee (*Apisdorsata*) are collected and eaten. Insects form a part of their diet, as they believe that insects contain rich proteins and vitamins. So, the bio-resources form an important part of their diet.

Ethnomedicine

Ethnomedicine refers to the study of traditional medical practice. It can encompass methods of diagnosis and treatment. In some cases it is associated with professional medicine men and women, in others with lay persons who have acquired knowledge from parents or relatives. Ethnomedicine is a sub-field of medical anthropology and deals with the study of traditional medicines. It may include not only those that have relevant written sources (e.g. Traditional Chinese Medicine, Ayurveda), but the knowledge and practices orally transmitted over the centuries. In the scientific arena, ethnomedical studies are generally characterized by a strong anthropological approach, more than a bio-medical one. The focus of these studies is then the perception and context of use of traditional medicines, and not their bio-evaluation. Traditional medicine has remained as the most affordable and easily accessible source of treatment in the primary healthcare system. In the tribal society the local therapy had been only means of medical treatment.

In Arunachal Pradesh, medicinal plants have been used as traditional medicine to treat different human ailments by the local people from time immemorial. These medicinal plants are estimated to be of numerous species. There is a high expectation of enormous traditional knowledge and use of medicinal plant species in state due to the existence of diverse cultures, languages and beliefs among the people. However, since cultural systems are dynamic, the skills are fragile and easily forgettable as most of the indigenous knowledge transfer in the state is based on oral transmission. The Akas are also practicing the knowledge of traditional medicinal plant since time immemorial. There are large number of valuable medicinal plants and herbs in the Aka area. They collect medicinal plants, roots, fruits, barks, etc. to heal variety of diseases and wounds. Thus, they have indigenous method of treatment for different kinds of diseases with the help of local herbal medicines (Plate 5.2). The knowledge of the traditional medicinal plants is restricted to the old aged people only. They use some parts of animals such as antelopes, bear, etc. for curing diseases of orthopedic, stomachache, etc. Consumption of some species of fish is also believed to be important for curing illness or diseases. The medicinal plants used for the curing of various diseases are given in Table 5.1.

Significance of Belief System in Forest Conservation

The Akas believe that the earth and the sky are the creators and worship them as their God. The strong linkages with the surrounding milieu have made them a strong believer of the nature. Their major festival is known as *Nyechidow* (which means to clean the village from evil spirits). All kinds of materials required for the successful completion of the festival depend on the available bio–resources of the forest. The priest (*mugouw*) holds important position in the society. The God (*Nyezino*) is appeased through the communion of the priest. The essential materials such as *duonyo* (plants, creepers, etc.) and *mthinye`* (altars) are collected from the forests. Besides, they use to celebrate in another occasion known as *Hu–Phu-kuwuow*, which means to worship the water and mountains of the village. The water and mountains are worshipped every year by sacrifice of animals. This is

Table 5.1
Ethnomedicinal Plants used by the Akas

Scientific Name	Local Name	Therapeutic indication	Mode of Use
1	2	3	4
Paederia foetida Linn. Rubiaceae	*Adraluhumbe*	Fire and Hot Water burns	10 gm of fresh leaves and stems are crushed in indigenous mortar and pestle, sieved with fine cloth and the juice is applied on the burns thrice a day.
Macaranga denticulata (Blume) Muell. Arg. Euphorbiaceae	*Liidzin*	Fire and Hot Water burns	Fresh resin is collected from the plant in bamboo tube and applied in the burns (anti-inflammatory) SOS.
Artemisia nilagirica (Clarke) pamp. Asteraceae	*Syowum*	Cough and fever	10 gm of fresh leaves and stems are crushed in indigenous mortar and pestle, sieved with fine cloth and the juice is applied on the burns thrice a day.
Begonia sp. Begoniaceae	*Pelowo*	Boil	Tender leaves are steamed and taken for quick recovery and lessening of pain and also used as blood purifier.
Ageratum conyzoides Linn. Asteraceace	*Pasong*	Cuts	Paste are prepared from leaves by hand squeezing method and applied in fresh cuts for clotting of blood and anti-microbial action.

Table 5.1 (Contd. . . .)

1	2	3	4
Curcuma sp. Linn. Zingiberaceae	*Kiistradu*	Stomachache	5 gm of clean rhizome are consumed twice a day for at least 3 days in severe stomach pain.
Dendrocalamus hamiltonni Poaceae	*Si-emnyo*	Cuts	With the help of dao / peeler the culm is peeled and powdery peel off is directly applied to fresh cut and injury for clotting of blood.
Zanthoxylum piperatum (L.) DC. Rutaceae	*Siina*	Labour pain	Dry fruits are fried in hot plate and taken with warm fermented local made alcohol *Tsii* (rice beer) mostly during labour pain and after delivery.
Clerodendrom colebrookianum Walp. Lamiaceae	*Droloin*	Diarrhoea	The tender leaves are steamed and consumed during diarrhoea and other indigestions.
Centella asiatica Linn. Apiaceae	*Syōwbo*	Jaundice	Raw roots and leaves are taken along with routine food during jaundice for appetizer.
Discorea sp. Dioscoreaceae	*Nyemumsi*	Dysentery	Cooked yam (both boil and burn) is consumed for curing dysentery. It is also applied to domestic animals for the same purposes.

Table 5.1 (Contd. . . .)

1	2	3	4
Ricinus cummunis Linn. Euphorbiaceae	*Migyim jyoksu*	Orthopaedic	10 – 20 gm of fresh leaves are made into paste and applied to fractured bones and joint pains. 2 – 3 leaves are slightly heated in fire and tied with a rope over the fractured part and kept for a week.
Costus specious (Koenig) Smith Zingiberaceae	*Rumo-sana-dugo*	Jaundice, gastric and eye infection	The juicy beat is chewed just like sugarcane during jaundice and gastric. 1–2 drops of the extracted juice from the stem is applied during eye infections twice a day for immediate relief and recovery.
Rhus javanica Linn. Anacardiaceae	*Subyutro*	Dysentery	In mild condition raw fruits are consumed directly. But during severe dysentery the juice is extracted from the fruit by squeezing method and taken 3–4 glass a day.
Unidentified	*Mechme*	Diarrhoea	2–3 leaves are consumed directly with water for at least 3 days.

Source: Field Survey, 2006 and 2008.

PLATE NO. 5.2
ETHNOMEDICINES AND MUSHROOMS

(a)

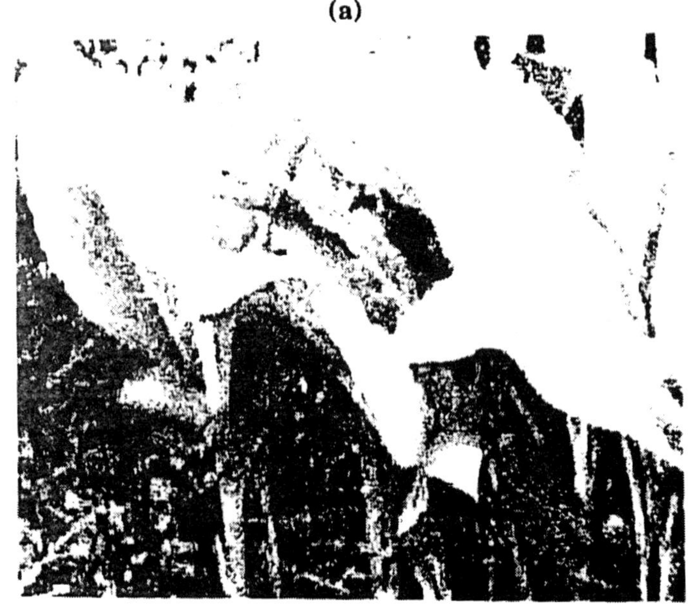

(b)

(c)

(d)

(e)

(f)

(g)

(h)

(i)

(j)

Photo : (a) *Ageratum conyzoides*, (b) *Curcuma sp.* Linn., (c) *Trichosanthes tricuspis*, (d) *Paederia-feotida*, (e) Unidentified medicinal plant locally known as *Mechime*, (f) *Cantherallus sp.*, (g) *Auricularia sp.*, (h) *Termitomyces sp.*, (i) *Ricinus cummunis*, (j) *Artemisia nilagirica*.

done for the betterment of the villagers and also for averting the natural calamities such as floods, earthquakes, landslides, etc. They worship the forests, mountains, water bodies, etc. for their well being in particular and the human world in general.

Conservation of Animal Resources

Conservation and management of plant and animal resources is not a new concept for the tribals. Rather, it is an integral part of the folk culture. Traditional modes of conservation and management of forest resources refer to the life long practices of mankind in relation to the optimal utilization of the plant and animal resources. It deals with the indigenous methods of conservation and management of plant and animal resources for the sustainable development in their economic system. Indigenous knowledge system of the tribe displays many traditional practices vital for conservation and management of forest resources. These include various faith and beliefs that are pertinent in protection of sacred-groves, from which extraction of plant material is restricted/restrained. The festivals are linked to the forests. Traditionally, they practice an annual hunting ritual after worshipping the forest god. During such hunting, they spare pregnant as well as immature animals. The herbal practitioners belonging to the community do not promote medicinal plants from over extraction/harvesting, fire and grazing (Gadgil, 1998).

Like many tribes of our country, tribal people of Arunachal Pradesh also depend on their surrounding forest ecosystem. They do not only use various plant and animal resources but also reflect heterogeneous beliefs and practices intricately associated with ecosystem. Study on such beliefs and practices have tremendous implications as these can be perceived in the process of natural resource management. Thus, it has vital significance in maintaining the bio-diversity of the region.

The Akas have their own indigenous knowledge system useful in the conservation of forest resources. Numerous species of plants are not extracted from the forests. Similarly, some animals are neither killed nor eaten by these people. As such, these people have developed an eco-friendly relation with the surrounding forest ecosystem. It is interesting to note that numerous species of animals are found in the area. The tradition and culture of these people were set on the lap of the nature. By trial or error method they got acquainted with do's and don'ts while interacting with the nature for sustainable development. Though, hunting and fishing are the primary occupation next to jhuming, people always restrain from killing of certain species of animals and contribute towards their conservation. Although, conservation in its strict sense is not practiced by the Akas, their traditional faith and beliefs indirectly help to conserve the forest resources. Some of the animals and birds are neither killed nor consumed such as tiger, elephant, wildcat, etc. Hunting of these animals involves substantial risk to their life as well. Birds such as crow, eagle, etc. are not killed and consumed because they are believed to be associated with the evil spirits and ghosts. Further, these birds have specific significance in cleansing the human/organic waste that eliminates the danger of spread of certain diseases. Glimpses of various species of animals and birds that are protected by them are given in table 5.2 and 5.3.

Concept of Sacred Groves

The concept of sacred groves finds mention in our literature throughout the length and breadth of India as Panchavati. It refers to five (*pancha*) groves (*vati*). *Panchavati*, therefore means a grove of five trees. These trees are the banyan, the peepal, the ashoka tree, the bela tree and the harada tree. These species of plants have their own significance; therefore, Hindus worship the plants that ultimately led to its conservation and protection. To Akas, the *Nowu-Husu yiew* means the forestland and ponds/lakes, which are believed to be sacred and have vital significance to the mankind in one way or the other, is used as substitute to term sacred groves. The areas where some trees grow in a grove, which bear a distinct character are protected. Any sort

Table 5.2
Traditional Practices in Conservation of Wild Animals

Local Name	*English Name*	*Scientific Name*	*Peoples beliefs*	*Mode of Management*
Hiitru	Tiger	*Panthera tigris*	The Akas believe that the tiger used to be afraid of man and vice-versa. People do not consume the flesh of tiger and therefore it is not killed. Killing of tiger is believed to be inauspicious and there is a long process of ritual performance for killing tiger.	As killing of the tiger involves such a long process of puja performance people do not went for hunting tiger and whenever on their way they meet any tiger they follow another path. When the tiger killed some villagers then all the villagers gather and tiger is being hunted. So, it is not killed by a normal man. Every one fear of killing tiger.
Achile	Elephant	*Elephus maximus*	Killing of elephant is restricted in the Aka area. It is killed only when it causes more damages and loses of life and property to the villagers. Killing of elephant requires members from at least ten villages. A piece of red thread is tied around the arrow of the person who is supposed to shoot the elephant. The priest will chant mantras that elephant has been killed by a man from other community and not by the Akas.	Any person who killed the elephant has to remain outside of the house for ten days. The Akas worship the elephants by burning incense (*syobrovji*). As the killing of elephant involves such a long process, people avoid killing the elephants. This is the reason that lots of elephants are found in the Aka inhabited forests.

Source : Field Survey, 2006.

Table 5.3
Traditional Practices in Conservation of Wild Birds

Local Name	*English Name*	*Scientific Name*	*People's Beliefs*	*Mode of Management*
Sujo	—	—	This bird is treated as equal to man. They believe that the chattering of this bird symbolizes the grief or sadness.	So this bird is not killed and conserved as because it is essential for the people to know about the bad times approaching them.
Gudruw Sugro	Hornbill Rufous-necked Wreated Great pied	*Accerao nipalensis Ryticeros undulats Buceros bicornis*	The Akas believe that this is the largest bird found in their area. The females are not allowed to eat the flesh of hornbill; therefore, it is not killed.	Management of this bird is done by imposing restrictions among the villagers. The fat of these birds is used by this people for curing chest pain, headaches and joints. So, it is only killed when it is required.
Pulwam	Crow	*Garcinia Periculeta*	These people believed that this bird carries numerous bad diseases.	Killing of this bird is restricted throughout the Aka villages. This is the reason why there are lots of crows in the area.
Asii-foki	—	—	They believe that this bird is the owner of the sacred thread, which is worn by the Akas in their right hand. They believe that this bird is related to the myth of the creation of the earth and sky.	These birds are never killed since long history of the Akas. Also they believe that they have never heard that somewhere, someone had killed this bird. In the forests, when they find this bird they always try to save the life of this bird by allowing it to fly away from those hunters who are not aware of the beliefs associated with this bird.

Source : Field Survey, 2006.

of interference to such grove would result in loss of human life. Further, they believe the presence of some unseen supernatural power *ubro* or *ubram* in such grove. As such, these areas remained free from human interference. These have made people exercise maximum restrain in the sacred grove and bears significance to conservation of forest resources.

The Aka inhabited area is generally characterised with hilly terrain and covered with very dense forest. To them forests, rivers, hills and so on are the creation of supernatural powers. So they worship the forests as *Thouw-gew*, meaning rearer and feeder. They also worship the mountains and rivers as *Huda kuwuow phuda kuwuow*. In fact, these people are the worshippers of nature. These people worships the nature and there are some areas at Palizi village, Nechiphu, etc., which are considered as sacred groves (Plate 5.3). Visiting and extraction of any kind of material from such groves are strictly prohibited because of its linkage with some beliefs and myths. The following places are believed as sacred places by Akas.

Wojo phu (Name of Mountain)

This mountain is considered as the highest mountain peak in the Aka area. The mountain is believed to be sacred. It is believed that this mountain is very far away from the human settlement and one has to struggle hard to reach there. Extraction of forest materials, collection of stones, hunting, etc. from this mountain is strictly prohibited to all the villagers. A saying goes 'if someone plucks some leaves or anything from the mountain, he/she will lose the way and suffer from dreadful diseases, which may result into bleeding from nose and mouth and ultimately loss of life. This belief of the people is so strong that even today also no one even dares to visit over there. Such beliefs have either directly or indirectly helped in the conservation of various forest products of the area which ultimately contributed to improvement of the quality of forest.

PLATE NO. 5.3
SACRED PLACES, BELIEFS, RITUALS AND FESTIVALS

(a)

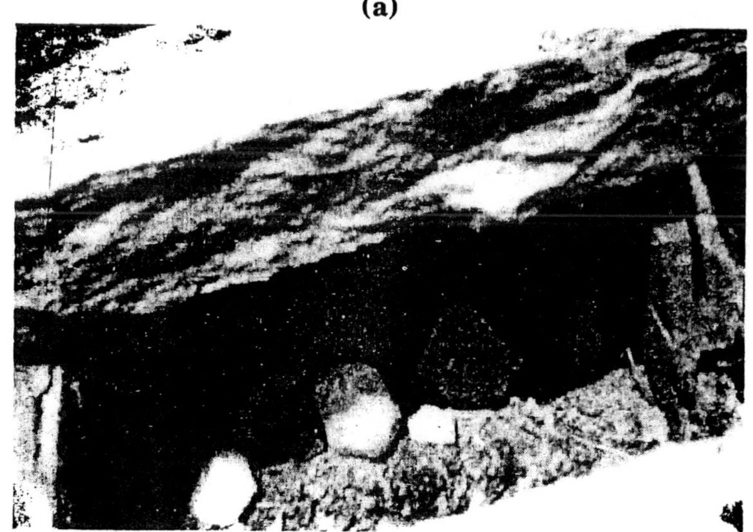

(b)

(c)

(d)

(e)

(f)

(g)

(h)

(i)

Photo : (a) *Nyezowo* (An isolated hill believed to be sacred at Jamiri village), (b) *Jyopsinfo* (Shining stones believed to be sacred near Prizin village), (c) *Vojophu* (A mountain believed to be sacred at Palizi village), (d) An elongated stone believed to be sacred near Kararamu village, (e) *Hugien* (Source of drinking water with puja altars at Yayong village), (f) *Nyetrii Psigha* (A sacred place where meetings and festivals are conducted at Yayong village, (g) *Suin* (Erection of stones as a mark of agreement between two parties), (h) The foundation stone of Thrizino festival ground, (i) *Kiyikhru* (A kind of ritual performed for the well-being of family).

Nearma *husu* (Name of Pond)

This pond is located near the Nechiphu pass, which is about 5,000 feet above mean sea level. This pond is situated on the top of mountain and has preponderance of betel nut tree and pan plants. These people go to worship at the pond. People visit this pond but plucking of any leaves from this pond is prohibited. They believe that if someone plucks leaves and wish to return home, he/she lost the way to home and would return the same place again and again. Only after leaving the plucked leaves on the pond he/she would get the lost way and will be able to return home safely. The extraction of forest resources from such sacred groves in any form is restricted for every individual throughout the area. The people have such a strong (superstitious) belief that even in this age of science and technology people restrain extraction of any forest items.

There are many myths, songs, folktales, proverbs, etc. regarding creation and existence of the forest resources. Detail description and interpretation of this myths, songs, folktales, proverbs, etc. is very difficult because it will take long time. Some examples may be cited as a reference, instead of its detail description. A song known as *Asi fokiyo* is related to a bird, named *Asi foki* and its contribution to existence of human beings. A folktale known as *chicho fumoji* is related to the evolution of a flower, etc. Besides, some areas such as *Jyopsinfo* at Prizin, *Nyezowoh* at Jamiri, *Paliri-Kunumro* at Palizi, etc. are being preserved and these have became a places of worship.

6 INFRASTRUCTURE

Infrastructure is generally a set of interconnected structural elements that provide the framework supporting an entire structure. The term has diverse meanings in different fields, but is perhaps most widely understood to refer to roads, airports, and utilities. These various elements may collectively be termed civil infrastructure, municipal infrastructure, or simply public works, although they may be developed and operated as private-sector or government enterprises. The more general use of the concept is that infrastructure provides organizing structure and support for the system or organization it serves, whether it is a city, a nation, or a corporation. Economically infrastructure could be seen to be the structural elements of an economy which allow for production of goods and services without themselves being part of the production process e.g. roads allows the transport of raw materials and finished products.

The word seems to have originated in 19th century France, and throughout the first half of the 20th century was used to refer primarily to military installations. The term came to prominence in the United States in the 1980s following publication of *America in Ruins* (Choate and Walter, 1981), which initiated a public-policy discussion of the nation's "infrastructure crisis," purported to be caused by decades of inadequate investment and poor maintenance of public works. That public-policy discussion was hampered by lack of a precise definition for infrastructure. US Senator Stafford commented at hearings before the Subcommittee on Water

Resources, Transportation, and Infrastructure (*Committee* on Environment and Public Works) that "probably the word infrastructure means different things to different people." The NRC (The U.S. National Research Council Committee) panel then sought to rectify the situation by adopting the term "public works infrastructure", referring to "...both specific functional modes - highways, streets, roads, and bridges; mass transit; airports and airways; water supply and water resources; wastewater management; solid-waste treatment and disposal; electric power generation and transmission; telecommunications; and hazardous waste management. A comprehension of infrastructure spans not only these public works facilities, but also the operating procedures, management practices and development policies. It interacts together with societal demand and the physical world to facilitate the transport of people and goods, provision of water for drinking and a variety of other uses, safe disposal of society's waste products, provision of energy where it is needed, and transmission of information within and between communities.

Rural infrastructure differs from urban infrastructure in the amount of public investment per unit of geographical area. In general, public investment in infrastructure tends to parallel the number of households in a geographical area. The funding of rural infrastructure is most often limited by the depth of the public revenue base in the area, which is often dependent on the presence or absence of industrial plants, other corporate employment nodes or community commerce. Although some publicly controlled assets critical to human survival exist in rural areas, utilities and transport tend to be much less extensive and thus less convenient or entirely unavailable to most of the general populace. Rural areas usually do not have extensive pipeline systems for distribution of potable water; inhabitants rely on nature's services for drinking, cooking and bathing water drawn from private wells or from streams, ponds and lakes. Private infrastructural capital such as dams, canals or irrigation ditches may be utilized for water diversion and supply. Rural societies seldom have community facilities for waste collection or treatment. Inhabitants must make their own arrangements for disposal of waste and rubbish; such private arrangements often produce conditions deleterious or dangerous to the local society, or even to neighbouring societies. Because the necessary capital investment is lower, systems for distribution of electricity and communications are more common in rural areas than systems for distribution of water or collection of waste. Rural areas tend to rely on community emergency response teams, such as volunteer firefighting organizations, rather than funding more costly fire and rescue departments comprised of full-time paid employees. The number of law enforcement personnel and frequency of patrols in rural areas tends to reflect population densities, the presence of public facilities or commercial enterprises and the volume of traffic along the area's surface transportation routes (Wikipedia, the free encyclopedia).

Most of the Aka settlements are rural excluding few locations that have little characteristics of urbanization namely – Thrizino, Bhalukpong, Jamiri and Yangsey (Plate 6.1). Some villages located along the main roads has better infrastructure than the villages in the heart of the area characterized by hilly terrain and inaccessibility. In this study the rural infrastructure forms the major emphasis for ascertaining the level of development in the area and the resultant changes therein. The following rural infrastructural facilities have been taken into consideration to analyze the level of infrastructure development in the area from 1971 to 2006:

- Educational
- Medical
- Drinking Water
- Post and Telegraph
- Transport and Communications
- Power Supply
- Banking Services

- Approach to Village
- Day or days of the Market
- Nearest Town and Distance (in km)

EDUCATIONAL

The word Education is derived from the Latin word 'Educare' which means 'to nourish' or 'to bring up'. Education encompasses teaching and learning specific skills, and also something less tangible but more profound: the imparting of knowledge, positive judgement and well-developed wisdom. Education has as one of its fundamental aspects the imparting of culture from generation to generation. It refers to draw out facilitating realizations of self-potential and latent talents of an individual. The education of an individual human begins at birth and continues throughout life. (Some believe that education begins even before birth, as evidenced by some parents' playing music or reading to the baby in the womb in the hope it will influence the child's development.) For some, the struggles and triumphs of daily life provide far more instruction than formal schooling does (thus Mark Twain's admonition to "never let school interfere with your education"). Family members may have a profound educational effect — often more profound than they realize — though family teaching may function very informally.

Educational institutions were introduced lately in the area, the census figures shows that during 1971 there was only four (4) Junior Basic Schools (JBS) and two (2) Middle Schools (Mid. S) in 32 villages of the Aka area. The proportion of total population and the number of educational institutions was poor leading to a lower literacy rate of just 12.11%. The number of institutions increased in the following decade of 1981, there was eleven (11) primary schools with three (3) adult literacy class centers attached and one (1) middle school at Buragaon in 45 villages. Consequently, there was a slight increase in the literacy rate i.e. 16.69% in 1981.

There were thirteen (13) primary schools, fourteen (14) adult literacy class centers and four (4) middle schools in the

PLATE NO. 6.1
INFRASTRUCTURAL FACILITIES

(a)

(b)

(c)

(d)

(e)

(f)

(g)

(h)

(i)

Photo : (a) Fencing along the footpath to Kararamu village, (b) Local made bridge across *Kadbiyo* nala, (c) A view of Nechiphu to Seppa metallic road, (d) Modern bridge constructed under Government scheme over *Hudii* nala, (e) Damaged hanging bridge over *Lusogo* nala, (f) A view of footpath (from Thissa to Karangania village), (g) A View of Govt. Middle School, Buragaon, (h) Concrete bridge over Tenga river at Jamiri, (i) Govt. Primary School, Thissa surrounded by herbs, shrubs and grasses.

area during 1991 in 48 villages that led to rapid increase in literacy rate. The literacy rate reached its highest at 39.95% during the last three decades.

In the absence of institutional figures of year 2001, it has been supplemented by the figures of field survey conducted in the year 2006. There were ten (9) community schools, fifteen (15) primary schools, four (4) middle schools, two (2) government secondary schools and eleven (11) adult literacy class centers attached to some of the schools in 39 villages. Some more private schools of the missionaries and other others had also come up at Palizi, Thrizino, Buragaon,

Bhalukpong and Yangsey. The Christian missionaries had established St. Xavier secondary school at Palizi village. Their branches are also extended to Thrizino and Buragaon, though these schools are at its initial stage of development. Apart from this there is a Navajyoti school and a primary missionary school at Bhalukpong. The increase in number of educational institutions had remarkable impact on literacy rate of the area. As per 2001 census the literacy rate was 44.75% and the male and female literacy was 52.88% and 27.84% respectively. The presence and absence of educational institutions in an area at a particular point of time determines the level of education or literacy rate. The proportion of educational institutions in the area since 1971 seems to be poor in compare to the other circles and the district headquarter hence the literacy rate remains low. There was no private schools, VKVs, Novadaya Vidhyalayas, etc. in the area until 1991, which might be responsible for lower literacy rate in the area.

Some schools at the remote villages exist for the sake of name only; there are no teachers, benches and chairs, since long time. Some of the schools like Yayong primary school, Thissa primary school are surrounded by jungles instead of the students. It has been revealed by the villagers that the schools stopped functioning since last 2 to 3 years and they are sending their children to Thrizino Secondary school which is about 15 to 20 kms away from the village. As a matter of fact the villages have a good proportion of population in the age group of 0 to 14 but the literacy rate in this age group is very poor.

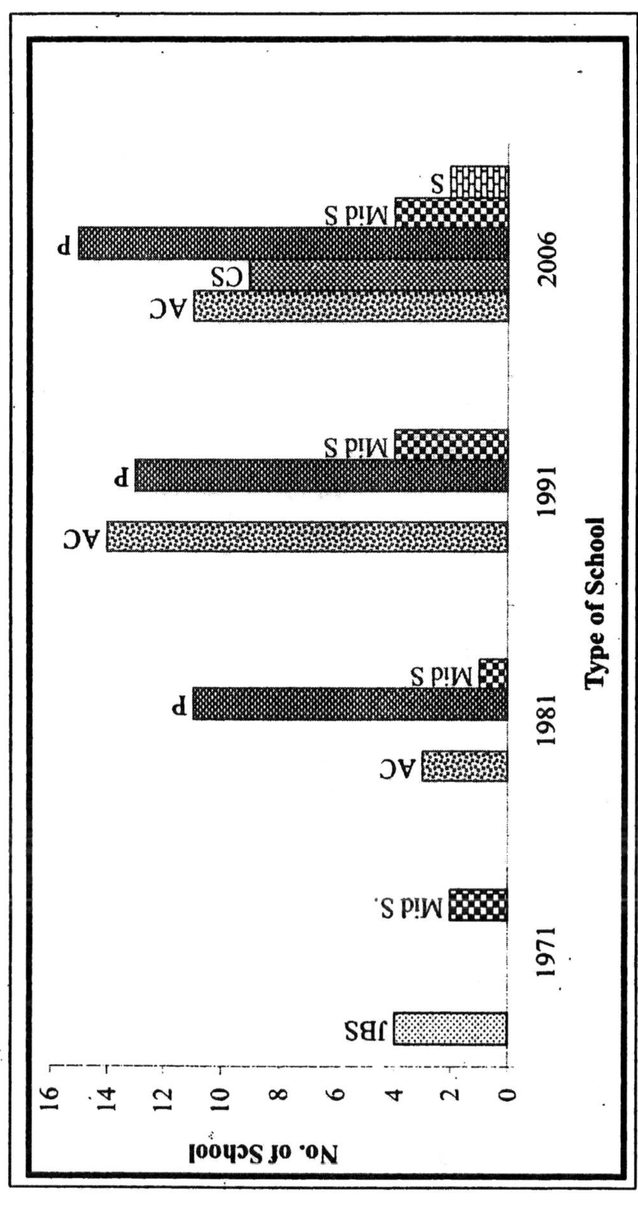

Fig. 6.1 : Village-wise educational institution (1971 to 2006).

JBS – Junior Basic School, AC – Adult Literacy Class/Centre, CS – Community School, P – Primary School, M – Middle School, S – Secondary School, S (P) – Secondary School Private.

Table 6.1
Village-wise Educational Institution (1971 to 2006)

Name of Village	1971	1981	1991	2006
1	2	3	4	5
Bana	Nil	AC	(-5 kms)	VDE
Bana Camp	Nil	P	P, M, AC	P, M, AC
Bhalukpong/Thrizino	Mid. S	P	P, M	P, M, S
Buragaon	Mid. S	P, M	P, M, AC	P, M, AC
Chizang	Nil	10+kms	P, AC	P, AC
Dedza	Nil	10+kms	(-5 kms)	(-5 kms)
Dijungania	JBS	P, AC	P, AC	P, AC
Gijiri	Nil	(-5 kms)	(-5 kms)	CS
Gohainthan	Nil	5-10 kms	5-10 kms	5-10 kms
Husigaon	Nil	10+kms	5-10 kms	5-10 kms
Jamiripoint/Noghupam	Nil	10+kms	5-10 kms	5-10 kms
Jamiri Village	Nil	10+kms	P, AC	P, AC
Karangania	JBS	P	P, AC	P, AC
Kararamu	Nil	(-5 kms)	(-5 kms)	P
Kichang	Nil	(-5 kms)	P, AC	P, AC
Morkha	Nil	5-10 kms	(-5 kms)	(-5 kms)
Palatari	Nil	P	P, AC	P, AC
Prizin	Nil	(-5 kms)	(-5 kms)	CS
Pichang	JBS	P, AC	P, AC	P, AC
Ramdagania	Nil	10+kms	P, AC	CS
Sakrin	JBS	5-10 kms	P, AC	P
Sessa	Nil	10+kms	10+kms	CS
Thisa	Nil	(-5 kms)	5-10 kms	P, AC
Yayong	Nil	P	P, AC	P, AC
Tania	Nil	5-10kms	VDE	(-5kms)
Tuluhu	VDE	10+kms	10+kms	CS
Thrizino (H.Q)	VDE	P	P, AC, M, S	P, AC, M, S
Elephant Flat	VDE	5-10 kms	5-10 kms	CS
Khamsiri	VDE	(-5 kms)	(-5 kms)	(-5 kms)
Khupi Forest office complex	VDE	10+kms	10+kms	P

1	2	3	4	5
Khupi Model Village	VDE	VDE	(-5 kms)	p
Khupi Det	VDE	VDE	10+kms	CS
Kimi	VDE	10+kms	10+kms	10+kms
Palizi	VDE	P	(-5 kms)	P, M, S (P)
Sopung	VDE	10+kms	5-10 kms	5-10 kms
Tipi	VDE	5-10 kms	P, AC	P,M
Yangsey	VDE	(-5 kms)	(-5 kms)	P
Bihupam	Nil	(-5 kms)	VDE	VDE
Tulu	Nil	5-10 kms	VDE	VDE
Kaya Valley Village	VDE	VDE	(-5 kms)	P
Nechiphu	VDE	VDE	5-10 kms	5-10 kms
New Sopung	VDE	VDE	(- 5kms)	CS
Pochong	VDE	VDE	P	P
Subu	VDE	VDE	10+kms	P
Baliphoo	VDE	VDE	VDE	VDE
Bhorali River Camp	VDE	10+kms	VDE	VDE
8 Km Point from Khuppi to Tenga River	VDE	10+kms	VDE	VDE
Huppipam/Dezling	Nil	VDE	VDE	VDE
Husugo	VDE	VDE	VDE	(-5 kms)
Humethu (under Jamiri)	VDE	VDE	VDE	5-10 kms
Jamiri H.Q.	VDE	VDE	VDE	CS
Linia	Nil	VDE	VDE	VDE
Labour camp at 2 km From Palizi towards Khupi (Hamlet)	VDE	VDE	10+kms	VDE
Mopgramo	VDE	(-5 kms)	VDE	VDE
Rogupam	Nil	VDE	VDE	VDE
Rabang Rugo L camp (Hamlet)	VDE	VDE	10+kms	5-10 kms
Saljipam (Hamlet)	VDE	VDE	5-10kms	5-10kms
7 km labour camp from Ziro point towards Khupi	VDE	VDE	5-10kms	10+kms
Rugugaon	Nil	VDE	VDE	VDE
Thesari	Nil	VDE	VDE	VDE
Sathi (64 KM)	VDE	5-10kms	VDE	VDE

1	2	3	4	5
3 KM Point towards Kimi	VDE	10+kms	VDE	VDE
34 KM Point from Nechiphu	VDE	10+kms	VDE	VDE
Tengadam site Labour Camp	VDE	VDE	10+kms	VDE

Source: Census of India, 1971, 1981, 1991 and Survey, 2006.

JBS – Junior Basic School, AC – Adult Literacy Class/Centre, CS – Community School, P – Primary School, M – Middle School, S – Secondary School, S (P) – Secondary School Private, VDE – Village Do not Exist.

MEDICAL

Medicine is concerned with the maintaining or restoring human health through its study, diagnosis and treatment. The term is derived from the Latin *ars medicina* which means *the art of healing*. The modern practice of medicine occurs at the many interfaces between *the art of healing* and various sciences. Medicine is directly connected to the health sciences and biomedicine. Broadly speaking, the term 'Medicine' today refers to the fields of clinical medicine, medical research and surgery, thereby covering the challenges of disease and injury. The medical profession is the social and occupational structure of the group of people formally trained and authorized to apply medical knowledge. Many countries and legal jurisdictions have legal limitations on who may practice medicine. Medical amenities form the basis of living for people in the modern world. The availability of medical facilities determines the overall development of people in any part of the world.

Medical amenities were few and developed very lately in the area. As per the census figures of 1971 there was only one VAC (Village Auxiliary Centre) at Bhalukpong/Thrizino and a health center at Buragaon in the total of 32 villages in the area. The decade of 1971 to 81 shows an increase of one Health Centre and up gradation of the VAC into Physical Health Centre, hence in 1981 census there were two health centre and a physical health centre. There was five villages that has accessibility to medical facilities in a distance of (-5 kms), 8 villages in a distance of 5 to 10 kms and rest of the villages had to travel for more than 10 kms for medical facilities. Such conditions had resulted in high mortality in these villages during the outbreak of epidemics.

During 1991 there were 3 Physical Health Sub-centre, 1 Health Centre and 5 Others (Pharmacy/supply of medicines in smaller quantity). About four villages has accessibility to medical facilities in a distance of (-5 kms), seven villages in a distance of 5 to 10 kms and rest of the villages in a distance of +10 kms. The area do not witnessed much improvement in the medical amenities at present also.

As per the survey conducted in 2006, there was no increase in the number of Physical Health Sub-Centre, it remained 3 and out of these the PHS of Thrizino has been taken up by an NGO Voluntary Health Association of India. There were 3 Physical Health Centre, 1 Others and 2 Health Centre (1 each of military at Sessa and NEEPCO at Kimi).

The figures reveal that the area has not advanced much in terms of medical amenities instead of increasing it had declined in the last few decades. However, due to advancement in transport system nowadays they are availing the facilities in the nearby towns and district headquarters. About 5 villages has accessibility in a distance of (-5 kms), 12 villages in a distance of 5 to 10 kms and rest of the villages in a distance of +10 kms. The area has lower proportion of medical amenities in compare to the surrounding areas which results in higher mortality rate in the area. As per the survey, the mortality rate of Aka population is 9.55% per 1000 persons, which is higher than the CDR of the state (5.0%) as well as the country (7.6%). Though, the numbers of medical centre are few but the growing health consciousness has led to the opening of more and more pharmacies in the area. The coming of missionaries, GREF personnel, military personnel and the NEEPCO had also helped to a greater extent in providingmedical facilities to the people.

Table 6.2
Village-wise Medical Amenities (1971 to 2006)

Name of Village	*1971*	*1981*	*1991*	*2006*
1	2	3	4	5
Bana	Nil	10+kms	10+kms	VDE
Bana Camp	Nil	10+kms	10+kms	PHC
Bhalukpong/Thrizino	VAC	PHC	PHS, O	PHS, O
Buragaon	HC	HC	PHS	PHS
Chizang	Nil	10+kms	10+kms	10+kms
Dedza	Nil	10+kms	10+kms	10+kms
Dijungania	Nil	5-10 kms	5-10 kms	10+kms
Gijiri	Nil	(-5 kms)	(-5 kms)	(-5 kms)
Gohainthan	Nil	5-10 kms	5-10 kms	5-10 kms
Husigaon	Nil	10+kms	10+kms	10+kms
Jamiripoint/Noghupam	Nil	10+kms	10+kms	10+kms
Jamiri Village	Nil	10+kms	10+kms	10+kms
Karangania	Nil	10+kms	5-10 kms	10+kms
Kararamu	Nil	5-10 kms	5-10 kms	5-10 kms
Kichang	Nil	(-5 kms)	10+kms	10+kms
Morkha	Nil	5-10 kms	10+kms	10+kms
Palatari	Nil	(-5 kms)	5-10 kms	5-10 kms
Prizin	Nil	(-5 kms)	(-5 kms)	(-5 kms)
Pichang	Nil	5-10 kms	HC	5-10 kms
Ramdagania	Nil	10+kms	O	10+kms
Sakrin	Nil	5-10 kms	O	5-10 kms
Sessa	Nil	10+kms	10+kms	HC Army
Thisa	Nil	10+kms	10+kms	10+kms
Yayong	Nil	10+kms	O	10+kms
Tania	Nil	10+kms	VDE	10+kms
Tuluhu	VDE	10+kms	O	5-10 kms
Thrizino (H.Q)	VDE	HC	PHS	PHS
Elephant Flat	VDE	5-10 kms	5-10 kms	5-10 kms
Khamsiri	VDE	10+kms	10+kms	10+kms
Khupi Forest office complex	VDE	10+kms	10+kms	10+kms

1	2	3	4	5
Khupi Model Village	VDE	VDE	10+kms	10+kms
Khupi Det	VDE	VDE	10+kms	10+kms
Kimi	VDE	10+kms	10+kms	HC Neepco
Palizi	VDE	10+kms	10+kms	PHC
Sopung	VDE	10+kms	10+kms	10+kms
Tipi	VDE	5-10 kms	5-10 kms	5-10 kms
Yangsey	VDE	10+kms	10+kms	(-5 kms)
Bihupam	Nil	(-5 kms)	VDE	VDE
Tulu	Nil	10+kms	VDE	VDE
Kaya Valley Village	VDE	VDE	10+kms	10+kms
Nechiphu	VDE	VDE	(-5 kms)	(-5 kms)
New Sopung	VDE	VDE	10+kms	10+kms
Pochong	VDE	VDE	10+kms	10+kms
Subu	VDE	VDE	10+kms	5-10 kms
Baliphoo	VDE	VDE	VDE	5-10 kms
Bhorali River Camp	VDE	10+kms	VDE	VDE
8 Km Point from Khuppi to Tenga River	VDE	10+kms	VDE	VDE
Huppipam/Dezling	Nil	VDE	VDE	VDE
Husugo	VDE	VDE	VDE	(-5 kms)
Humethu (under Jamiri)	VDE	VDE	VDE	5-10 kms
Jamiri H.Q.	VDE	VDE	VDE	PHC
Linia	Nil	VDE	VDE	VDE
Labour camp at 2 km From Palizi towards Khupi (Hamlet)	VDE	VDE	10+kms	VDE
Mopgramo	VDE	10+kms	VDE	VDE
Rogupam	Nil	VDE	VDE	VDE
Rabang Rugo L camp (Hamlet)	VDE	VDE	10+kms	5-10 kms
Saljipam (Hamlet)	VDE	VDE	10+kms	10+kms
7 km labour camp from Ziro point towards Khupi	VDE	VDE	(-5 kms)	10+kms
Rugugaon	Nil	VDE	VDE	VDE
Thesari	Nil	VDE	VDE	VDE

1	2	3	4	5
Sathi (64 KM)	VDE	10+kms	VDE	VDE
3 KM Point towards Kimi	VDE	10+kms	VDE	VDE
34 KM Point from Nechiphu	VDE	10+kms	VDE	VDE
Tengadam site Labour Camp	VDE	VDE	10+kms	VDE

Source: Census of India, 1971, 1981, 1991 and Survey, 2006.

VAC – Village Auxiliary Centre, HC – Health Centre, PHC – Primary Health Centre, PHS – Primary Health Sub-Centre, O – Others, VDE – Do not Exist.

Drinking Water

Drinking water is water that is intended to be ingested by humans. Water of sufficient quality to serve as drinking water is termed potable water whether it is used as such or not. Although many sources are utilized by humans, some contain disease vectors or pathogens and cause long-term health problems if they do not meet certain water quality guidelines. Water that is not harmful for human beings is sometimes called safe water, water which is not contaminated to the extent of being unhealthy. The available supply of drinking water is an important criterion of carrying capacity, the population level that can be supported by planet Earth.

Water is essential for all life on Earth, including mammals and by extension mankind. Humans can survive for several weeks without food, but for only a few days without water. A constant supply is needed to replenish the fluids lost through normal physiological activities, such as respiration, sweating and urination. Water generated from the biochemical metabolism of nutrients provides a significant proportion of the daily water requirements for some arthropods and desert animals, but provides only a small fraction of a human's necessary intake. There are a variety of trace elements present in virtually all potable water, some of which play a role in metabolism; for example sodium, potassium and

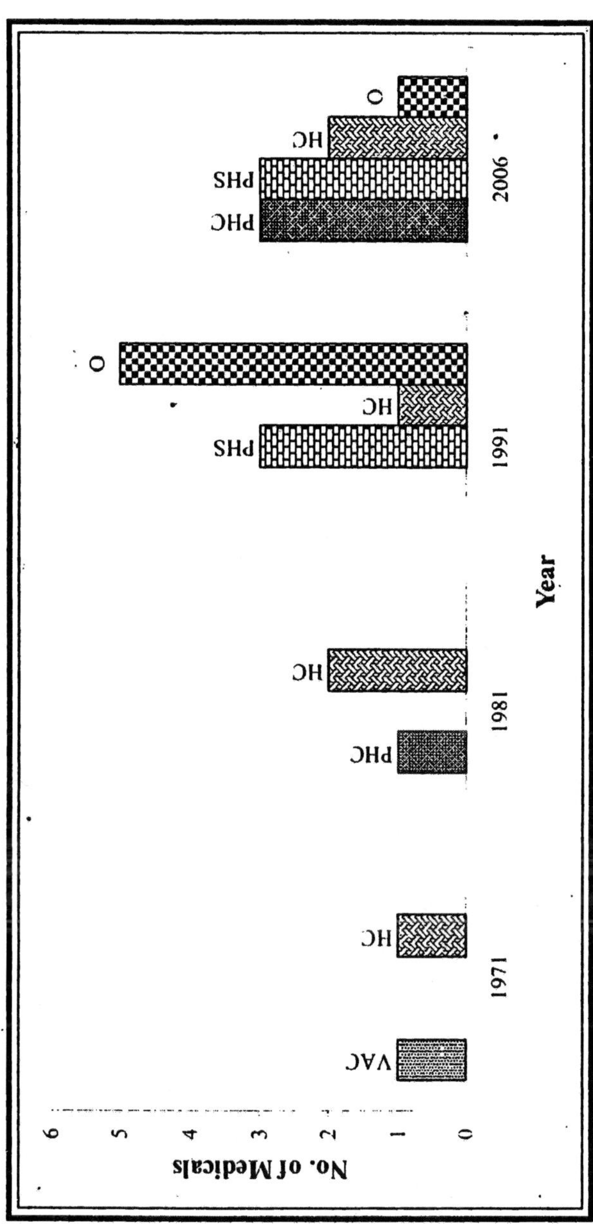

Fig. 6.2 : Village-wise Medical Amenities (1971 to 2006).

VAC – Village Auxiliary Centre, HC – Health Centre, PHC – Primary Health Centre, PHS – Primary Health Sub-Centre, O – Others.

chloride are common chemicals found in very small amounts in most waters, and these elements play a role (not necessarily major) in body metabolism. Other elements such as fluoride, while beneficial in low concentrations, can cause dental problems and other issues when present at high levels. As a country's economy becomes stronger (as its GNP per capita or PPP rise) a larger percentage of its people tend to have access to drinking water and sanitation. Access to drinking water is measured by the number of people who have a reasonable means of getting an adequate amount of water that is safe for drinking, washing, and essential household activities. It reflects the health of a country's people and the country's capacity to collect, clean, and distribute water to consumers. According to the World Health Organization (WHO) more than one billion people in low and middle-income countries lack access to safe water for drinking, personal hygiene and domestic use. These numbers represent more than 20 per cent of the world's people. In addition nearly 2 billion people did not have access to adequate sanitation facilities. While the occurrence of waterborne diseases in developed countries is generally low due to a generally good system of water treatment, distribution and monitoring, waterborne diseases are among the leading causes of morbidity and mortality in low- and middle-income countries, frequently called developing countries. According to the United Nations about 1.1 billion people are currently without safe drinking water. The lack of water and the lack of hygiene is one of the biggest problems that many poor countries have encountered in progressing their way of life. The problem has reached such endemic proportions that 2.2 million deaths per annum occur from unsanitary water - ninety per cent of these are children under the age of five.

As an inhabitant of the mountains drinking water was availed by the people from the nearby rivers and streams since a long time. However, the outbreak of water borne diseases prevailed in the area due to the lack of necessary treatment of the water. As per the 1971 census figures there was only 2 villages where the drinking water was supplied through tape water. There are 13 villages in which drinking water was collected from the fountain and the rest of 17 villages collect drinking water from the nearby rivers.

By 1981 about 11 villages have access to drinking water through tape water, 13 villages through spring, 4 villages through river, 3 through canal, 1 through fountain,10 through others, and 1 from a distance of (-5kms).

The number of villages connected by tape water increased in 1991. There was 12 villages that collect drinking water from spring, 1 village from canal and rest of the 34 villages were connected with water pipelines for tape water facility. Out of these villages Bhalukpong has both tape water as well as spring water facility.

Table 6.3
Village-wise Drinking Water Facilities (1971 to 2006)

Name of Village	*1971*	*1981*	*1991*	*2006*
1	2	3	4	5
Bana	F	S	T	VDE
Bana Camp	F	R	T	T
Bhalukpong/Thrizino	T	S	S,T	S,T
Buragaon	T	T	T	T
Chizang	F	T	T	T
Dedza	F	R	T	T
Dijungania	R	T	T	T
Gijiri	R	T	T	T
Gohainthan	F	O	T	T
Husigaon	F	O	T	T
Jamiripoint/Noghupam	F	R	T	T
Jamiri Village	R	F	T	T
Karangania	R	O	T	T
Kararamu	R	O	T	T
Kichang	F	T	T	T
Morkha	R	O	T	T
Palatari	R	O	T	T
Prizin	R	T	T	T

1	2	3	4	5
Pichang	F	T	T	T
Ramdagania	F	O	T	T
Sakrin	R	O	T	T
Sessa	F	C	T	T
Thisa	R	S	T	T
Yayong	R	T	T	T
Tania	R	S	VDE	T
Tuluhu	VDE	S	S	T
Thrizino (H.Q)	VDE	T	T	T
Elephant Flat	VDE	C	T	T
Khamsiri	VDE	S	S	T
Khupi Forest office complex	VDE	S	T	T
Khupi Model Village	VDE	VDE	S	T
Khupi Det	VDE	VDE	T	T
Kimi	VDE	S	S	T
Palizi	VDE	T	T	T
Sopung	VDE	(-5 kms)	T	T
Tipi	VDE	C	T	T
Yangsey	VDE	S	T	T
Bihupam	R	O	VDE	VDE
Tulu	R	S	VDE	VDE
Kaya Valley Village	VDE	VDE	T	T
Nechiphu	VDE	VDE	S	T
New Sopung	VDE	VDE	S	T
Pochong	VDE	VDE	T	T
Subu	VDE	VDE	C	T
Baliphoo	VDE	VDE	VDE	T
Bhorali River Camp	VDE	R	VDE	VDE
8 Km Point from Khuppi to Tenga River	VDE	O	VDE	VDE
Huppipam/Dezling	R	VDE	VDE	VDE
Husugo	VDE	VDE	VDE	T
Humethu (under Jamiri)	VDE	VDE	VDE	T
Jamiri H.Q.	VDE	VDE	VDE	T

1	2	3	4	5
Linia	R	VDE	VDE	VDE
Labour camp at 2 km From Palizi towards Khupi (Hamlet)	VDE	VDE	S	VDE
Mopgramo	VDE	S	VDE	VDE
Rogupam	R	VDE	VDE	VDE
Rabang Rugo L camp (Hamlet)	VDE	VDE	S	S
Saljipam (Hamlet)	VDE	VDE	S	T
7 km labour camp from Ziro point towards Khupi	VDE	VDE	S	S
Rugugaon	F	VDE	VDE	VDE
Thesari	F	VDE	VDE	VDE
Sathi (64 KM)	VDE	S	VDE	VDE
3 KM Point towards Kimi	VDE	T	VDE	VDE
34 KM Point from Nechiphu	VDE	S	VDE	VDE
Tengadam site Labour Camp	VDE	VDE	S	VDE

Source: Census of India, 1971, 1981, 1991 and Survey, 2006.

T – Tape Water, R – River Water, F – Fountain, S – Spring, C– Canal, O – Others VDE – Do not Exist.

During the last decade or the survey data of 2006 reveals that almost all the villages now have tape water facility. There are only 2 villages that collect drinking water from nearby spring in the absence of the tape water facility. Though, the villages have tape water facility but, it sometimes give rise to water borne diseases especially to the children. Proper treatment of water is lacking in the area, excepting the circle headquarters and some important villages most of the settlements do not have access to healthy drinking water.

Banking

A bank is a commercial or state institution that provides financial services, including issuing money in form of coins, banknotes or debit cards, receiving deposits of money, lending money and processing transactions. A commercial bank

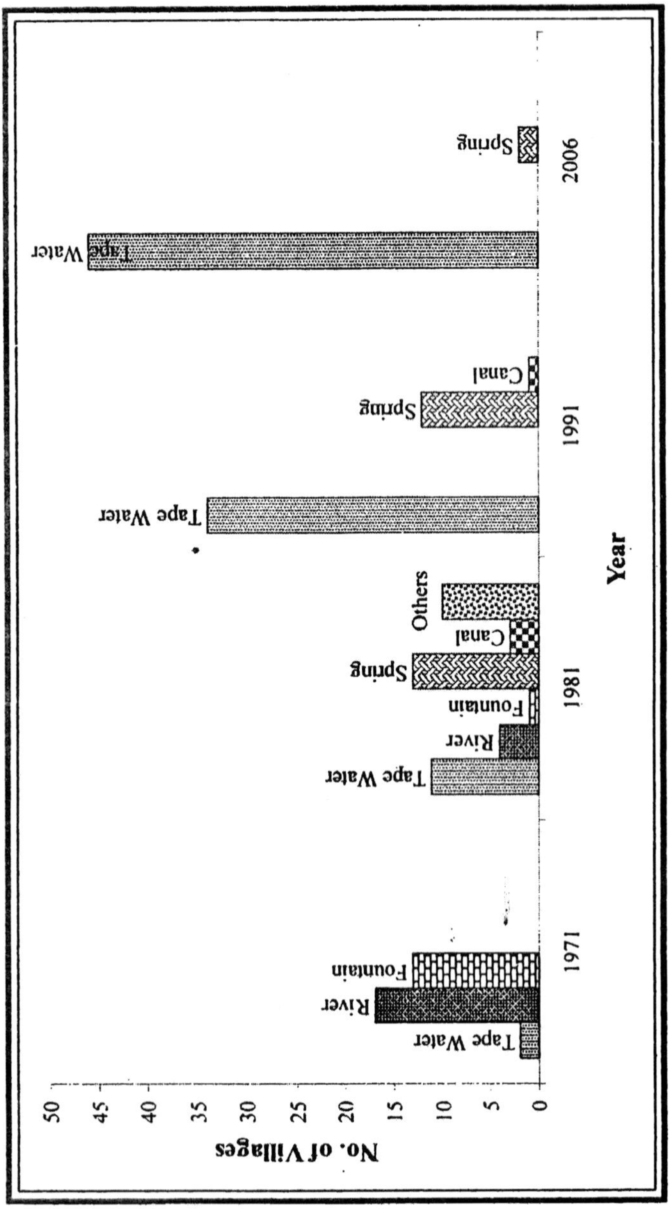

Fig. 6.3 : Village-wise Drinking Water Facilities (1971 to 2006).

accepts deposits from customers and in turn makes loans based on those deposits. Some banks (called Banks of issue) issue banknotes as legal tender. Many banks offer ancillary financial services to make additional profit; for example, most banks also rent safe deposit boxes in their branches.

During the early days the concept of banking was not significant to the villagers but the introduction of market or money economy do not let them to isolate from banking activities. There is no records of banks either government or private in the whole area in the census of 1971, 1981 and 1991. They are totally dependent on the State Bank of India branch located at Bomdila, the district headquarters of West Kameng and Seppa, the district headquarters of East Kameng. Later on the establishment of a State Bank of India branch at Chindit Top near Tenga had also served as an important bank source for the people. At present there is a State Bank of India branch at Bhalukpong, which is the only bank located in the study area. All kinds of money transactions of the people are dependent on this bank. Banking is an important activity in the modern days, hence more banks either government or private is of great need in the area.

Post and Telegraph

A post office also called postal service is a facility authorized by a postal system for the posting, receipt, sorting, handling, transmission or delivery of mail. Post offices offer mail-related services such as post office boxes, postage and packaging supplies. In addition, some post offices offer non-postal services such as passport applications and other government forms, money orders, and banking services. Post offices also rent post-office boxes to people and businesses, who prefer not to have mail delivered to their home or office, or who live or stay at addresses to which mail delivery is not available.

Post and Telegraph a facility in the area was very poor during 1970s. There was only one Post Office throughout the study area. The lone Post Office was located at Bhalukpong/ Thrizino the headquarters of the Thrizino Buragaon CD block.

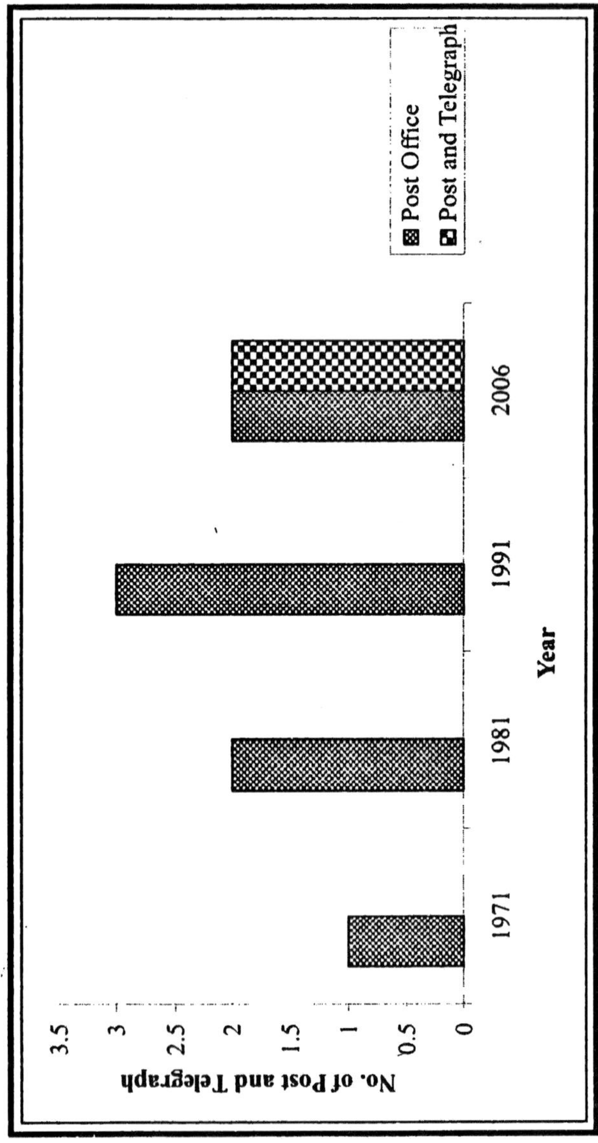

Fig. 6.4 : Village-wise Posts and Telegraph (1971 to 2006).

The number increased to 2 in 1981 one each at Bhalukpong and Thrizino. There were 4 villages that has access to Post Office within a distance of (-5 kms), 4 villages in a distance of 5-10 kms and rest of the villages in a distance of +10 kms.

In 1991 one more Post Office came up at Bana camp raising the number to three in the total villages of 48. There were 6 villages that had access to Post Office within a distance of less than 5 kms, 8 villages in a distance of 5 to 10 kms and rest of the villages in a distance of more than 10 kms.

The survey data of 2006 reflects 2 Post Offices (one each at Bana camp and Tipi) and 2 Post and Telegraph Offices (one each at Bhalukpong and Thrizino). Apart from this there is Post and Telegraph facility at Kimi that is being provided by the NEEPCO personnel undertaking the Kameng Hydel Power Project. There were 6 villages located within less than 5 kms from the Post Offices, 8 villages in a distance of 5 to 10 kms and rest within a distance of more than 10 kms. The figures cited above point towards the slower pace of development in post and telegraph facilities in the area.

Table 6.4
Village-wise Posts and Telegraph (1971 to 2006)

Name of Village	*1971*	*1981*	*1991*	*2006*
1	2	3	4	5
Bana	Nil	10+kms	(-5 kms)	VDE
Bana Camp	Nil	10+kms	PO	PO
Bhalukpong/Thrizino	PO	PO	PO	PTO
Buragaon	Nil	10+kms	10+kms	10+kms
Chizang	Nil	10+kms	10+kms	10+kms
Dedza	Nil	10+kms	5-10 kms	(-5 kms)
Dijungania	Nil	5-10kms	5- 10kms	10+kms
Gijiri	Nil	(- 5kms)	(- 5kms)	(-5 kms)
Gohainthan	Nil	10+kms	10+kms	10+kms
Husigaon	Nil	10+kms	10+kms	10+kms
Jamiripoint/Noghupam	Nil	10+kms	10+kms	10+kms

1	2	3	4	5
Jamiri Village	Nil	10+kms	10+kms	10+kms
Karangania	Nil	10+kms	5-10 kms	10+kms
Kararamu	Nil	10+kms	5-10 kms	5-10 kms
Kichang	Nil	10+kms	10+kms	10+kms
Morkha	Nil	10+kms	10+kms	10+kms
Palatari	Nil	(-5 kms)	5-10 kms	5-10 kms
Prizin	Nil	(-5 kms)	(-5 kms)	(-5 kms)
Pichang	Nil	10+kms	10+kms	10+kms
Ramdagania	Nil	10+kms	10+kms	10+kms
Sakrin	Nil	5-10 kms	(-5 kms)	5-10 kms
Sessa	Nil	10+kms	5-10 kms	5-10 kms
Thisa	Nil	10+kms	10+kms	10+kms
Yayong	Nil	10+kms	10+kms	10+kms
Tania	Nil	10+kms	VDE	10+kms
Tuluhu	VDE	10+kms	10+kms	5-10 kms
Thrizino (H.Q)	VDE	PO	PO	PTO
Elephant Flat	VDE	5-10 kms	5-10 kms	5-10 kms
Khamsiri	VDE	10+kms	10+kms	10+kms
Khupi Forest Office Complex	VDE	10+kms	10+kms	10+kms
Khupi Model Village	VDE	VDE	10+kms	10+kms
Khupi Det	VDE	VDE	10+kms	10+kms
Kimi	VDE	10+kms	10+kms	PTO Neepco
Palizi	VDE	10+kms	10+kms	10+kms
Sopung	VDE	10+kms	10+kms	10+kms
Tipi	VDE	5-10 kms	5-10 kms	PO
Yangsey	VDE	(-5 kms)	(-5 kms)	(-5 kms)
Bihupam	Nil	10+kms	VDE	VDE
Tulu	Nil	10+kms	VDE	VDE
Kaya Valley Village	VDE	VDE	10+kms	10+kms
Nechiphu	VDE	VDE	10+kms	10+kms
New Sopung	VDE	VDE	(-5 kms)	(-5 kms)
Pochong	VDE	VDE	10+kms	10+kms

1	2	3	4	5
Subu	VDE	VDE	10+kms	10+kms
Baliphoo	VDE	VDE	VDE	10+kms
Bhorali River Camp	VDE	10+kms	VDE	VDE
8 Km Point from Khuppi to Tenga River	VDE	10+kms	VDE	VDE
Huppipam/Dezling	Nil	VDE	VDE	VDE
Husugo	VDE	VDE	VDE	(-5 kms)
Humethu (under Jamiri)	VDE	VDE	VDE	5-10 kms
Jamiri H.Q.	VDE	VDE	VDE	10+kms
Linia	Nil	VDE	VDE	VDE
Labour camp at 2 km From Palizi towards Khupi (Hamlet)	VDE	VDE	10+kms	VDE
Mopgramo	VDE	10+kms	VDE	VDE
Rogupam	Nil	VDE	VDE	VDE
Rabang Rugo L camp (Hamlet)	VDE	VDE	10+kms	5-10 kms
Saljipam (Hamlet)	VDE	VDE	10+kms	10+kms
7 km labour camp from Ziro point towards Khupi	VDE	VDE	10+kms	10+kms
Rugugaon	Nil	VDE	VDE	VDE
Thesari	Nil	VDE	VDE	VDE
Sathi (64 KM)	VDE	10+kms	VDE	VDE
3 KM Point towards Kimi	VDE	10+kms	VDE	VDE
34 KM Point from Nechiphu	VDE	10+kms	VDE	VDE
Tengadam site Labour Camp	VDE	VDE	10+kms	VDE

Source : Census of India, 1971, 1981, 1991 and Survey, 2006.

PO – Post Office, PTO – Post and Telegraph, VDE – Do not Exist.

Transport and Communication

Transport or transportation is the movement of people and goods from one place to another. The term is derived from the Latin *trans* ("across") and *portare* ("to carry"). The field of transport has several aspects: loosely they can be divided into a triad of infrastructure, vehicles and operations. Infrastructure includes the transport networks (roads, railways, airways, waterways, canals, pipelines, etc.) that are used, as well as the nodes or terminals (such as airports, railway stations, bus stations and seaports). The vehicles generally ride on the networks, such as automobiles, bicycles, buses, trains, airplanes. The operations deal with the control of the system, such as traffic signals and ramp meters, railroad switches, air traffic control, etc. as well as policies, such as how to finance the system (for example, the use of tolls or gasoline taxes).

The term transport and communication has been generally used to denote available infrastructure in the present study. The roads, bus stations, nearest town and distance, etc. have been given emphasis to highlight the available transport and communication amenities in the area from 1971 to 2006. During 1971 there was no Bus station throughout the area and only Bana camp was connected with Katcha Road. Excepting two villages i.e. Bana camp and Bhalukpong/Thrizino all other villagers had to travel for more than 10 kms distance in order to get access to bus station. There were 14 villages connected with foot track and 17 villages connected with porter track that is evident of poor transport and communication facilities in the area.

In 1981 census there was at least 15 villages that has either bus stations or access to bus stations. The rest of 28 villages do not possess bus stations and the villagers have to travel for +10 kms for bus facilities. Bhalukpong, Jamiri point, Elephat flat, Sessa, Dedza and Bana camp villages located in the roadside towards Bomdila, the headquarters of West Kameng district and Seppa, the headquarters of East Kameng district were connected with Pucca road. There were 17 villages that were connected with katcha road and 20 villages with foot-paths.

The number of villages having access to bus stations increased to 19 in 1991 census. There were 4 settlements

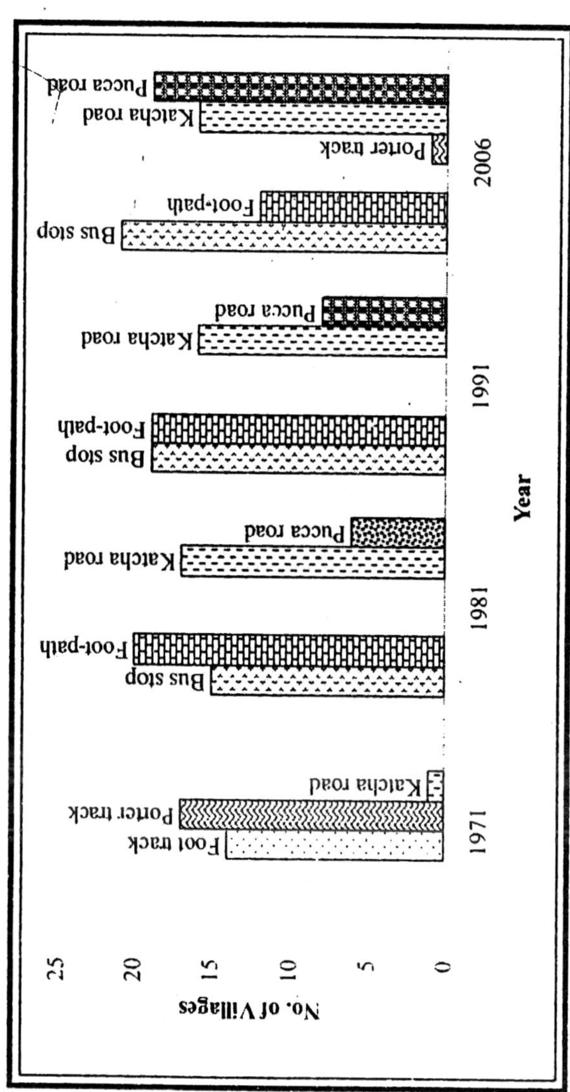

Fig. 6.5 : Village-wise Communications and Approach to Village (1971 to 2006).

that have access to bus stations within a distance of less than 5 kms, 3 villages within 5 to 10 kms and rest 21 villages in a distance of more than 10 kms. About 8 villages were connected with pucca roads, 16 villages with katcha roads and 19 villages with foot-paths.

During 2006 about 21 villages out of the total 48 villages had bus stations or access to bus stations while 3 settlements are located within a distance of less than 5 kms from the bus stations, 6 villages in a distance of 5 to 10 kms and the rest of the villages in a distance of more than 10 kms. About 19 villages were connected by pucca roads, 16 villages by katcha roads, 12 villages by foot-path and 1 village by porter track. Majority of the villages are connected by either katcha roads or foot-path and porter track which is a hurdle in the development of the area. The katcha roads are totally damaged and movement of vehicles during the rainy season is almost impossible.

Table 6.5
Village-wise Communications and Approach to Village (1971 to 2006)

Name of Village	*1971*	*1981*	*1991*	*2006*
1	2	3	4	5
Bana	10+kms, PT	10+kms, KR	(- 5kms), KR	VDE
Bana Camp	(- 5kms), KR	BS, PR	BS, PR	BS, PR
Bhalukpong/ Thrizino	(- 5kms), FT	BS, PR	BS, PR	BS, PR
Buragaon	10+kms, PT	10+kms, FP	10+kms, FP	10+kms, KR
Chizang	10+kms, PT	10+kms, KR	10+kms, KR	10+kms, FP
Dedza	10+kms, PT	BS, PR	BS, PR	BS, PR
Dijungania	10+kms, FT	10+kms, FP	10+kms, FP	10+kms, KR
Gijiri	10+kms, FT	10+kms, FP	10+kms, FP	(- 5kms), KR
Gohainthan	10+kms, PT	10+kms, FP	10+kms, FP	10+kms, KR
Husigaon	10+kms, FT	10+kms, FP	10+kms, FP	10+kms, KR
Jamiripoint/ Noghupam	10+kms, PT	BS, PR	BS, PR	BS, PR
Jamiri Village	10+kms, FT	10+kms, KR	10+kms, KR	10+kms, KR

1	2	3	4	5
Karangania	10+kms, FT	10+kms, FP	5-10 kms, FP	10+kms, FP
Kararamu	10+kms, PT	10+kms, FP	5-10 kms, FP	5-10 kms, FP
Kichang	10+kms, PT	10+kms, KR	10+kms, PR	10+kms, FP
Morkha	10+kms, FT	10+kms, FP	10+kms, FP	10+kms, FP
Palatari	10+kms, FT	10+kms, FP	5-10 kms, FP	5-10 kms, FP
Prizin	10+kms, FT	10+kms, FP	10+kms, FP	10+kms, FP
Pichang	10+kms, PT	10+kms, KR	10+kms, KR	10+kms, PT
Ramdagania	10+kms, PT	BS, FP	BS, KR	BS, PR
Sakrin	10+kms, PT	10+kms, FP	(- 5kms), FP	5-10 kms, KR
Sessa	10+kms, PT	BS, PR	BS, PR	BS, PR
Thisa	10+kms, PT	10+kms, FP	10+kms, FP	10+kms, FP
Yayong	10+kms, FT	10+kms, FP	10+kms, FP	10+kms, FP
Tania	10+kms, FT	10+kms, FP	VDE	10+kms, FP
Tuluhu	VDE	10+kms, FP	(- 5kms), FP	5-10 kms, KR
Thrizino (H.Q)	VDE	BS, KR	BS, KR	BS, KR
Elephant Flat	VDE	BS, PR	BS, PR	BS, PR
Khamsiri	VDE	10+kms, FP	10+kms, FP	10+kms, FP
Khupi Forest office complex	VDE	BS, KR	BS, KR	BS, PR
Khupi Model Village	VDE	VDE	BS, FP	BS, PR
Khupi Det	VDE	VDE	BS, KR	BS, PR
Kimi	VDE	BS, KR	BS, KR	BS, PR
Palizi	VDE	BS, KR	BS, KR	BS, PR
Sopung	VDE	10+kms, KR	10+kms, KR	5-10 kms, PR
Tipi	VDE	BS, KR	BS, PR	BS, PR
Yangsey	VDE	10+kms, KR	BS, KR	BS, PR
Bihupam	10+kms, PT	10+kms, FP	VDE	VDE
Tulu	10+kms, FT	10+kms, FP	VDE	VDE
Kaya Valley Village	VDE	VDE	10+kms, FP	10+kms, KR
Nechiphu	VDE	VDE	BS, KR	BS, PR

1	2	3	4	5
New Sopung	VDE	VDE	10+kms, KR	BS, PR
Pochong	VDE	VDE	BS, KR	BS, KR
Subu	VDE	VDE	10+kms, FP	BS, KR
Baliphoo	VDE	VDE	VDE	BS, KR
Bhorali River Camp	VDE	BS, KR	VDE	VDE
8 Km Point from Khuppi to Tenga River	VDE	10+kms, KR	VDE	VDE
Huppipam/ Dezling	10+kms, PT	VDE	VDE	VDE
Husugo	VDE	VDE	VDE	(-5 kms), KR
Humethu (under Jamiri)	VDE	VDE	VDE	BS, PR
Jamiri H.Q.	VDE	VDE	VDE	(-5 kms), KR
Linia	10+kms, FT	VDE	VDE	VDE
Labour camp at 2 km From Palizi towards Khupi (Hamlet)	VDE	VDE	10+kms, KR	VDE
Mopgramo	VDE	10+kms, FP	VDE	VDE
Rogupam	10+kms, FT	VDE	VDE	VDE
Rabang Rugo L camp (Hamlet)	VDE	VDE	10+kms, KR	5-10 kms, PR
Saljipam (Hamlet)	VDE	VDE	10+kms, FP	10+kms, FP
7 km labour camp from Ziro point towards Khupi	VDE	VDE	BS, KR	10+kms, PR
Rugugaon	10+kms, PT	VDE	VDE	VDE
Thesari	10+kms, PT	VDE	VDE	VDE
Sathi (64 KM)	VDE	10+kms, KR	VDE	VDE
3 KM Point towards Kimi	VDE	BS, KR	VDE	VDE

1	2	3	4	5
34 KM Point from Nechiphu	VDE	BS, KR	VDE	VDE
Tengadam site Labour Camp	VDE	VDE	(-5 kms), KR	VDE

Source : Census of India, 1971, 1981, 1991 and Survey, 2006.

BS – Bus Stop, FP – Foot-path, FT – Foot Track, PT – Porter Track, KR – Katcha Road, PR – Pucca Road, VDE – Do not Exist.

The nearest town and distance in kms is given in Table–6.6. Most of the settlements are located far away from the town/city viz. Bomdila, Seppa, Balipara and Rangapara. Such a remote location is a major hurdle in the availability of modern essential commodities to the villagers.

Table 6.6
Village-wise Nearest Town and distance (in km) from 1971 to 2006

Name of Village	*1971*	*1981*	*1991*	*2006*
1	2	3	4	5
Bana	Sepla, 34	Bomdila, 121	Bomdila, 121	VDE
Bana Camp	Sepla, NA	Bomdila, 117	Bomdila, 117	Seppa, 34
Bhalukpong/ Thrizino	Bomdila, 84	Rangapara, 45	Rangapara, 45	Balipara, 38
Buragaon	Bomdila, 63	Bomdila, 60	Bomdila, 60	Bomdila, 60
Chizang	Sepla, 43	Bomdila, 132	Bomdila, 132	Seppa, 43
Dedza	Bomdila, 39	Bomdila, 36	Bomdila, 36	Bomdila, 36
Dijungania	Bomdila, 90	Bomdila, 122	Bomdila, 122	Bomdila, 122
Gijiri	Bomdila, 84	Bomdila, 121	Bomdila, 112	Bomdila, 112
Gohainthan	Bomdila, 59	Bomdila, 57	Bomdila, 57	Bomdila, 57
Husigaon	Bomdila, 59	Bomdila, 49	Bomdila, 49	Bomdila, 49
Jamiripoint/ Noghupam	Bomdila, 42	Bomdila, 38	Bomdila, 38	Bomdila, 38
Jamiri Village	Bomdila, 84	Bomdila, 41	Bomdila, 41	Bomdila, 41
Karangania	Bomdila, 78	Bomdila, 133	Bomdila, 132	Bomdila, 132

1	2	3	4	5
Kararamu	Bomdila, 79	Bomdila, 129	Bomdila, 126	Bomdila, 126
Kichang	Sepla, 35	Bomdila, 125	Bomdila, 125	Seppa, 35
Morkha	Bomdila, 48	Bomdila, 68	Bomdila, 68	Bomdila, 68
Palatari	Bomdila, 70	Bomdila, 132	Bomdila, 134	Bomdila, 134
Prizin	Bomdila, 81	Bomdila, 126	Bomdila, 120	Bomdila, 140
Pichang	Sepla, NA	Bomdila, 122	Bomdila, 122	Seppa, 45
Ramdagania	Bomdila, 103	Bomdila, 91	Bomdila, 91	Bomdila, 91
Sakrin	Bomdila, 82	Bomdila, 126	Bomdila, 179	Bomdila, 136
Sessa	Bomdila, 72	Rangapara, 75	Rangapara, 75	Balipara, 68
Thisa	Bomdila, 62	Bomdila, 138	Bomdila, 140	Bomdila, 140
Yayong	Bomdila, 90	Bomdila, 134	Bomdila, 138	Bomdila, 138
Tania	Bomdila, 93	Bomdila, 118	VDE	Bomdila, 118
Tuluhu	VDE	Bomdila, 116	Bomdila, 121	Bomdila, 121
Thrizino (H.Q)	VDE	Bomdila, 122	Bomdila, 122	Bomdila, 122
Elephant Flat	VDE	Rangapara, 60	Rangapara, 60	Balipara, 53
Khamsiri	VDE	Bomdila, 144	Bomdila, 144	Bomdila, 144
Khupi Forest office complex	VDE	Bomdila, 97	Bomdila, 97	Bomdila, 68
Khupi Model Village	VDE	VDE	Bomdila, 144	Bomdila, 60
Khupi Det	VDE	VDE	Bomdila, 92	Bomdila, 72
Kimi	VDE	Bomdila, 100	Bomdila, 100	Bomdila, 100
Palizi	VDE	Bomdila, 105	Bomdila, 105	Bomdila, 105
Sopung	VDE	Bomdila, 102	Bomdila, 102	Seppa, 42
Tipi	VDE	Rangapara, 50	Rangapara, 50	Balipara, 43
Yangsey	VDE	Bomdila, 182	Bomdila, 182	Seppa, 32
Bihupam	Bomdila, 70	Bomdila, 62	VDE	VDE
Tulu	Bomdila, 90	Bomdila, 113	VDE	VDE
Kaya Valley Village	VDE	VDE	Bomdila, 122	Bomdila, 122
Nechiphu	VDE	VDE	Bomdila, 53	Bomdila, 53
New Sopung	VDE	VDE	Bomdila, 104	Seppa, 40
Pochong	VDE	VDE	Bomdila, 168	Seppa, 37
Subu	VDE	VDE	Bomdila, 116	Bomdila, 113
Baliphoo	VDE	VDE	VDE	Bomdila, 112
Bhorali River Camp	VDE	Bomdila, 89	VDE	VDE

1	2	3	4	5
8 Km Point from Khuppi to Tenga River	VDE	Bomdila, 76	VDE	VDE
Huppipam/ Dezling	Bomdila, 74	VDE	VDE	VDE
Husugo	VDE	VDE	VDE	Bomdila, 123
Humethu (under Jamiri)	VDE	VDE	VDE	Bomdila, 45
Jamiri H.Q.	VDE	VDE	VDE	Bomdila, 40
Linia	Bomdila, 97	VDE	VDE	VDE
Labour camp at 2 km From Palizi towards Khupi (Hamlet)	VDE	VDE	Bomdila, 76	VDE
Mopgramo	VDE	Bomdila, 140	VDE	VDE
Rogupam	Bomdila, 60	VDE	VDE	VDE
Rabang Rugo L camp (Hamlet)	VDE	VDE	Bomdila, 107	Bomdila, 107
Saljipam (Hamlet)	VDE	VDE	Bomdila, 150	Bomdila, 150
7 km labour camp from Ziro point towards Khupi	VDE	VDE	Bomdila, 73	Bomdila, 73
Rugugaon	Bomdila, 58	VDE	VDE	VDE
Thesari	Bomdila, 65	VDE	VDE	VDE
Sathi (64 KM)	VDE	Bomdila, 82	VDE	VDE
3 KM Point towards Kimi	VDE	Bomdila, 84	VDE	VDE
34 KM Point from Nechiphu	VDE	Bomdila, 84	VDE	VDE
Tengadam site Labour Camp	VDE	VDE	Bomdila, 94	VDE

Source : Census of India, 1971, 1981, 1991 and Survey, 2006.

VDE – Village Do not Exist, NA – Information Not Available.

Power Supply

A power supply (sometimes known as a Power Supply Unit or PSU) is a device or system that supplies electrical or other types of energy to an output load or group of loads. The term is most commonly applied to electrical energy supplies, less often to mechanical ones, and rarely to others. This term covers the mains power distribution system together with any other primary or secondary sources of energy such as:

- Conversion of one form of electrical power to another desired form and voltage. This typically involves converting 120 or 240 volt AC supplied by a utility company (see electricity generation) to a well-regulated lower voltage DC for electronic devices. For examples, see switched-mode power supply, linear regulator, rectifier and inverter (electrical).
- Batteries
- Chemical fuel cells and other forms of energy storage systems
- Solar power
- Generators or alternators (particularly useful in vehicles of all shapes and sizes, where the engine has rotational power to spare or in semi-portable units containing an internal combustion engine and a generator). Low voltage, low power DC power supply units are commonly integrated with the devices they supply, such as computers and household electronics.

Constraints that commonly affect power supplies are the amount of power they can supply, how long they can supply it for without needing some kind of refueling or recharging, how stable their output voltage or current is under varying load conditions, and whether they provide continuous power or pulses. The regulation of power supplies is done by incorporating circuitry to tightly control the output voltage and/or current of the power supply to a specific value. The specific value is closely maintained despite variations in the load presented to the power supply's output, or any reasonable voltage variation at the power supply's input. This kind of regulation is commonly categorized as a stabilized power supply.

The area was in total darkness during 1971 and 1981, there was not a single settlement that has power supply of any form in these two decades. Power supply in the area was started in 1991, there was 7 settlements namely - Bhalukpong, Tipi, Elephant flat, Sessa, Jamiri point, Dedza and Jamiri village that has power supply for various domestic uses. The remaining 41 villages were under darkness till 1991.

Table 6.7
Village-wise Power Supply (1971 to 2006)

Name of Village	*1971*	*1981*	*1991*	*2006*
Bana	Nil	Nil	Nil	VDE
Bana Camp	Nil	Nil	Nil	ED
Bhalukpong/Thrizino	Nil	Nil	ED	EA
Buragaon	Nil	Nil	Nil	ED
Chizang	Nil	Nil	Nil	ED
Dedza	Nil	Nil	ED	ED
Dijungania	Nil	Nil	Nil	ED
Gijiri	Nil	Nil	Nil	ED
Gohainthan	Nil	Nil	Nil	ED
Husigaon	Nil	Nil	Nil	ED
Jamiripoint/Noghupam	Nil	Nil	ED	EA
Jamiri Village	Nil	Nil	ED	ED
Karangania	Nil	Nil	Nil	ED
Kararamu	Nil	Nil	Nil	ED
Kichang	Nil	Nil	Nil	ED
Morkha	Nil	Nil	Nil	ED
Palatari	Nil	Nil	Nil	ED
Prizin	Nil	Nil	Nil	ED
Pichang	Nil	Nil	Nil	ED
Ramdagania	Nil	Nil	Nil	ED
Sakrin	Nil	Nil	Nil	ED
Sessa	Nil	Nil	ED	EA

1	2	3	4	5
Thisa	Nil	Nil	Nil	ED
Yayong	Nil	Nil	Nil	ED
Tania	Nil	Nil	VDE	ED
Tuluhu	VDE	Nil	Nil	ED
Thrizino (H.Q)	VDE	Nil	Nil	ED
Elephant Flat	VDE	Nil	ED	ED
Khamsiri	VDE	Nil	Nil	Nil
Khupi Forest office complex	VDE	Nil	Nil	ED
Khupi Model Village	VDE	VDE	Nil	ED
Khupi Det	VDE	VDE	Nil	ED
Kimi	VDE	Nil	Nil	ED
Palizi	VDE	Nil	Nil	ED
Sopung	VDE	Nil	Nil	ED
Tipi	VDE	Nil	ED	EA
Yangsey	VDE	Nil	Nil	ED
Bihupam	Nil	Nil	VDE	VDE
Tulu	Nil	Nil	VDE	VDE
Kaya Valley Village	VDE	VDE	Nil	ED
Nechiphu	VDE	VDE	Nil	ED
New Sopung	VDE	VDE	Nil	ED
Pochong	VDE	VDE	Nil	ED
Subu	VDE	VDE	Nil	ED
Baliphoo	VDE	VDE	VDE	ED
Bhorali River Camp	VDE	Nil	VDE	VDE
8 Km Point from Khuppi to Tenga River	VDE	Nil	VDE	VDE
Huppipam/Dezling	Nil	VDE	VDE	VDE
Husugo	VDE	VDE	VDE	ED
Humethu (under Jamiri)	VDE	VDE	VDE	ED
Jamiri H.Q.	VDE	VDE	VDE	ED
Linia	Nil	VDE	VDE	VDE
Labour camp at 2 km from Palizi towards Khupi (Hamlet)	VDE	VDE	Nil	VDE

1	2	3	4	5
Mopgramo	VDE	Nil	VDE	VDE
Rogupam	Nil	VDE	VDE	VDE
Rabang Rugo L camp (Hamlet)	VDE	VDE	Nil	Nil
Saljipam (Hamlet)	VDE	VDE	Nil	ED
7 km labour camp from Ziro point towards Khupi	VDE	VDE	Nil	Nil
Rugugaon	Nil	VDE	VDE	VDE
Thesari	Nil	VDE	VDE	VDE
Sathi (64 KM)	VDE	Nil	VDE	VDE
3 KM Point towards Kimi	VDE	Nil	VDE	VDE
34 KM Point from Nechiphu	VDE	Nil	VDE	VDE
Tengadam site Labour Camp	VDE	VDE	Nil	VDE

Source: Census of India, 1971, 1981, 1991 and Field Survey, 2006.

ED – Electricity for Domestic use, EA – Electricity for all purpose, VDE – Do not Exist.

Electric supply had improved tremendously during the last decade; almost all the villages have power supply for domestic uses during the months of when there is abundance of power supply from the Elephant flat hydel power plant. But, it is mostly absent for majority of the months when there is shortage in electricity due to reduced level of water in the hydel power plant. Bhalukpong, Tipi, Sessa and Jamiri point has power supply for all purposes i.e. use of power in saw mills, distilleries, plywood industries, etc.

Market

A market is a social arrangement that allows buyers and sellers to discover information and carry out a voluntary exchange of goods or services. It is one of the two key institutions that organize trade, along with the right to own property. In everyday usage, the word "market" may refer to the location where goods are traded, sometimes known as a marketplace, or to a street market. The function of a market requires, at a minimum, that both parties expect to become better off as a result of the transaction. Markets generally rely on price adjustments to provide information to parties engaging in a transaction, so that each may accurately gauge the subsequent change of their welfare. In less sophisticated markets, such as those involving barter, individual buyers and sellers must engage in a more lengthy process of haggling in order to gain the same information.

Although many markets exist in the traditional sense—such as a flea market—there are various other types of markets and various organizational structures to assist their functions. A market can be organized as an auction, as a shopping center, as a complex institution such as a stock market, and as an informal discussion between two individuals.

In economics, a market that runs under laissez-faire policies is a free market. It is "free" in the sense that the government makes no attempt to intervene through taxes, subsidies, minimum wages, price ceilings, etc. Market prices may be distorted by a seller or sellers with monopoly power, or a buyer with monopsony power. Such price distortions can have an adverse effect on market participant's welfare and reduce the efficiency of market outcomes. Also, the level of organization or negotiation power of buyers, markedly affects the functioning of the market. Markets where price negotiations do not arrive at efficient outcomes for both sides are said to experience market failure.

Most markets are regulated by state wide laws and regulations. While barter markets exist, most markets use currency or some other form of money. Markets of varying types can spontaneously arise whenever a party has interest in a good or service that some other party can provide. Hence there can be a market for cigarettes in correctional facilities, another for chewing gum in a playground, and yet another for contracts for the future delivery of a commodity. There can be black markets, where a good is exchanged illegally and virtual markets, such as eBay, in which buyers and sellers do not physically interact. There can also be markets for goods under a command economy despite pressure to repress them.

As an inhabitant of the high hills, they descend down the plains of Assam every season to collect the essential commodities like cloths, salt, betel nuts, etc. Markets were almost nil throughout the area in 1971 and 1981 census. Except Bhalukpong where there is a weekly market on every Thursday. The other villagers had to travel more than 10 kms for marketing purposes. There were daily markets in three village viz. Bhalukpong, Thrizino and Palizi in 1991. The daily market at Bhalukpong was of greater magnitude in comparison to the markets at the other two settlements because they are located at the heart of the area. Most of the commodities are collected from the market at Bhalukpong. Apart from these villages, 3 villages had access to markets within a distance of less than 5 kms, 3 villages at a distance of 5 to 10 kms and rest of the villages at a distance of more than 10 kms. As per the survey 2006, Bhalukpong, Tipi, Kimi (NEEPCO), Palizi, Thrizino and Yangsey villages have daily markets. Three settlements have markets at a distance of (-5 kms), 9 villages at a distance of 5 to 10 kms.

Table 6.8
Village wise Day/days of the Market (1971 to 2006)

Name of Village	*1971*	*1981*	*1991*	*2006*
1	2	3	4	5
Bana	10+kms	10+kms	10+kms	VDE
Bana Camp	10+kms	10+kms	10+kms	10+kms
Bhalukpong/ Thrizino	Thursday	Thursday	Daily market	Daily market
Buragaon	10+kms	10+kms	10+kms	10+kms
Chizang	10+kms	10+kms	10+kms	10+kms
Dedza	10+kms	10+kms	(-5 kms)	(-5 kms)
Dijungania	10+kms	10+kms	10+kms	10+kms
Gijiri	10+kms	10+kms	10+kms	(-5 kms)
Gohainthan	10+kms	10+kms	10+kms	10+kms

1	2	3	4	5
Husigaon	10+kms	10+kms	10+kms	10+kms
Jamiripoint/ Noghupam	10+kms	10+kms	10+kms	10+kms
Jamiri Village	10+kms	10+kms	10+kms	10+kms
Karangania	10+kms	10+kms	5-10 kms	10+kms
Kararamu	10+kms	10+kms	5-10 kms	5-10 kms
Kichang	10+kms	10+kms	10+kms	10+kms
Morkha	10+kms	10+kms	10+kms	10+kms
Palatari	10+kms	10+kms	10+kms	10+kms
Prizin	10+kms	10+kms	5-10 kms	5-10 kms
Pichang	10+kms	10+kms	10+kms	10+kms
Ramdagania	10+kms	10+kms	10+kms	10+kms
Sakrin	10+kms	10+kms	(-5 kms)	5-10kms
Sessa	10+kms	10+kms	10+kms	10+kms
Thisa	10+kms	10+kms	10+kms	10+kms
Yayong	10+kms	10+kms	10+kms	10+kms
Tania	10+kms	10+kms	VDE	10+kms
Tuluhu	VDE	10+kms	(- 5kms)	5-10 kms
Thrizino (H.Q)	VDE	10+kms	Daily market	Daily market
Elephant Flat	VDE	10+kms	10+kms	10+kms
Khamsiri	VDE	10+kms	10+kms	10+kms
Khupi Forest Office Complex	VDE	10+kms	10+kms	10+kms
Khupi Model Village	VDE	VDE	10+kms	10+kms
Khupi Det	VDE	VDE	10+kms	10+kms
Kimi	VDE	10+kms	10+kms	Daily market
Palizi	VDE	10+kms	Daily market	Daily market
Sopung	VDE	10+kms	10+kms	5-10 kms
Tipi	VDE	10+kms	10+kms	Daily market
Yangsey	VDE	10+kms	10+kms	Daily market
Bihupam	10+kms	10+kms	VDE	VDE

1	2	3	4	5
Tulu	10+kms	10+kms	VDE	VDE
Kaya Valley Village	VDE	VDE	10+kms	10+kms
Nechiphu	VDE	VDE	10+kms	10+kms
New Sopung	VDE	VDE	10+kms	10+kms
Pochong	VDE	VDE	10+kms	10+kms
Subu	VDE	VDE	10+kms	5-10 kms
Baliphoo	VDE	VDE	VDE	5-10 kms
Bhorali River Camp	VDE	10+kms	VDE	VDE
8 Km Point from Khuppi to Tenga River	VDE	10+kms	VDE	VDE
Huppipam/ Dezling	10+kms	VDE	VDE	VDE
Husugo	VDE	VDE	VDE	(-5 kms)
Humethu (under Jamiri)	VDE	VDE	VDE	5-10 kms
Jamiri H.Q.	VDE	VDE	VDE	10+kms
Linia	10+kms	VDE	VDE	VDE
Labour camp at 2 km From Palizi towards Khupi (Hamlet)	VDE	VDE	10+kms	VDE
Mopgramo	VDE	10+kms	VDE	VDE
Rogupam	10+kms	VDE	VDE	VDE
Rabang Rugo L camp (Hamlet)	VDE	VDE	10+kms	5-10 kms
Saljipam (Hamlet)	VDE	VDE	10+kms	10+kms

1	2	3	4	5
7 km labour camp from Ziro point towards Khupi	VDE	VDE	10+kms	10+kms
Rugugaon	10+kms	VDE	VDE	VDE
Thesari	10+kms	VDE	VDE	VDE
Sathi (64 KM)	VDE	10+kms	VDE	VDE
3 KM Point towards Kimi	VDE	10+kms	VDE	VDE
34 KM Point from Nechiphu	VDE	10+kms	VDE	VDE
Tengadam site Labour Camp	VDE	VDE	10+kms	VDE

Source: Census of India, 1971, 1981, 1991 and Survey, 2006.

VDE – Village Do not Exist.

7 ECONOMY

The word *economy* can be traced back to the Greek word *oikonomos*, "one who manages a household," derived from *oikos*, "house," and *nemein*, "to manage." From *oikonomos* was derived *oikonomiā*, which had not only the sense "management of a household or family" but also senses such as "thrift," "direction," "administration," "arrangement," and "public revenue of a state." *Economy* is later recorded in other senses shared by *oikonomiā* in Greek, including "thrift" and "administration." What is probably our most frequently used current sense, "the economic system of a country or an area," seems not to have developed until the 19th or 20th century. The large set of inter-related economic production and consumption activities which aid in determining how scarce resources are allocated. The economy encompasses everything related to the production and consumption of goods and services in an area.

The tribal economy without plants and animals is quite unthinkable. As such the economic organization of the Akas revolves around jhum/shifting cultivation which is locally known as *Vee*. Other subsidiary means like collection of forest products, fishing and hunting also forms a part of their economy. Forest and forest resources have a profound influence on the economy of the Akas. Forest is the most valuable source of timber, animals, birds, reptiles, fish flowers, orchids, etc. It forms the base of economic activities in a tribal inhabited area.

Agriculture

The term 'Agriculture' is not an easy term to define precisely; it involves the deliberate effort to modify a portion of the earth's surface through the cultivation of crops and the rearing of livestock for sustenance or economic gain. Thus, agriculture originated prior to the domestication of plants and animals by humans for their use. According to Carl Sauer, a prominent cultural geographer, the earliest form of plant cultivation consisted of vegetative planting. He defined vegetative planting as the reproduction of plants by direct cloning from existing plants, such as cutting stems and dividing roots. Seed agriculture that involves the reproduction of plants through the annual introduction of seed, which result from sexual fertilization, came later. The farmers all over the world practice forms of agriculture unique to their area in spite of the increased knowledge of alternatives. The physical characteristics of the environment continue to influence the type of agriculture, but areas with similar climates often show different agricultural practices because of their unique cultural traits. Many analysts have attempted to classify the world's major types of agriculture into meaningful regions. The classification made by Whittlesey in the year 1936 has been accepted by many modern geographers with some modification.

The five important type of agriculture in developing countries are, shifting cultivation, intensive subsistence with wet rice dominance, intensive subsistence without wet rice dominance, pastoral nomadism and plantation agriculture. Shifting cultivation forms the important type of agriculture among the tribes inhabiting the state. Subsistence agriculture in the form of terrace cultivation and wet rice agriculture has been also taken up by some of the tribes inhabiting the lower reaches of the state. The Akas are mostly shifting cultivators during the post independence period, but the later periods of statehood reveals some percentage of area under wet rice cultivation amongst them (Plate 7.1). During the recent decade horticulture activities in the form of pine apple, orange, kiwi, etc. has been started either by the farmers themselves or with the assistance of the various schemes of horticulture department. The changes in the agricultural practices of Akas are shown in Table – 7.1 and Figure – 7.1.

Table 7.1
Types of Agriculture

Period	*Jhumming*	*Jhumming, Wet Rice Cultivation*	*Jhumming, Wet Rice Cultivation and Horticulture*
Post Independence	862 (100%)	—	—
Statehood Onwards	729 (84.6%)	3 (0.3%)	130 (15.1%)
2000 Onwards	—	2 (0.2%)	860 (99.8%)

Source: Field Survey, 2006.

Jhum/Shifting Cultivation (*Vee*)

Shifting cultivation is an agricultural system in which plots of land are cultivated temporarily, and then abandoned. This system often involves clearing of a piece of land followed by several years of wood harvesting or farming until the soil loses fertility. Once the land becomes infertile for crop production, it is left to be reclaimed by natural vegetation. This system of agriculture is often practiced at the level of an individual or family, but sometimes may involve an entire village. An estimated world population exceeding 250 million people derives subsistence from the practice of shifting cultivation, and ecological consequences are often deleterious. In general, many people practice slash-and-burn as one element of their farming cycle. Others employ land clearing without any burning, and some cultivators are purely migratory. Sometimes no slashing at all is needed where re-growth is purely of grasses.

Shifting cultivation is found in much of the world's tropical regions, which have relatively high temperatures and abundant rainfall. It is mostly dominant in three tropical regions viz. the Amazon area of South America, Central and West Africa, and Southeast Asia. Shifting cultivation is an integral part of tribal culture, as it affects all the spheres of

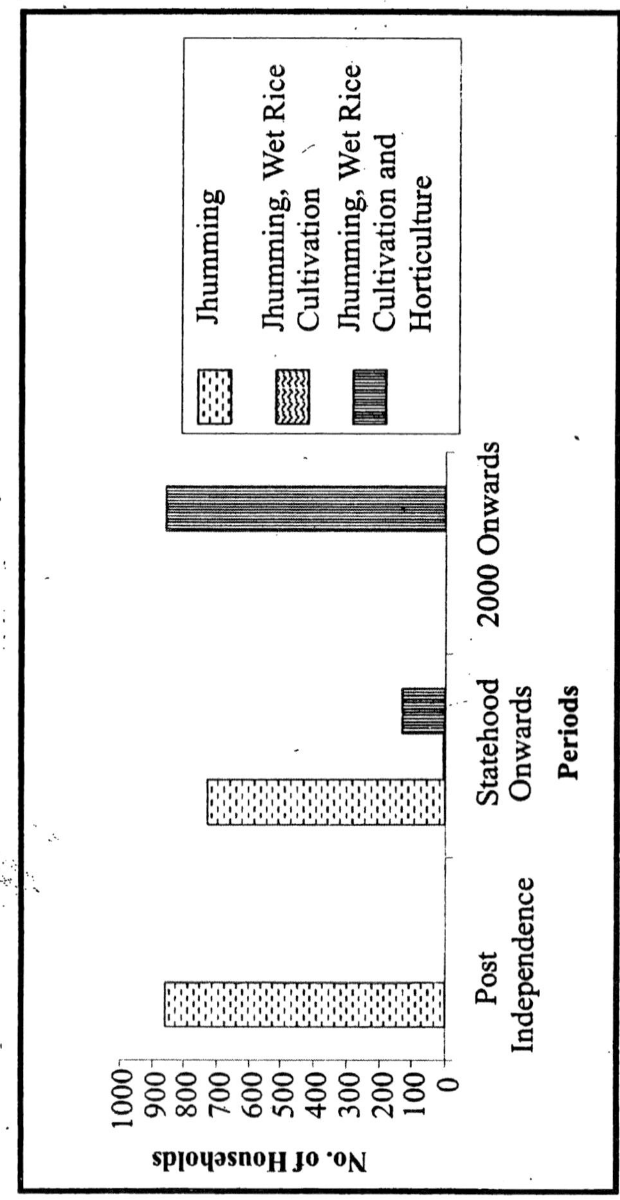

Fig. 7.1 : Types of Agriculture.

PLATE NO. 7.1
TYPES OF AGRICULTURE

(a)

(b)

(c)

(d)

(e)

(f)

(g)

(h)

(i)

Photo : (a) Traditional Jhum fields (new and old) (b) Patches of Jhum fields along the slopes of Yayong village (c) A view of jhum and terrace cultivation (d) A small area under Wet Rice Cultivation (e) Modern Terrace Cultivation (f) Potato cultivation along the slopes (Contour cultivation), (g) Standing maize crops in a Jhum field (h) Patches of Jhum fields and a small hamlet (i) Orange cultivation at Sopung village.

their cultural life. The tribes, which prefer shifting cultivation, deliberately choose hilly and forested areas for their habitats. They venerate the spirits of mountains, rocks, rivers, lakes and trees. They pay special veneration to the fertile soil, the Earth Mother, with offerings of domestic animals *viz.* chicken, goats, pigs, *mithuns*, etc. Shifting cultivation is firmly rooted in the religion and mythology of tribals (Deb Nath, *et.al.,* 1998).

The Akas are essentially agricultural people. The undulating terrain with higher slope characteristics in the hilly areas naturally demands the jhum or shifting type of cultivation. A tract of land ranging from 2 to 5 acres is selected by each and every household for *jhuming*. The dense forest cover (*Noke*) or vegetation growth over the area is usually cleared in the month of January (*Liiga*), which continues up to the month of March (*Munyomu*). Slashed trees, bushes and grasses are left at least for two months to be completely dry-up. It is put to fire (*Vee Fow*) in the month of April (*Gyeo*) and the half burnt logs are cut again and removed to separate places (*Ghra Dow*). First of all, the maize (*sibe*) seeds are sown over the ash in the field in the month of May (*Kheo*), followed by arum (*truo*), ginger (*tiikrin*), pumpkin (*drubji*), cucumber (*migyi*), sweet potato (*jimchio alu*), *sawo*, saje, etc. Another important crop is paddy which is sown in this month. The season of sowing crops are identified by the flowering of an orchid on the trees, locally known as *chichow-eba*. Common pulses such as *urad* or *mas* (*shapoo*) and other similar crops locally known as *labiunsu* and *libji* are sowed in the month of June (*Chiyiew*). Millet seeds are broadcasted in the month of July (*Wuju*). French bean (*laprapra*), maize, *shapiu, pemdu*, etc. are sown in the month of August (*Dosa*). The September (*Domuhu*) month is considered to be bad month for germination of any crop. The October (*ledishi*) month is marked by the sowing of motor (*pulbji*) as well as potato (*lasaneksi*) in the fields for consumption. Harvesting of paddy takes place in the month of November (*Wugiehu*). The month of December (*Nuchohu*) is reserved for collection and storing of the crops. After the harvesting of paddy, every household invite the villagers for the first toast of the new grain. This occasion is known as *Ope Tsao*, which is mandatory for all the villagers after the harvesting of new food crops especially paddy. Again in the month of January people start to clear forests for new agricultural land or may retain the same land for the succeeding year also.

Agriculture of this type involves hard labour and thus often necessitates corporate activity. Men and women join together to share the toil. During the clearing of land for agriculture field both men and women go together to the forest; soon after reaching the spot, the division of labour among them begins. Men occupy the more arduous tasks involving physical labour, such as felling of big trees and removing the logs, while women are given lighter tasks like clearing the small plants and weeds. The equipments used are axe (*puwje*), and *dao* (*Vetsii*). These people divide the land in to three types i.e. *Noke* (dense forestland), *Nowdii* (fallow land left for at least 5 years), and *Veeto* (continuation of a same land for 2 to 3 years). It takes about three to four weeks to finish the entire process of clearing forest. The daily work during this period usually starts in the early hours of morning and continues till late in the evening. Boys and girls of over ten to twelve years also sometimes take part in this work. Burning of the slashed forest is essentially a man's job. Sowing of seed, which is less difficult, is usually entrusted to women. Seeds are sown by women using dibbling technique. The seeds sown on the field are required to keep a casual watch for protecting it from the wild birds. This task is usually entrusted to the grown up children of the house, who learn from their very early life to live in the secluded parts of forest, away from their home. They may stay in the temporary huts made for them locally known as *Tuwonye*. Often the parents now and then use to visit them to take necessary care.

When the seeds sprout they keep a strict and constant vigilance over the plants to check the ravages to the growing crops by the wild, domesticated and semi-domesticated animals. Fencing of bamboo or of wooden logs is made around the field to protect the crop against animals. The harvesting of crops is done by means of a common *dao*. The harvested crop is gathered at the *Tuwonye*. It is primarily women's job, though men also sometimes assist them. The men and women collectively carry the grains in the village and store in the granary. Each house builds its own granary (*nyechi*) close to it.

Shifting cultivation is the principal and the only method of agriculture for the Akas, though some people, at present, are adopting wet rice cultivation where plain areas are available. Agriculture is the main source of livelihood for the people, and thus to ensure its success, some rites are being performed by the Akas before the beginning of agricultural process. Thus, forest plays an important role in determining the economic activities of the Akas. Since the Akas are nurtured in the lap of the nature their subsistence pattern is highly influenced by forest ecology.

Size of Jhum Field

The living of the people is highly dependable to the jhum fields and other subsidiary means of sustenance viz. hunting, fishing and food gathering. Jhum field is the main source of food crops and vegetables. Generally, the size of jhum field is determined by the number of family members present in a household as well as the strength of the individual farmer in managing the agricultural field. Sometimes a farmer with few family members also goes for a larger agricultural field in comparison to a big family. Normally, the average size of jhum fields ranges from 1 to 5 acres, but sometimes it ranges up to 5 to 10 acres also.

Table 7.2 and Figure 7.2 given below shows that during the post independence period majority of them use to select 1 to 5 acres of land every year for jhum field, but in exceptional cases it use to be up to 10 acres. In the later decades of statehood and 21st century most of them select jhum field of less than 1 acre. During the post independence they were totally dependent on the agricultural field, but with the introduction of education system some of them are in services and even the children who help the parents in one way or other in carrying out various agricultural activities are sent to school. Therefore, the size of jhum field had drastically declined to less than 1 acre at present. It may even decline in days to come because more and more people are engaging themselves in other sectors of economy.

Table 7.2
Size of Jhum Field in the Aka Area (in Acres)

Period	*Less than 1 acres*	*1 – 5 acres*	*5 – 10 acres*
Post Independence	—	760 (88.3%)	101 (11.7%)
Statehood Onwards	760 (88.3%)	101 (11.8%)	—
2000 Onwards	861 (100%)	—	—

Source : Field Survey, 2006.

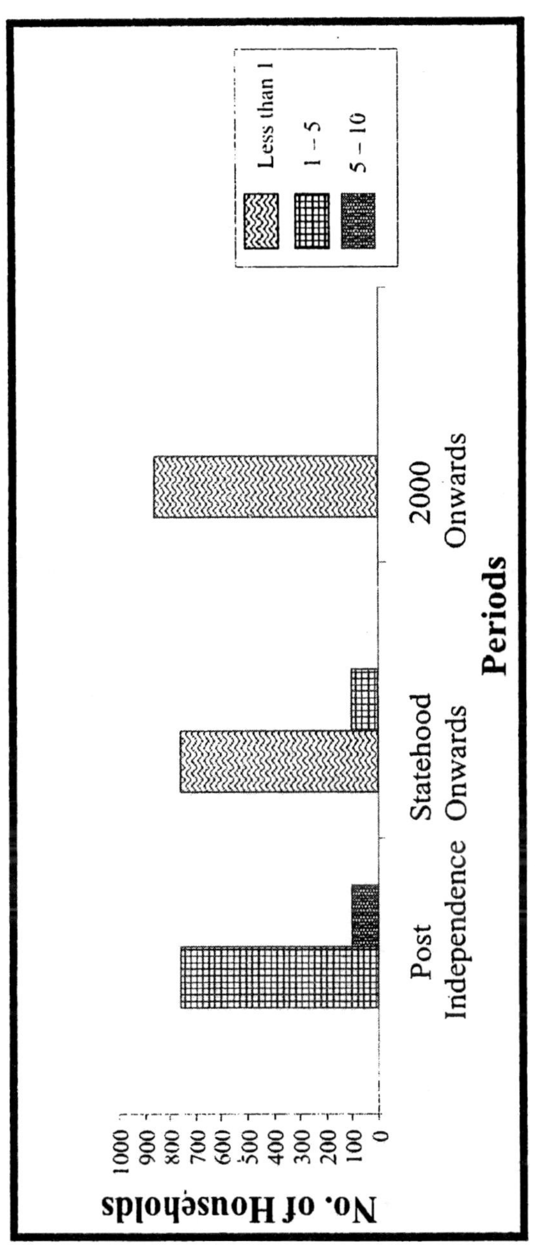

Fig. 7.2 : Size of Jhum field.

Jhum Cycle

Shifting agriculture involves clearing a patch of forest land. In shifting cultivation a patch of forest land is used for agriculture for two to three years and then abandoned it for 10 to 20 years to allow the natural forest to grow back to regain its fertility. The cycle of cultivation, leaving it fallow and coming back to it for cultivation is called the Jhum cycle. Traditionally, a village community owns/controls the forest land and decides the piece of land to be used for such cultivation in rotation. Thus, the community cultivates land for livelihood while practicing conservation and taking care of the ecological balance. However, due to the population pressure, communities have to grow more food crops by clearing the greater chunks of forest lands. The length of the fallow phase between two successive cropping has come down to even two to three years in some places. This has led to soil degradation, fall in yield, and reduction in green cover. Forests are also exploited for timber and hills are being disturbed for the quarry of soil and stones. The state government has come out with various schemes to provide the jhumias an alternate means of livelihood and wean them away from jhuming. However the needs of the jhum cultivators have not been assessed rightly and these schemes have met with limited success or have completely failed. The concept of jhum cycle is not strictly followed by them. Basically, a jhum field is left out until the regeneration of trees. During the olden days the same field is not selected until and unless it became dense forest land (*Noke*), which used to take at least a period of 5 to 10 years. Nowadays, due to increase in population the ratio

Table 7.3
Changes in the Jhum Cycle

Period	*Less than 3 years*	*3 – 5 years*	*5 – 10 years*
Post Independence	—	180 (20.9%)	682 (79.1%)
Statehood Onwards	180 (20.9%)	682 (79.1%)	—
2000 Onwards	862 (100%)	—	—

Source: Field Survey, 2006.

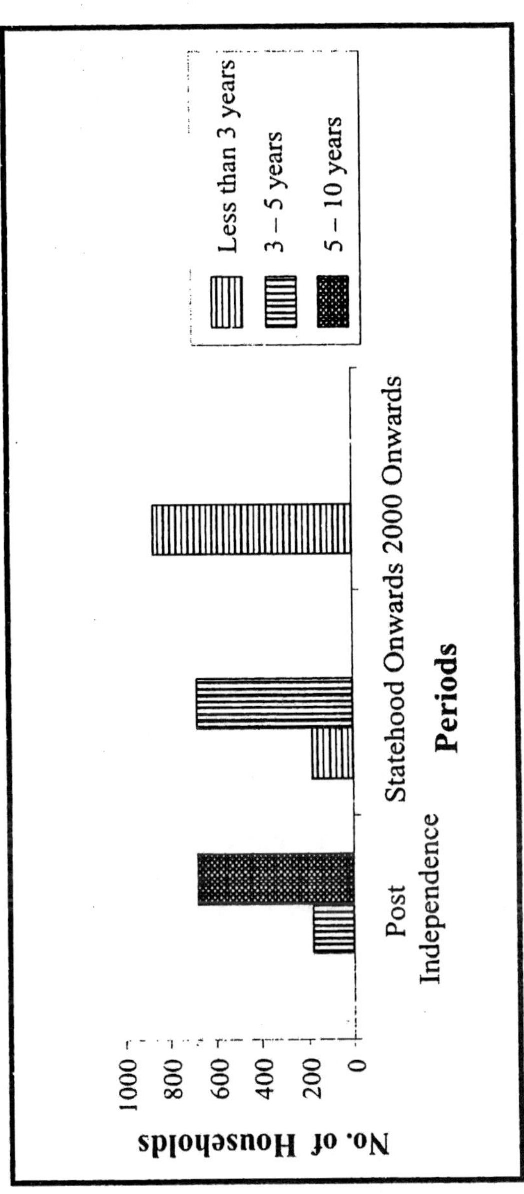

Fig. 7.3 : Jhum Cycle.

of suitable area for jhum to the total population has become much lesser, which had reduced the length of jhum cycle to less than 3 years. A field left out for 10 years to regenerate during the post independence period is left out for less than 3 years that has resulted in rapid loss of soil fertility and higher degree of deforestation in the recent decades.

Crop Combination

Crop combination is an important aspect of agricultural geography because it provides a good basis for agricultural regionalization. Generally, crops are grown in combination and one can experience rarely that a particular crop is occupying a position of total isolation from other crops in a given areal unit at a given point of time.

Crop combination is a possible concomitant element of shifting cultivation. At first paddy (*o)* and maize (*sibe*) seeds are sown over the burnt ash in the field in the month of May (*Kheo*), followed by arum (*truo*), ginger (*tiikrin*), pumpkin (*drubji*), cucumber *(miyi*), sweet potato (*jimchio alu*), *nyekhsii, sawo, saje*, etc. Common pulses such as *urad* or *mas* (*shapoo*) and other similar crops locally known as *labiunsu* and *labji* are sowed in the month of June (*Chiyiew*). Millet seeds are broadcasted in the month of July (*Wuju*). French bean (*laprapra*), maize, *shapoo, pemdu*, etc. are being sowed in the month of August (*Dosa*). The September (*Domuhu*) month is considered to be bad month for germination of any crop. The October (*ledishi*) month is marked by the sowing of motor (*pulbj)* as well as potato (*lasaneksi*) in the fields for early consumption. Hence, they practice crop combination of paddy, maize, millet, vegetables, chili, and spices in a year. The combination of crop is done for the sustenance of the family because apart from the food grains, which form meal for one time the other crops like arum, *nyekhi, sawo, saje,* pumpkin, etc. forms the meal for another time in a day. Besides, the vegetables and spices are the added requirements of their food habits; therefore, these crops are grown in combination to meet the requirements of the family.

The recent survey of the area reveals that majority of them go for combination of paddy, maize and millet in the jhum fields. A separate small field is maintained for the requirements of vegetables and other crops. Nowadays the concept of kitchen garden gaining momentum and people mostly grow vegetables and other crops in kitchen gardens. The jhum fields are mostly left for major food crops – paddy and maize. Farmers are becoming more conscious and cropping pattern is also changing due to the increasing importance of the requirement of food grains. The shortage of food grains during the rainy season forced them to grow more and more food crops in place of vegetables and other crops.

Table 7.4
Various Crops Grown in Jhum Fields

Local Name	*English Name*	*Scientific Name*
Siibe	Maize	*Zea mays*
O	Paddy	*Oryza sativa*
Kiitse	Millet	*Setaria sp.*
Tro	Arum	*Colocassia sp.*
Nyeksi	Yams	*Dioscorea opposita*
Sawo	Yams	*Dioscorea sp.*
Saje	Yams	*Dioscorea sp.*
Drubzii	Pumpkin	*Cucurbita sp.*
Miyi	Cucumber	*Cucumis sativa*
Shapoo	Pulses	*Vigna sp.*
Labionsu	Pulses	*Vigna sp.*
Labji	Soyabean	*Glycine max*
Laprapra	French bean	*Phaseolus sp.*
Pemdu	Laisak	—
Pulbji	Pea	*Pisum sativum sp.*
Lasanyeksii	Potato	*Solanum tuberosum*
Tiikrin	Ginger	*Zingiber sp.*
Adii	Chili	*Capsicum sp.*
Mufu	Roots	—
Miisi	Roots	—

Source: Field Survey, 2006.

Area under Wet Rice Cultivation

Wet rice cultivation spreads over a very large area in Asia - it is cultivated in India, Japan, Malaysia, Indonesia Thailand and China. This distribution is influenced by physical (climate, relief and soils), economic and social factors. The synonyms of wet rice cultivation are wet-rice farming, wet-rice society, wet-rice growing, and wet-rice technology. It is a type of farming in which paddy is grown in level, flooded fields in southern and eastern Asia. Wet-rice cultivation is the most prevalent method of farming in the Far East, where it utilizes a small fraction of the total land yet feeds the majority of the rural population. Rice was domesticated as early as 3500 BC, and by about 2,000 years ago it was grown predominantly in deltas, floodplains and coastal plains, and some terraced valley slopes. Although rice can also be grown under dry conditions, wet-rice cultivation in paddy fields is much more productive. The fields can be flooded naturally or by irrigation channels, and are kept inundated during the growing season. About a month before harvesting, the water is removed and the field left to dry.

This type of agriculture was not known to the people during the past until the post independence period. During the post independence period also such agriculture was not practiced by the people. However, the early period of statehood shows little area under wet rice cultivation. Due to the increased knowledge of wet rice cultivation about 1 to 2 acres of land in the river valleys and foothills has been devoted to this type of agriculture by the people since the statehood period. The higher yields and use of scientific tools had also encouraged them to carry out wet rice cultivation to a larger extent. Nowadays almost every household is in search of flat plain or little flat area for either wet rice cultivation or terrace rice cultivation to enhance the production of rice. The irrigational facilities in the form of canals had also contributed in transforming the type of agriculture in the area. All these changes had relieved a little pressure on the land caused by the higher rate of shifting cultivation.

HUNTING (*FU SOW*)

Hunting is the practice of pursuing animals for food, recreation, trade or for their products. In modern use, the term refers to regulated and legal hunting, as distinguished from poaching, which is the killing, trapping or capture of animals contrary to law. Hunted animals are referred to as game animals, and are usually large mammals or migratory birds. By definition, hunting strictly speaking, excludes the killing - though similar techniques may be used - of individual protected animals, such as bears which have become dangerous to humans, as well as the killing of non-game animals, domestic animals, or vermin as a means of pest control. Hunting can be a component of modern wildlife management maintaining a population of healthy animals within an environment's ecological carrying capacity. In the United States, wildlife managers are frequently part of hunting regulatory and licensing bodies, where they help to set rules on the number, manner and conditions in which game may be selected for culling.

Even agriculture and animal husbandry become more prevalent, hunting often remains a part of human cultures where the environment and social conditions allow. Hunting may be used to kill animals that prey upon domestic animals or to extirpate native animals seen as competition for resources such as water or forage. As hunting moved from a subsistence activity to a social one, two trends emerged. One was that of the specialist hunter: rather than a general masculine task, hunting became one of many trades pursued by those with special training and equipment. The other was the emergence of hunting as a sport for those of a higher social class. Historical, subsistence and sport hunting techniques can differ radically, with modern hunting regulations often addressing issues of where, when and how hunts are conducted. Techniques may vary depending on government regulations, a hunter's personal ethics, local custom, firearms and the animal being hunted. Often a hunter may use a combination of more than one technique as mentioned below:

- Baiting – is the use of decoys, lures, scent or food to attract animals.
- Blind or Stand hunting – is waiting for animals from a concealed or elevated position.
- Calling – is the use of animal noises to attract or drive animals.
- Camouflage – is the use of visual concealment (or scent) to blend with the environment.
- Dogs may be used to help flush, herd, drive, track, point at, pursue or retrieve prey.
- Driving – is the herding of animals in a particular direction, usually toward another hunter in the group.
- Flushing – is the practice of scaring animals from concealed areas.
- Glassing – is the use of optics (such as binoculars) to more easily locate animals.
- Netting – is the active netting with the use of cannon nets and rocket nets.
- Scouting – is a variety of tasks and techniques for finding animals to hunt.
- Spotlighting – is the use of artificial light to find or blind animals before killing.
- Staling – is the practice of walking quietly, often in pursuit of an identified animal.
- Still hunting -- is the practice of walking quietly in search of animals.
- Tracking – is the practice of reading physical evidence in pursuing animals.
- Trapping – is the use of devices (snare, pits, deadfalls) to capture or kill an animal.

The Akas go for hunting whenever they have time and convenience (Plate 7.2). Hunting is an important part of their life. The most commonly used weapons for hunting during the past are the bow and arrow (*Kiyi, Mudra, Muchi* or *Mu*).

PLATE NO. 7.2
HUNTING AND FISHING TOOLS AND TECHNIQUES

(a)

(b)

(c)

(d)

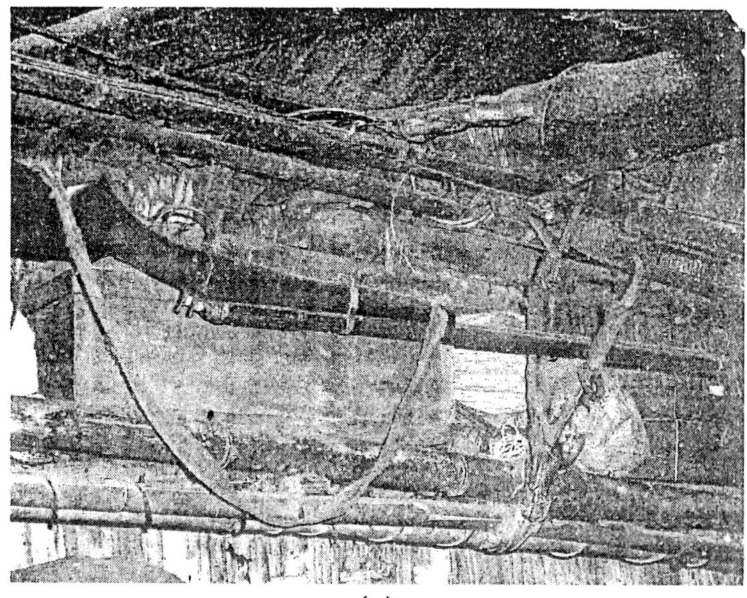

(e)

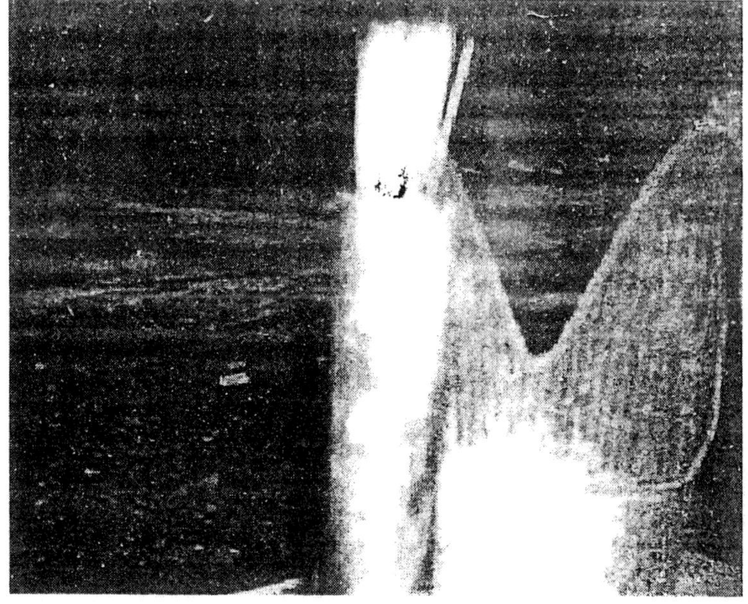

(f)

(g)

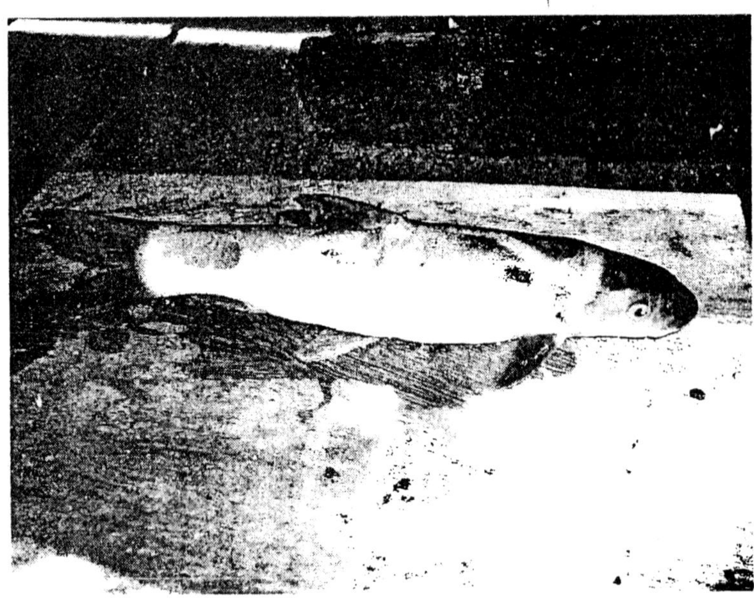

(h)

(i)

Photo : (a) *Ghyi* (*Derris scandens*) – a creeper used as fish poison, (b) *Fuhuliitrii* (*Amphineuron extensus*) – a shrub used as fish poison, (c) *Wukupa* (*Acasia sp.*) – a thorny creeper used as fish poison, (d) *Thuvo Kiyi* – Traditional bow and quiver, (e) *Mubyo* – Local made gun, (f) *Khriiyi* – Indigenous technique of using rubber for killing birds, (g) Decoration of the teeth of hunted wild boar in the front of house, (h) *Chimnu* – fish species considered to be the cleanest among all, (i) *Chilvu* – fish species do not consumed by all.

The bow and arrows are made out of a hard species of bamboo and the rope for bow and arrow are collected from a bark of small tree known as *Mumdra*. The arrows are kept in a quiver, made of bamboo and locally known as *Thuvou*. The arrows are poisoned (aconite) on the front part, which is known as *Mukhu*. This poison plant (aconite) is not available in the Aka area; hence it is collected from far places locally known to be *Lasa-Sigyeng*. The arrows are divided into two types: (i) arrows that are used for shooting birds, such types are not poisoned and (ii) arrows which are used for big game hunting, such types are always being poisoned by fitting with tips of iron and smeared with aconite poison. The feathers of the arrows are collected from a plant known as *Kiigatsho*.

Hunting is done by three methods i.e. individual hunting (*Siim Dow/Jiw*), group hunting (*Fu Sow*) and community hunting (*Fu Sow*). Individual hunting is done up to a distance of 10 kms. The equipments/weapons used for such type of hunting are the common bow and poisoned arrow (*Kiyi, Moo* and *Muchi*), spear (*Kriiju*), gun (*Mubeo*) and *Dao* (*Vetsii*). Deer, wild pig, monkey, bear, etc. are the important animals hunted. In such kind of hunting, if the person uses others gun or bow and arrow then a portion of the animal hunted is given to him and rest is retained by the person. If he had used his own weapons, then he may distribute some pieces of meat to his clan members and relatives. Trapping can also be put under this category of hunting that involves killing of animals through indigenous techniques. They prepare numerous types of traps for hunting with the help of plants and stones. A kind of trap for hunting big animals such as beer, wild pig, deer, monkey, etc. is known as *Tshe*, which is completely a work of woods, stones and ropes collected from the forest. It is prepared on the path of the animal and as the animal passes through this trap, it falls upon the animal and kills the same. A second type of trap is known as *Yetu*, which is prepared with the help of a hard rope. A hard rope is used to tight on the top of a hardwood pole, then stretches it and fixed on the ground by some technique. If animals happen to pass through this trap, it will hang the animal on the pole. A third type of trap is known as *Mudru*, which is also done by the women folk. It is prepared with the help of a rope made of *Mumdra*. It is prepared for hunting birds and rats. The same technique of *Yetu* is applied here as well but it is smaller than the *Yetu*. Another type of trap is known as *Muju*, which is prepared with the help of a stone, two pieces of wood, a rope of bamboo and a piece of insect. When the bird tries to eat the insect, the bird will be trapped there. The local rubber is also used for killing birds. Some 50 to 100 pieces of small sticks of bamboo are prepared and the rubber is poured on the sticks in a bamboo tube and mixed-up completely. These sticks are placed on the branches of the wild fruits, early in the morning. As soon as the bird's tries to eat fruits, they will be trapped on the rubber and fall down on the ground. This rubber is known as *Sejyen-kseo*.

Group hunting is done up to 25 to 30 kms away from the village. This type of hunting may last for 3 to 4 days. Animals found on the way are being hunted and the intestine, liver, etc. are cooked and consumed on the forest itself. The animals hunted are equally distributed amongst the members and dried to take home. The participating member ranges from about ten years young boys to old people. The young boys are given the task of shouting with the dogs, so that the animals may run to the place where the hunters are hiding to shoot.

Community hunting is performed up to a distance of 10 kms away from the village. It is organized to hunt specific animal required for puja performance of certain rituals. It is also done when a priest (*Mugow*) tells after performing rituals that if a particular animal is killed then the sufferings will be cured and evil spirit will be driven away from the village. The common animals and birds hunted in all types of hunting are given in table – 5.5 and 5.6.

Table 7.5
Name of Common Wild Animals Hunted

Local Name	*English Name*	*Scientific Name*	*How Consumed*
1	*2*	*3*	*4*
Fumi	Deer	*Cervulus mutijac*	Roasting, directly burning on the fire and also after boiling/frying.
Sucho	Bear	*Melursus ursinus Sclenarctos thibetanus*	-Do-. Not eaten by the women.
Fuhu	Wild boar	*Sus scrofa*	-Do-
Fumi-cho	Reindeer	*Axis axis*	-Do-
Wofu	—	—	-Do-
Siije	—	—	-Do-

1	*2*	*3*	*4*
Syofu	Monkey	*Macaca radiate*	-Do-. Not eaten by the women.
Mthifu	Wild mithun	*Bos fontalis*	-Do-
Fuggi	—	—	-Do-
Wuve	—	—	-Do-
Mujo	Porcupine	*Porcupine hystrix*	-Do-
Muju	Pangolin/ Scaly anteater	*Manis tricupis*	-Do-
Pse	Squirrel of big size	*Dremomys lokriah*	Roasting as well as smoked dry. Not eaten by the women.
Psesinsa	Squirrel	*Funambulus*	Smoked dry mostly after roasting and boil. Not eaten by the women.
Rumo inyigro	Rat (wild)	*Ratus ratus*	Smoked dry, roasting and boil. Not eaten by the women.

Source : Field Survey, 2006.

Table 7.6
Name of Common Birds Hunted

Local Name	*English Name*	*Scientific Name*	*How Consumed*
1	*2*	*3*	*4*
Kesajyo	Wild chicken	—	Roasting, smoked dry, boil/ fry and burning directly on the fire. Consumed by all.
Thiirii	Wild chicken	—	-Do-
Sujo	—	—	-Do-
Diigj	—	—	-Do-
Siiwbam	—	—	-Do-
Futuchem	—	—	-Do-
Liidam	—	—	-Do-
Psiglu	Bulbul	*Molpastes cafer*	-Do-

1	2	3	4
Pacho	Parrot	*Psittacula eupatricia*	-Do-
Siise	—	—	-Do-
Drain-dradum	—	—	-Do-
Subeau	Wild pigeon		-Do-
Subeau-jim	—	—	-Do-
Subeau-kro	—	—	-Do-
Salvo	—	—	-Do-. Not eaten by the women.
Gudru/ Sugrow	Hornbill Rufous necked Wreated Great pied	*Aceroa nipalensid* *Ryticeros undulats* *Buceros bicornis*	-Do-

Source: Field Survey, 2006.

The thick forests around allow them to move constantly and the urges for defense against the wild life have made them good archers. Hunting is a part of their life and through this they supplement their shortage of food supply. It is a subsidiary means of sustenance for them that fulfil the requirement of flesh for consumption. Tribal people all around the globe do hunting in one form or the other. Hunting is done throughout the year except for two months June (*Chiyiw*) and July (*Wusu*) because these months are believed to be *Hubey-suyuw* (bad months) and hunting during these months may cause accident and loss of life.

FISHING

Fishing is the activity of hunting for fish by hooking, trapping, or gathering. The term fishing is applied to pursuing other aquatic animals such as various types of shellfish, squid, octopus, turtles, frogs, and some edible marine invertebrates. The term *fishing* is not usually applied to pursuing aquatic mammals such as whales, where the term "whaling" is more appropriate, or to commercial fish farming. Fishing is an ancient and worldwide practice with various techniques and traditions and it has been transformed by modern technological developments. In addition to providing food through harvesting fish, modern fishing is both a recreational and professional sport.

Fishing forms a part of their economic life. People go for fishing almost throughout the year, except the two months of June and July. These two months are believed to be *Hubey-suyuw* (bad months). In these months no fish can be fished and there is a risk of get drowned in the river and loss of life. So, usually people do not go for fishing in these months. The maximum fishing is done in the months of December and January and these months are known as *Hubey-sivjiw* (good month). Fish formed an important diet for these people. Fishing can be done by individual, group and community. Usually, man goes for fishing. But, in group or community fishing the interested women's may also take part. In such case also the womenfolk were given the work, which involves less hard work. The important species of fishes are given in Table – 7.7.

Techniques of Fishing

The Akas evolved and adopt a variety of indigenous techniques of fishing. Fishing in any form is restricted in the flooded streams probably due to anticipated risk of getting drowned in the river and loss of life. The following are the various indigenous techniques of fishing practiced by them:

- *Tromo-mo* (netting)
- *Akiighii-jyo* (angling)
- *Hu-view* (damming of the rivers)
- *Gyi-guw* – use of herbal poisons.
- *Tuvo-peo* (use of bamboo traps)
- *Huji-dow* (Community fishing – diversion of big river course
- *Chi-kuluw*

- *Chi-suw*
- *Miinow* (baiting)

Various herbal poisons are collected from the forests and used in small streams and after diversion of rivers/streams. The common herbal poisons are *Gyi* (*Derris scandens*) plate no. 7.2 (a), *Fuhuliitrii* (*Amphineuron*) *extensus* plate no. 7.2 (b) and *Wukupa* (*Acasia sp.*) plate no. 7.2 (c). A community fishing is done when a large river course is to be diverted (*Huji-dow*). Each and every household has to send one member each in performing this type of fishing because this type of fishing involves hard labour. The uses of indigenous techniques of fishing burdened with imperfection have proved significant in meeting their needs and requirements as well as checking the depletion of fish species. Use of blasting and chemical poisons is not allowed in the area. Anyone practicing this mode of fishing is against the customary laws however nowadays, a punishment up to 6 months imprisonment and an amount of Rs. 5,000/- is proposed as fine by the villagers. Thus, methods of fishing that are adopted in the area are eco-friendly. They spare the small fishes and some fish species are not consumed due to social beliefs attached to them. However, the modern technology has provided lots of fishing options to the people that has assured them easy fishing but more destruction to the aquatic lives. The traditional techniques of fishing are eco-friendly and helped them in their sustenance for hundreds and thousands of years. The introduction of new techniques of fishing like blasting, chemical poisoning, use of electric current, etc. had led to higher loss of aquatic lives in the last few decades. The most recent technique of fishing that has penetrated in the area is the use of electric current in the river. This new method is frequently practiced by the people to earn money by killing enormous fish that led to depletion of fish species as well as other organisms present in the river. Traditionally, fishing was done for self consumption, social occasions, festivals, etc. Sometimes, people who are running short of food grains exchange fish with food grains through the process of barter trade. Nowadays some vested persons are engaged in large scale fishing by applying wrong methods of fishing to sell and earn huge amount of money. The tradition of fishing has become a business for some people who are always engaged in fishing almost throughout the year. Though, tradition prohibits people from any kind of fishing in the months of June and July but, such restrictions has lost its significance and unable to make a mark in the minds of the younger generation hence fishing is carried out round the year.

Table 7.7
Species of Fishes Caught for Consumption

Local Name	*English Name*	*Scientific Name*	*How Consumed*
1	2	3	4
Bebeau	—	—	This is very big fish. It is consumed by roasting as well as boiling. Now-a-days it is rarely found.
Chikpem	—	—	This is the largest fish found in the Aka inhabited area. It weights up to 25-30 kg. It is found occasionally, while diverting the river course. Eaten by roasting, boiling and burning on the fire.
Gnawo	—	*Labeo pangsu*	It is found abundantly in netting.
Sla-lusu	—	—	It is a big fish and not found abundantly. Eaten as her same process the others are being taken.
Silache	Rohu	*Rohita sp.*	Most commonly found species of fish is in the Aka area. This fish is not consumed by the women folk of higher status.
Ludo	—	*Labeo sp.*	Another kind of fish consumed by all boiled form with other vegetables.

1	2	3	4
Chimnu/Chische	—		This fish is considered to be the cleanest among the different species of fishes and consumed by all men and women.
Chilvu	—	*Glyptothrox sp.*	It is a medium sized fish which is not consumed by the women.
Mumuin	—	*Garra sp.*	Seasonal fish eaten by the same process.
Humey	—	*Abriricthes sp.*	It is a seasonal small fish mostly found in the mouths of September and October in small streams and *nalas*.
Chibeau	Eel	*Anguilla japonica*	It is taken by burning on the fire and after boil/fry. Consumption of this fish is considered to be useful during the fire burnt on any part of the body.
Fusiu	Prawn	*Panoles sp.*	Consumed by burning on the fire and boil/fry.
Ghji	Crab	*Cancer sp.*	Consumed by burning on the fire and boil/fry.

Source: Field Survey, 2006.

Ownership Issues of Rivers for Fishing

The ownership system of rivers for fishing has been practiced by the people since the olden days. The general agreement of the people on the ownership of rivers is made by counting the rivers that are falling in the boundary as marked through any physical features like mountain pass, peak, rivers, stone, etc. In case of the major rivers that traverse the two villages on the opposite banks, the ownership is done by dividing the bank of rivers on either side. The total length of river that flows from the upper boundary to the lower boundary will be owned by the villagers of that area. No outsiders from other villages/places are allowed fishing of any form in the rivers owned by a particular village. If some one found doing illegal fishing will be brought under the traditional village council for discussion and punishment and fine will be imposed. Apart from the major rivers, some small streams are cleared and maintained by either an individual or by the clan. The small streams are important for catching small seasonal fishes like *Mumun* and *Humey.* These seasonal fishes lay their eggs in the source of the small streams. Such streams are owned by the members of a clan in the village, but sometimes it is also owned by an individual family. Small huts are constructed near the streams and it is cleared during the season when the fish lay eggs in the source to catch them for consumption. Other members of the village except the clan members are not restricted from any kind of fishing in these streams. The ownership issue nowadays has been relaxed up to certain extent. The openness of the society with the other societies and cultural exchanges had loosened the tightened hands of rules and regulations of the people. The development of friendly relations with other villagers has increased the chances of fishing and hunting together without any restrictions and fine. The indigenous methods of fishing like angling and netting are relaxed to all sections of people, but chemical poisoning, blasting, etc. are still strictly prohibited to others.

Food Gathering

Food gathering is an important part of their occupation and a supplementary source of livelihood. The Akas mainly depend on the nearby forests for their requirement of vegetables, fruits, barks, edible plants and leaves, fruits, etc. The collections of forest produce *i.e.* vegetables, mushrooms, etc. falls within the province of womenfolk. Collection of fruits, tree barks, edible plants, etc. which involves hard work are done by men. Some of these forest produce are being collected throughout the year, some of which are collected for six months and some of which are collected for only one or two months. The food gathering pursuits among the Akas, however, do not involve co-operative actively among the premier food gathers of the country. Women or girls in small groups, or even individually, collect the vegetables from the forest whenever they need.

Table 7.8
Wild Vegetables and Mushrooms Collected from the Forests

Local Name	*English Name*	*Scientific Name*	*How Consumed*
1	2	*4*	*5*
Siiga	Bamboo shoot	*Dendocalamus hamiltonni*	Consumed in both form - raw and dry. Raw form by boiling with chili and salt and dry form is called *suhu*. It is also consumed by keeping in raw form either in jungle or home by packing in leaves and placing big stones over it locally called as *spshii*.
Wolbu	Banana flower/ inflore-cence	*Musa paradisiaca*	Used for vegetable purpose by burning on the fire as well as boiling it.
Fumpem	—	—	It is small plant and its leaves are consumed while boiling with other vegetables.
Pesa	—	*Pouzolzia viminea*	It is also a leafy vegetable and is somewhat slippery in nature and consumed in boil form.
Pedba	—	*Piper pedicellatum*	Widely found in the Aka area and consumed with dal and bamboo shoot.
Husa-pemdu	—	—	It is found in the banks of small streams and taken through boiling process.
Pelowo	—	—	It is a creeper and not found abundantly.
Malasi	—	—	It is a creeper and not found abundantly.
Wulo chanchi	—	*Piplazium esculantum*	It is found abundantly on the roadsides and consumed after boiling/frying.
Droloin	—	*Clerodendrom colebrookianum*	It is eaten by streaming process.

1	2	4	5
Huju	—	*Alocasia sp.*	It is a wild *kochu* the tender leafs are collected and eaten after boiling.
Pyen	—	—	Consumed through steaming and boiling process.
a. *Lumyogji*	Mushrooms	*Temitomyces sp.*	Consumed by burning in the fire as well as boiling. Some of the mushrooms are eaten in raw forms.
b. *Lumyo-tiinta*	—	*Contherallus sp.*	
c. *Lumyo-kiila*	—	—	
d. *Lumyo-fusi*	—	*Schizophyllum*	
e. *Lumyoji*	—	—	
f. *Lumyo-fu*	—	*Pleurotus*	
g. *Tasilii*		*pulmonarius* *Auricularia sp.*	

Source: Field Survey, 2006.

The edible plants collected in the month of January includes wild plants locally known as *husa-pendu, malasi, pesu, pesa*, etc. and the fruits collected are locally known as *syochulje, syotro, kfsjein, emdyin*, etc. Different varieties of mushrooms locally known as *lumyoji, lumyofu, lumyotinta, lumyofusiw, tasilii*, etc. were collected by women/girls in the month of February. In this month other vegetables such as banana flower (*wolbu*), *pedba, miithi-troksi, and wulochanchi* are also gathered. The same vegetables are used to collect in the next month also i.e. March. The two months i.e. April and May are restricted months and no forest produce are being collected because in these months the plants are not fit for consumption. So, these people fully depend on their jhum fields for vegetables in these two months. In the month of June vegetables known as *fumpem*, mushroom (*lumyogji*), bamboos (*bjechi*) are gathered from the forests. Fruits locally known as *lugi, kotocovo, sejilafo syovaji*, etc. are collected to meet the food shortage in the month of June. Some species of bamboo such as *siiga, miisajo, giidri*, are collected in the month of July and also fruits known as *giijey, syobee, wotro*, are gathered in the same month. No vegetables or edible plants are available in the forest in the months of August and September. So, these people depend on the jhum fields

Table 7.9
Wild Fruits Collected from the Forests

Local Name	*English Name*	*Scientific Name*	*How Consumed*
Munyumu	Bansum	*Phoebe* spp.	This is a big tree mostly used for timber. On the same time fruits are collected and outer cover of it is consumed in raw form with chilly and salt.
Kotocovo	Wild lichi	*Myristica fragrance*	It is somewhat similar to lichi. It is consumed by removing the outer cover.
Syobrolofsin	—	—	Inner portion is eaten.
Niuyi	—	*Ficus semichordata*	Cleaned by water and the whole parts are eaten in raw form.
Syobee	—	—	Outer cover is eaten with chilly and salt.
Luduje	—	—	Outer thorny portion is removed and inner portion is eaten.
Lugie	—	—	Consumed by boiling, raw and streaming.
Giijey	—	*Hodgsonia macrocarpa*	Consumed by smoked dry.
Kusuwun	Wild Strawberry	*Rubus sp.*	Eaten in raw form and by putting on the bamboo cups.
Kusukabro	-Do-	*Rubus niveus*	Eaten in raw form and by putting on the bamboo cups.
Kumu	-Do-	*Rubus ellipticus*	Eaten in raw form and by putting on the bamboo cups.
Lufuje	—	*Ficus hispida*	Inner parts are eaten.
Wusa	Wild banana	*Musa sp.*	Eaten by removing the seeds.
Syotro	—	—	A kind of fruit, which is soar in taste. And inner portion is eaten.

Source: Field Survey, 2006.

for their requirement of vegetables in these months. Another important edible wild plant locally known as *siim-neksi* is gathered during the period of shortage in food. Also, there are other edible plants known as *sawo, saje, gudrolu, lumo,* etc. which are collected for consumption to compensate the shortage of food in off seasons. This way almost throughout the year they collect vegetables, fruits, etc. from the nearby forests. In this process a good deal of relationship with the forest ecology has been developed by them.

Table – 7.10

Various Basketry Works of the Akas

Local Name	*English Name*	*Raw materials use*	*Purpose*
Biyo	Basket	Cane, bamboo	It is used for carrying paddy, maize and other allied materials by the women folk.
Mo	Basket	Bamboo	Mainly used for carrying firewood.
Tragdu	—	Bamboo, cane	Mainly used for cooling the hot rice and keeping the local beer for maturing.
Migyi	Winnowing pan	Cane, bamboo	It is used for cleaning rice, maize, millets, vegetables, etc.
Pusey	—	Cane, bamboo	It is used for cleaning vegetables.
Kiitse-lagje	Drying pan	Bamboo, cane	It is used for drying bamboo shoot or any other items, which were wet.
Gja	—	Cane, bamboo	It is used for filtering the local wine.
Sunu	Strainer	Cane	It is used for straining rice beer.
Jyoksu	—	Bamboo	It is used for keeping chickens.
Hutriing	—	Cane	It is put on by the men while going to jungle.
Gtrii	Mat	Cane, bamboo	It is used for sleeping and drying paddy.

Source: Field Survey, 2006.

PLATE NO. 7.3
VARIOUS BASKETRY WORKS OF CANE AND BAMBOO

(a)

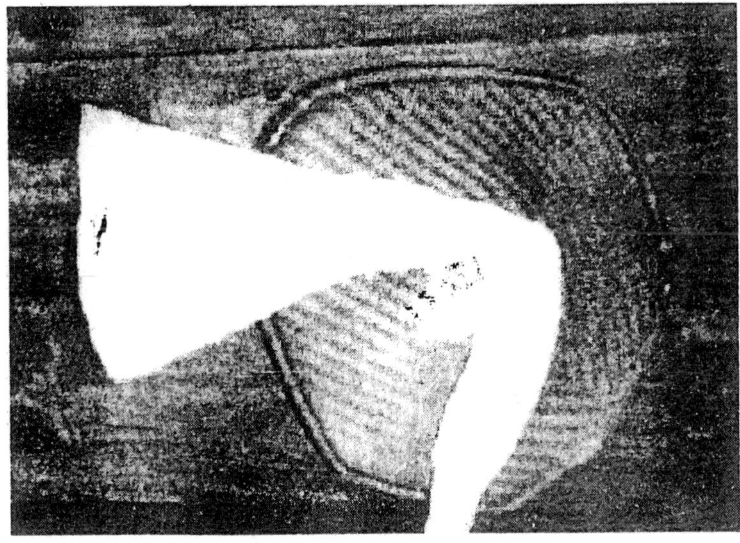

(b)

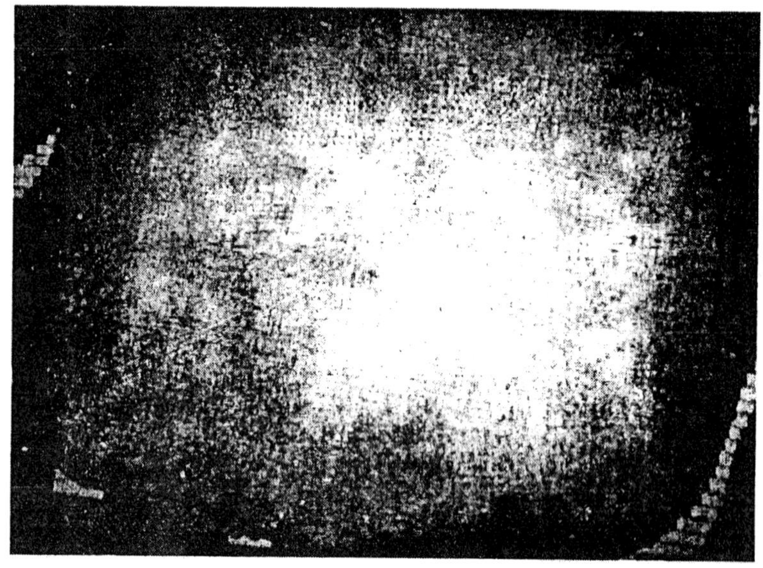

(c)

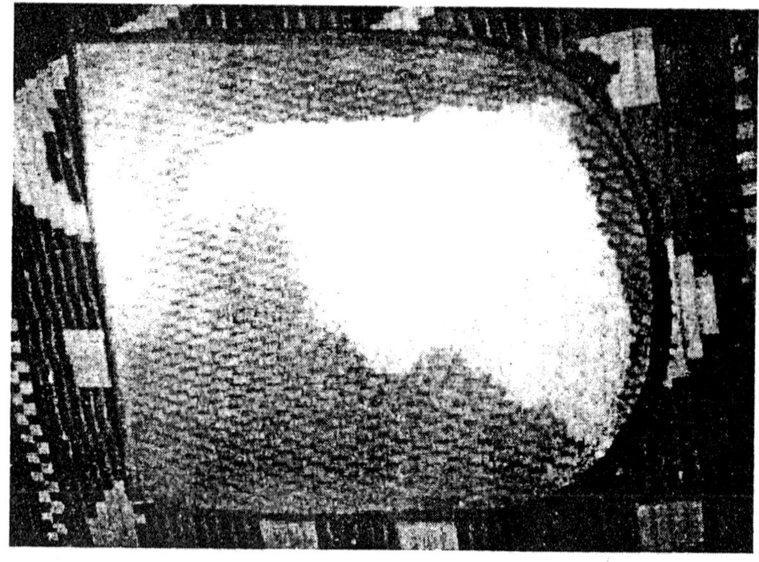

(d)

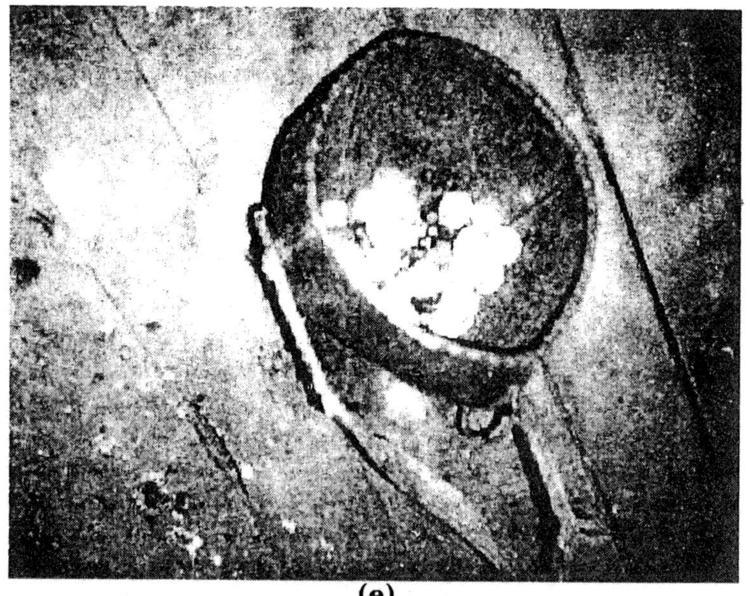

(e)

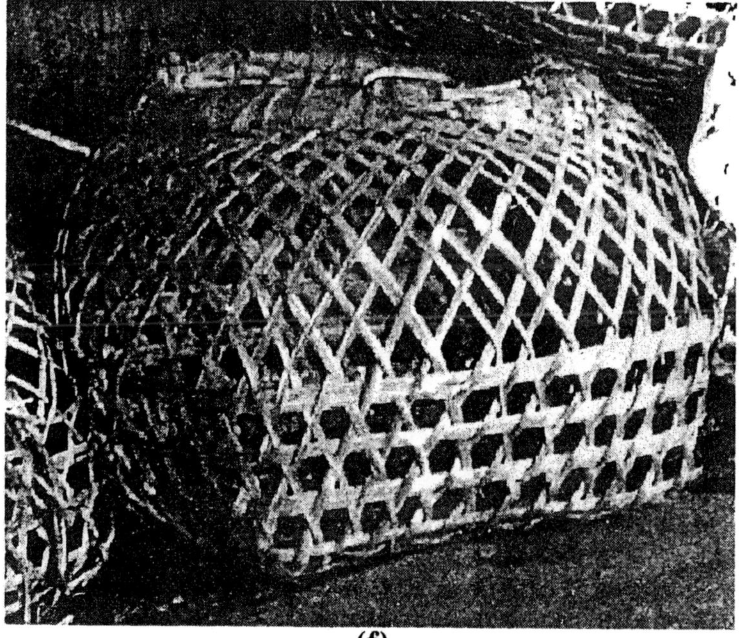

(f)

(g)

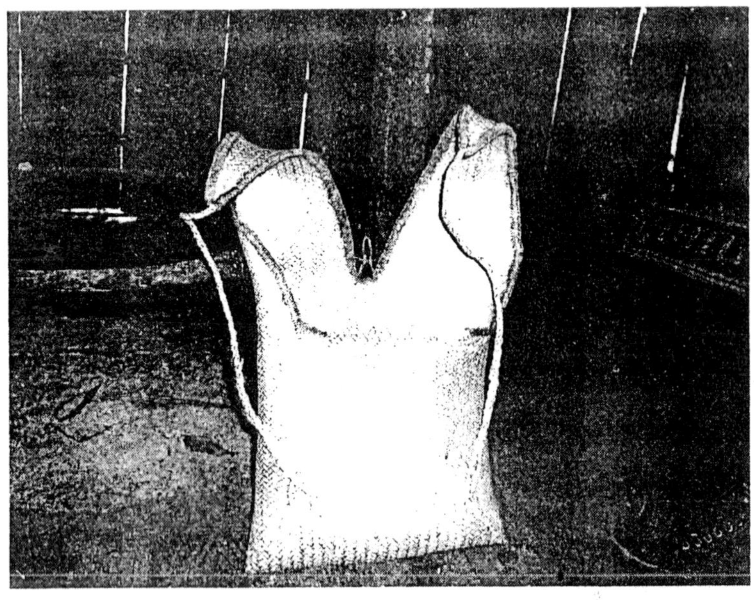

(h)

(i)

Photo : (a) *Pusey* – a circular bamboo pan used for cleaning vegetables, (b) *Ghje Sunu* – strainers used for straining rice beer, (c) *Tragdu* – a bamboo drying pan, (d) Winnowing pan made of cane and bamboo, (e) Conical basket used for carrying vegetables, (f) *Jyoksu* – chicken cage made of bamboo, (g) Bamboo tube used for storing rice beer, (h) *Hütriin* – Traditional bag prepared by modern materials (nylon), (i) *Wulu Miyi* – Wooden Mortar and Pestle.

Basketry and Weaving

Basketry is the craft or process of making baskets or objects woven like baskets. Basketry is also known as basketwork, basket weaving and basket making. Most of the domestic items are made of bamboo and cane therefore, basketry has an important place among the Akas (Plate 7.3). People believe that basketry is an art which is not known to all. Hence, this art is mostly confined to the matured and old people only. The perfection in this art is attained by the experience achieved as one grows older and older. Traditionally, the knowledge of basketry was more widespread as people totally depend on these basketries for domestic uses. The perfection of the work remained in few hands which led to the exchange of baskets with other important materials during the past. A demand of such baskets is made to the person who has better products in exchange of items that are in need of him. Therefore, basketry played a significant role in the barter trade among the people. Nowadays, basketry works are limited to those villages which are far from the roads or located in the heart of the jungles. The traditional baskets are being replaced by the market products with better designs that had pushed the traditional basketry towards the interior villages. The knowledge is now confined to very few people only and it may dwindle in the decades to come, if the present rate of avoiding basketry works by the people continues. Some villagers having good knowledge of basketry are earning money by selling baskets. Though, it is confined to very few people but contributes in their overall economic development.

On the other hand, weaving is the use of wool, cotton, silk, flax, or some other plant or animal fibre yarn or thread to produce textiles of various sorts by criss-crossing the yarns together in at least two directions. *Warp* threads are those which run up and down the length of a piece of textile, *weft* threads are those that run across the weave at right angles to the warp. Many different patterns are possible, producing different kinds of textile and styles of weave. Patterns can be introduced by using different coloured threads in a set order.

The earliest evidence of weaving is that represented as textile and flexible basketry impressions on burnt clay from Pavlov in the Czech Republic which date to between 25, 000 and 23, 000 BC. The oldest woven cloth so far discovered is made from flax, dates to about 7000 BC, and comes from Çayönü, Turkey.

The Akas use to weave some clothes in the past known as *Pasa*. A bark of a small plant known as *mumdra* is used for making yarns. The bark of the plant is taken out in form of long ribbons and left in the sunlight for several days so that it may dry out completely. These dried ribbons were used for preparing yarns. The womenfolk use to weave clothes from these yarns by using a traditional instrument known as *ge-triiw ganyi*. The process of weaving is known as *pasa-triiw* or *ge-triiw*. The use of looms for weaving purpose was not known to them. The clothes weaved by this process was very simple and used for the protection of body only. Another plant known as *wuma* was also used for weaving clothes by applying the same process. Trade in any form was not practiced for these clothes because its production involves hard work and takes more time for making a single piece of cloth. The production was used by the family members only. Before coming in contact with the plains people, weaving was important for them and every household use to weave clothes one way or the other. The Ahom-Aka relations appeared to be a landmark in the traditional weaving practices of the Akas. The system of *Posa* was introduced by the Ahom king Pratap Singha (1603 – 41) to deal effectively with Akas to maintain peace and order in the country which was later followed by the British for many years. As per the records of 1825, the Akas were entitled to receive from each house of their allotted *Khels* 'one portion of a female dress, one bundle of cotton thread, and one cotton handkerchief'. Such a right given to them had made them totally dependent on the Ahom people for their requirement of cloths and slowly the art of weaving has lost its significance among the people. The Aka dress for both male and female is mostly a work of endi cloth (woven from the thread made out of cocoon of a worm called Endi) produced by the Ahoms. Hence, the old records reveal that the art of weaving among the Akas do not hold much significance due to its availability in the nearby plains of Assam. However, it is not abandoned by the people completely and some ladies still weave *Srasi Polu* (a jacket worn by men and women), *Tsupeo* (a long cloth worn around the waist by men and women as a part of the dress), and *Kapgha* (Bags). Some modified dresses are also weaved in the form of the *Gales* as worn by the Tani group of tribes. The introduction of craft centers by the government had encouraged them to learn the art of weaving and start their own small scale industries. It has succeeded in some areas and enabled them to carry out their own craft centers but, it has also helped in the total eradication of the traditional art of weaving because the machine made clothes are available in these craft centers and the indigenous method of weaving has been neglected.

Status of Barter Trade (*Miidrng*)

Barter is a type of trade that doesn't use any medium of exchange, in which goods or services are exchanged for other goods and/or services. It can be bilateral or multilateral as trade. Barter and money are different means of balancing an economic exchange. Barter is used in societies where no monetary system exists. It is the oldest and simplest way of doing business on the planet. It provides the means for a business/person to acquire goods or services through a medium where cash is not a requirement for a transaction to take place. Since the beginning of civilization, mankind has bartered and traded goods and services for those skills or items owned by another. But, today's companies barter for a number of reasons, from getting rid of excess inventory and finding new customers to conserving cash and supporting the local economy.

Exchange of materials either domestic or forest product is practiced by the Akas for acquiring the needs and requirements of such products, which are not available in a particular area or village. For example, the villagers of Palizi exchange a species of bamboo shoot with other neighbouring villagers where it is not available and in return they demand green vegetables from them. In this way each and every village lacks in some kind of forest products, which they use to manage through the exchange of these products and such a tradition is locally known as *miidrng-jiw*. In some occasions they also exchange dried meat and fish also. The most important barter items during the past includes – food grains (paddy, maize, millet), vegetables, roots, tubers, fruits, spices, bamboo shoot, mushrooms, endi cloths, brass plates, beads, swords, etc. Barter trade during the past was exchange of materials that are not available in a particular village. This was the only method of trade followed by them to meet the necessity of clothing, betel nuts and salt from the plains people. Another form of trade during the past was known as *Bjiwu*. Some families of the neighbouring tribes like Miji, Sherdukpen, Monpa, Sartang, Bugun, Bangni, etc. were made friends known as *Bjiwu* by a particular clan or family or sometimes even the whole villagers. All kinds of materials (eatables to material culture) are exchanged in such kind of trade. This practice is also used to be helpful during the visits to far off places where there are no arrangements to stay. As per the old narrations they use to visit their friends in Assam which they call as *Nyuksutro* by carrying, goats, chicken, vegetables and pulses for them and in return they receive betel nuts, cloth, salt, etc. Therefore, the status of barter trade was significant during the past decades, which was maintained by them until the development of modern amenities in the area. People still practice the barter system among them in the far off villages.

The traditional barter trade in which no money was involved has been modified in the recent days. Money is paid for the commodities these days if a person is an employee in lieu of the material given by the person.

Workers and Non-workers

Work is defined as participation in any economically productive activity with or without compensation, wages or profit. Such participation may be physical and/or mental in nature. Work involves not only actual work but also includes effective supervision and direction of work. It even includes part time help or unpaid work on farm, family enterprise or in any other economic activity. All persons engaged in 'work' as defined above are workers. Persons who are engaged in cultivation or milk production even solely for domestic consumption are also treated as workers. Reference period for determining a person as worker and non-worker is one year preceding the date of enumeration. According to the Census of India' 2001 the workers are classified into:

Main Workers

Those workers who had worked for the major part of the reference period (i.e. 6 months or more) are termed as Main Workers.

Marginal Workers

Those workers who had not worked for the major point of the reference period (i.e. less than 6 months) are termed as Marginal Workers. Further, the main and marginal workers are classified into occupational categories based on work performed, skills, education, training and credentials.

Cultivator

For purposes of the census a person is classified as cultivator if he or she is engaged in cultivation of land owned or held from Government or held from private persons or institutions for payment in money, kind or share. Cultivation includes effective supervision or direction in cultivation. A person who has given out her/his land to another person or persons or institution(s) for cultivation for money, kind or share of crop and who does not even supervise or direct cultivation in exchange of land, is not treated as cultivator. Similarly, a person working on another person's land for wages in cash or kind or a combination of both (agricultural labourer) are not treated as cultivator. Cultivation involves ploughing, sowing, harvesting and production of cereals and millet crops such as wheat, paddy, jowar, bajra, ragi, etc., and other crops such as sugarcane, tobacco, ground-nuts, tapioca, etc., and pulses, raw jute and kindred fibre crop, cotton, cinchona and other medicinal plants, fruit growing, vegetable growing or keeping orchards or groves, etc. Cultivation does not include the following plantation crops - tea, coffee, rubber, coconut and betel-nuts (areca).

Agricultural Labourers

A person who works on another person's land for wages in money or kind or share is regarded as an agricultural labourer. (S) He has no risk in the cultivation, but merely works on another person's land for wages. An agricultural labourer has no right of lease or contract on land on which (s) he works.

Household Industry Workers

Household Industry is defined as an industry conducted by one or more members of the household at home or within the village in rural areas and only within the precincts of the house where the household lives in urban areas. The larger proportion of workers in the household industry consists of members of the household. The industry is not run on the scale of a registered factory which would qualify or has to be registered under the Indian Factories Act. The main criterion of a Household industry even in urban areas is the participation of one or more members of a household. Even if the industry is not actually located at home in rural areas there is a greater possibility of the members of the household participating even if it is located anywhere within the village limits. In the urban areas where organized industry takes greater prominence, the Household Industry is confined to the precincts of the house where the participants live. In urban areas, even if the members of the household run an industry by themselves but at a place away from the precincts of their home, it is not considered as a Household Industry. It should be located within the precincts of the house where the members live in the case of urban areas. Household Industry relates to production, processing, servicing, repairing or making and selling (but not merely selling) of goods. It does not include professions such as a Pleader, Doctor, Musician, Dancer, Waterman, Astrologer, Dhobi, Barber, etc., or merely trade or business, even if such professions, trade or services are run at home by members of the household.

Other Workers

All workers i.e., those who have been engaged in some economic activity during the last one year, but are not cultivators or agricultural labourers or in Household Industry, are 'Other Workers (OW)'. The type of workers that come under this category of 'OW' include all government servants, municipal employees, teachers, factory workers, plantation workers, those engaged in trade, commerce, business, transport, banking, mining, construction, political or social work, priests, entertainment artists, etc. In effect, all those workers other than cultivators or agricultural labourers or household industry workers are 'Other Workers'.

Work Participation Rate

Work participation rate is defined as the percentage of total workers (main and marginal) to total population.

$$\text{Work Participation Rate} = \frac{\text{Total Workers (Main + Marginal)}}{\text{Total Population}} \times 100$$

$$= \frac{2052}{5027} \times 100$$

$$= 40.82\%$$

Non-workers

Non–workers are defined as those who have been not participated or have been unable to participate in any economically productive activity during the last one year preceding the date of enumeration. The non-workers are again categorized into the following seven heads :

- *Household duties* - This covers all persons who are engaged in unpaid home duties and who do no work or have not done any work at all during the last one year.
- *Students* - This covers all full time students and children attending school. In most houses the daughters

help in the household work though they are studying full time. In such cases, they are recorded as students and not as engaged in household duties.

- *Dependents* - This category includes all dependents such as infants or children not attending school or a person permanently disabled from work because of illness or old age. Dependents will include even able bodied persons who cannot be categorized in any other category of non–workers but are dependent on others. However, if such a person who is dependent on others for subsistence is seeking work, he or she will be categorized as other non – workers.
- *Retired Persons or Rentiers* - A person who has retired from service and is doing no other work i.e. not employed again in some economic activity for some part of the year, or a person who is a rentier or living on agricultural or non-agricultural royalty, rent or dividend, or any other person having an independent means of earning an income for which he/she does not have to work, will come under this category.
- *Beggars, etc* - This covers beggars, vagrants or those persons without indication of source of income and also those with unspecified sources of subsistence who are not engaged in any economically productive work.
- *Inmates of Institutions* - This covers convicts in jails or inmates of penal, mental or charitable institutions, even if such persons are compelled to do some work, such as, carpentry, carpet weaving, vegetable growing, etc. in such institutions. But, in the case of the under trial prisoners in a jail, for the work he/she was doing before he/she was apprehended is recorded for their work or economic activity. Similarly, a person temporarily in a hospital or similar institution is categorized according to the kind of work he/she was doing before he/she was admitted into the hospital or institution. But for a long-term under trial prisoner, or convict in a prison, or for a long-term inmate of penal or charitable or mental

institution, the person's previous work is not recorded but he/she is treated as non–worker under the category of inmates of institutions. A person is considered for long term if he or she is in such an institution for 6 months or more.

The village wise distribution of workers and non–workers in the Aka area since 1971 to 2001 is shown in Tables–7.11, 7.12, 7.13 and 7.14

The 1971 census recorded a total of 2046 workers (2012 males and 340 females) and 2046 non–workers (711 males and 1335 females). The workers and non–workers were recorded equal, however there is a marked variation in the sex composition. The higher number of people in the non-worker category is evident of higher dependency ratio in the area. The majority of workers were classified as other services numbering 1359 with 1232 males and 127 females. It was followed by cultivators numbering 941 with 733 males and 208 females.

There were 32 persons engaged in trade and commerce and 11 agricultural labourers with 6 males and 5 females. The categories like household industry (5), constructions (3) and livestock, forestry, fishing, hunting and plantations, orchards and allied activities (1) has very less share in the occupational structure. About 50% of the population was non–worker, which was the result of shift in the approach to the concept of workers in 1971 census. The census considered only the main workers as workers and marginal workers + non–workers as non–workers which had its impact at the national level as well. The workers at the national level were 175 million in 1971, which was less than the number of workers of 182.5 million in 1961 census. This shift in the approach might have resulted in the higher percentage of non – workers in the area. The location of villages determines the workers engaged in different occupations. The villages situated in the interior area were mostly engaged in cultivation whereas the villages located near the roads and administrative headquarters have more people engaged in other services. The total main worker in 1981 census was 3152 with 2103 males and 1049 females respectively.

Table 7.11
Table Showing Total Workers and Non-workers of the Aka Villages 1971

	Total Workers		*Cultivators*		*Agricultural Labourers*		*Livestock, Forestry, Fishing, Hunting and Plantations, Orchards and allied activities*		*Household Industry*	
Village	*M*	*F*	*M*	*F*	*M*	*F*	*M*	*F*	*M*	*F*
1	2	3	4	5	6	7	8	9	10	11
Bana	18	15	18	15	..	..	..	..	..	..
Bana Camp	57	7					..		..	
Bhalukpong/Thrizino	529	65					..		5	
Bihupam	7		7							
Buragaon										
Chizang	44	32	42	29	2	3				
Dedza	81	..	..	..	..	..				
Dijangania	89	2	83	1	3	1				
Gijiri	17	..	17	..	..	..	..	..	..	..

Table 7.13 (Contd. . . .)

1	2	3	4	5	6	7	8	9	10	11
Gohainthan	18	..	18	..	..	..	..	..	..	..
Huppipam/Dezling	457	38	21	4	..	..	..	..	..	..
Hussigaon	38	3	22	1	..	..	..	..	..	..
Jamiripoint/Noghupam	76	10	7	..	..	..	..	1	..	..
Jamiri Village	28	..	24	..	..	..	..	..	..	..
Karangania	31	..	30	..	..	..	..	..	..	..
Kararamu	13	..	13	..	..	..	..	..	..	..
Kichang	35	36	34	35	1	1	..	..	..	..
Linia	7	..	7	..	..	..	..	..	..	..
Moracca	10	..	10	..	..	..	..	..	..	..
Palatari	44	..	44	..	..	..	..	..	..	..
Pharizing	15	..	15	..	..	..	..	..	..	..
Pichang	131	121	102	121	..	..	..	..	..	..
Ramdagania	52	..	47	..	..	..	..	..	..	..
Rogupam	7	..	7	..	..	..	..	..	..	..
Rugugaon	4	..	4	..	..	..	..	..	..	..
Sakrin	54	..	53	..	..	..	..	..	..	..
Sessa	42	9	..	..	..	..	..	..	..	..
Tania	17	1	17	1	..	..	..	..	..	..
Thesa	46	..	46	..	..	..	..	..	..	..
Thesari	9	..	9	..	..	..	..	..	..	..
Tulu	22	1	22	1	..	..	..	..	..	..
Yayong	14	..	14	..	..	..	..	..	..	..
Total	2012	340	733	208	6	5	0	1	5	0

Table 7.13 (Contd. . . .)

Village	Other than Household Industry		Constructions		Trade and Commerce		Other Services		Non-Workers	
	M	F	M	F	M	F	M	F	M	F
	12	13	14	15	16	17	18	19	20	21
Bana	..	..	..	..	..	..	..	..	19	16
Bana Camp	..		..		..		57	7	9	9
Bhalukpong/Thrizino			1		7		516	65	70	130
Bihupam									11	14
Buragaon										
Chizang					..		..		26	33
Dedza					3		78		..	..
Dijangania							3		50	146
Gijiri									14	29
Gohainthan			..				..	..	15	33
Huppipam/Dezling			1				435	34	43	71
Hussigaon	..		..		..		16	2	14	43
Jamiripoint/Noghupam	..	..	1	..	3	..	64	10	30	31

Table 7.13 (Contd. . . .)

	12	13	14	15	16	17	18	19	20	21
Jamiri Village	..	..	..	..	..	..	4	..	28	53
Karangania	..	..	..	..	..	..	1	..	24	53
Kararamu	..	..	..	..	..	..	..	..	17	26
Kichang	..	..	..	..	..	..	..	..	36	25
Linia	..	..	..	..	..	..	..	..	5	18
Moracca	..	..	..	..	..	..	..	..	3	19
Palatari	..	..	..	..	..	..	..	..	31	74
Pharizing	..	..	..	..	..	..	..	..	13	33
Pichang	..	..	..	..	..	..	29		71	64
Ramdagania	..	..	..	..	3	..	2	..	25	70
Rogupam	..	..	..	..	..	..	..	..	8	16
Rugugaon	..	..	..	..	..	..	..	..	5	9
Sakrin	..	..	..	..	..	..	1	..	41	110
Sessa	..	..	..	..	16	..	26	9	10	17
Tania	..	..	..	..	..	..	..	..	23	23
Thesa	..	..	..	..	..	..	..	..	24	86
Thesari	..	..	..	..	..	..	..	..	5	14
Tulu	..	..	..	..	..	..	..	..	29	42
Yayong	..	..	..	..	..	..	..	..	12	28
Total	0	0	3	0	32	0	1232	127	711	1335

Source: Census of India, 1971.

Table 7.12
Table Showing Total Workers and Non-workers of the Aka Villages 1981

	Total Main Workers (I-IX)		*Cultivators (I)*		*Agricul-turals Labourer (II)*		*Household Industry, Manufactu-ring, Processing, Servicing and Repairs {V(a)}*		*Other Workers {III, IV, V (b) and VI to IX)*		*Marginal Workers*		*Non Workers*	
Village	M	F	M	F	M	F	M	F	M	F	M	F	M	F
1	2	3	4	5	6	7	8	9	10	11	12	13	14	15
Bana	30	32	29	32	..	..	..	..	1	..	..	..	19	10
Bana Camp	38	4	13	2			1	1	24	1	1		35	40
Bhalukpong (HQ)	251	17					2		249	17	..		93	188
Bhorali River Camp	14	2	..	..					14	2			..	3
Bihupam	7	9	7	9					..	..		..	8	6
Buragaon	56	1	23	..					33	1		19	55	69
Chijang	39	36	39	36			..		..	..		..	26	19
Dedza	31	9	..	..	..	..	2		29	9			19	41
Dizangania	77	72	49	58	14	14	..	..	14	..	..	..	51	45

Table 7.14 (Contd. . . .)

1	2	3	4	5	6	7	8	9	10	11	12	13	14	15
8 KM Point from Khuppi to Tenga River	43	5	1	2	..	..	..	..	42	3		..	10	20
Elephant Flat	50	15	..	..	6	3	..	..	44	12	..	..	12	14
Giziri	13	20	13	20	..	..	..	..	..	..	..	..	9	14
Gohainthan	26	15	15	15	..	..	..	..	11	..	..	..	7	4
Husigaon	32	15	13	10	..	..	..	..	19	5	..	..	9	9
Jamiri	452	152	46	55	..	..	..	..	406	97	..	..	106	132
Jamiri Point	57	7	1	1	..	..	8	..	48	6	..	25	51	26
Karangonia	31	43	28	43	..	..	..	..	3	..	..	..	36	35
Kararamu	13	18	13	18	..	..	..	..	..	..	..	..	15	15
Khamsiri	14	14	14	14	..	..	..	..	..		..	..	7	16
Khuppi – A	14	..	1	..	..	..	..	..	13	..	..	..	6	15
Khuppi – B	28	7	..	..	..	..	..	..	28	7	..	..	20	19
Kitchang	41	43	40	43	..	..	..	..	1	..	6	13	26	14
Kimi	14	10	11	10	..	..	..	..	3	..	..	..	5	7
Mopgromo	6	10	6	10	..	..	..	..	..	..	..	..	10	13
Morakaha	15	14	15	14	..	..	..	..	..	..	..	..	15	18
New Kaspi	18	8	10	8	..	..	..	..	8	..	3	..	11	6
Palatari	49	57	44	57	..	..	..	..	5	..	..	..	44	33
Palizi	66	13	41	9	..	..	..	..	25	4	..	..	61	100

Table 7.14 (Contd. . . .)

1	2	3	4	5	6	7	8	9	10	11	12	13	14	15
Phrizing	20	24	20	24	..	..	..	..	..	..	..	..	21	16
Pitchang	75	98	69	98	..	..	..	..	6	..	1	..	71	60
Ramdagania	23	12	19	11	..	..	..	..	4	1	..	..	15	19
Sakrin	50	65	49	65	..	..	..	..	1	..	..	..	44	30
Sapung	24	24	24	24	..	..	..	..	..	..	..	..	14	13
Sathi (64 KM)	1	3	1	3	..	..	..	..	..	..	..	..	3	1
Sessa	92	36	..	..	22	7	1	..	69	29	..	..	35	33
Tania	20	20	16	20	..	..	..	..	4	..	..	..	6	8
Thessa	15	18	15	18	..	..	..	..	..	..	..	..	11	16
3 KM Point towards Kimi	17	8							17	8			4	9
34 KM Point from Nechiphu	2	2	1	2	..	..	..	..	1	..	..	..	..	1
Thrizino (H.Q)	100	20	9	19	..	..	..	..	91	1	..	..	64	94
Tipi	26	1	..	..	..	..	..	..	26	1	..	..	6	16
Tulu	38	22	21	21	..	..	..	..	17	1	..	..	7	11
Tuluhu	4	8	..	7	..	..	..	..	4	1	..	..	4	4
Yashey	41	14	17	14	..	..	..	..	24	..	..	..	22	43
Yayong	30	26	27	26	..	..	..	..	3	..	..	..	18	26
Total	2103	1049	760	818	42	24	14	1	1197	296	11	57	1111	1331

Source: Census of India, 1981.

I – Cultivators, II – Agricultural Labourers, III – Livestock, Forestry, Fishing, Hunting, and Plantation, Orchards and allied activities, IV – Mining and Quarrying, V(a) – Household Industry, V(b) – Other than Household Industry, VI – Constructions, VII – Trade & Commerce, VIII – Transport, Storage and Communications, IX – Other Services, X – Non-workers.

Table 7.13
Table Shwoing Total Workers and Non-workers of the Aka Villages 1991

Village	Total Workers		Cultivators		Agricultural Labourers		Livestock, Forestry, Fishing Hunting and Plantations, Orchards and allied activities		Household Industry		Other than Household Industry	
	M	F	M	F	M	F	M	F	M	F	M	F
1	2	3	4	5	6	7	8	9	10	11	12	13
Bana Camp	171	44	32	31	..	..	57	..	4	1	1	..
Bana Village	18	23	17	23								
Buragaon	97	61	44	51	..	..						
Chijong	45	44	42	42	1	1	..					
Dedza	72	14	..	..			4					
Dizangoniapam (Hamlet)	6	8	6	8			..				..	..
Elephant Flat	128	32	2	3			2				1	2
Giziri	12	..	9	..	..							
Gohainthan	10	13	9	13	1	..	..	..	..	..	..	..

Table 7.15 (Contd. . . .)

1	2	3	4	5	6	7	8	9	10	11	12	13
Hussigaon	24	18	13	18	..	..	..	..	..	..	..	..
Jamiri Point	195	28	8	11	..	..	..	..	..	..	4	..
Jamiri Village (including labour camp at 3 Km)	65	50	37	44	..	..	..			..		
Karangonia	21	15	19	15	..	..	..			..		
Kararamu	13	2	10	2	1	..	..			..		
Kaya Valley	27	34	24	34	..	..	..			..		
Khamsiri (Hamlet)	2	1	2	1	..	..	..			..		
Khupi Det	9	4	2	2	..	..	..			..		
Khupi Forest office complex	30	14	1	3	..	..	..			2		
Khupi Model village	25	20	25	20	..	..	..			..		
Kimi Forest office complex	22	..	..	..	..	..	6			..		
Kitchang	31	25	22	24	..	..	..			..		
Labour camp at 2 km from Palizi towards Khupi (Hamlet)	6	5	..	..			..	..	..	..	..	
L. Bhalukpong	369	66	1	1			54	29	7	3	49	
Moorakka	8	4	8	4			..	..	..	..	..	
Nechiphu Camp (including labour camp at .5 Km)	15	11	..	..	..	..	..	..	1	1	..	..
New Sapung	21	19	12	13	..	..	1	..	..	..	..	..
Old Kaspi (Hamlet)	1	2	1	2	..	..	..	..	..	..	..	..

Table 7.15 (Contd. . . .)

1	2	3	4	5	6	7	8	9	10	11	12	13
Palatary	30	2	18	1	6	..	..	..	..	..	..	..
Palizi	100	25	31	13	5	1	1	..	..	1	13	1
Phirizin	14	..	14	..	..	..	..	..	..	..	..	..
Pitchang	58	63	42	62	10	1	..	..	..	..	..	..
Pochung	10	11	9	11	..	..	..	..	..	..	..	..
Rabong Rugo L camp (Hamlet)	2	1	2	1	..	..	..	..	..	..	..	..
Ramdagonia	25	15	17	14	..	..	..	..	..	..	..	..
Sakrin	40	4	37	4	..	..	..	..	..	..	..	..
Saljipam (Hamlet)	5	7	5	7	..	..	..	..	..	..	..	..
Sapung	20	21	20	21	..		..	..	..	..	..	..
Sessa	204	13	..	..	..	..	11	..	..	..	1	..
Sobu	47	..	44	..	..	..	..	..	..	..	..	..
Thesa	34	27	31	23	..	..	..	..	..	..	..	..
Thrizino (H.Q)	184	56	16	16	..	..	13	1	..	..	14	..
Tipi	286	44	..	..	..	..	9	..	..	..	25	2
Tuluhui	20	..	19	..	..	..	..	..	..	..	..	..
U. Bhalukpong (H.Q)	521	40	..	..	..	..	3	..	..	..	4	..
Yangse	119	40	51	25	8	10	..	..	1	..	15	..
Yayung	24	16	22	16	..	..	..	..	..	..	..	..
Total	3186	942	724	579	32	13	161	30	13	8	127	5

Table 7.15 (Contd. . . .)

Village	*Constructions*		*Trade and Commerce*		*Transport, Storage and Communi-cations*		*Other Services*		*Marginal Workers*		*Non-workers*	
	M	F	M	F	M	F	M	F	M	F	M	F
	14	15	16	17	18	19	20	21	22	23	24	25
Bana Camp	29	4	8	4	1	..	39	4	..	..	131	137
Bana Village	..	..	1	..	..		..	..			18	18
Buragaon	28	4			2		23	6			82	105
Chijong	..		..		..		2	1			40	36
Dedza	2		8		5		53	14			61	94
Dizangoniapam (Hamlet)	..	..	..		..		..	..			2	4
Elephant Flat	98	26	..		2		23	1			29	68
Giziri			..				3				14	32
Gohainthan			..		..		..				7	10
Hussigaon	..		10	..	..		1	..			17	18
Jamiri Point	2		30	3	3		148	14			69	123
Jamiri Village (including labour camp at 3 Km)	2	..	..	..	..	..	26	6	..	..	52	61

Table 7.15 (Contd. . . .)

	14	15	16	17	18	19	20	21	22	23	24	25
Karangonia	..	..	..	..	..	..	2	..	..	..	23	41
Kararamu	..	..	..	..	..	..	2	..	..	..	14	40
Kaya Valley	..	..	..	..	..	..	3	..	..	..	31	23
Khamsiri (Hamlet)	..	..	..	..	..	..	..	..	..	..	2	5
Khupi Det	..	..	3	..	..	..	4	2	..	..	5	14
Khupi Forest office complex	..	..	1	..	..	..	28	9	..	..	12	10
Khupi Model village		..	..	..	..	..	..	..	..	..	12	14
Kimi Forest office complex		..	..	..	5	..	11	..	..	..	4	7
Kitchang		..	8	1	..	..	1	..	..	..	39	21
Labour camp at 2 km from Palizi towards Khupi (Hamlet)	..	..	..	..	..	..	6	5			7	7
L. Bhalukpong	48	6	31	1	57	1	122	25			210	355
Moorakka	..	..	..	..	..	..	..	..			3	4
Nechiphu Camp (including labour camp at .5 Km)	..	..	9	7	..	..	5	3	..	3	59	106
New Sapung	..	..	..	..	..	..	8	6	..	..	16	19
Old Kaspi (Hamlet)	..	..	..	..	..	..	..	..	..	..	2	1
Palatary	..	..	..	..	..	..	6	1	..	..	43	60
Palizi	9	2	10	1	1	..	30	6	..	..	75	149
Phirizin	..	..	..	..	..	..	..	..	..	..	20	28

Table 7.15 (Contd. . . .)

	14	15	16	17	18	19	20	21	22	23	24	25
Pitchang	..	..	..	..	..	..	6	..	..	..	43	61
Pochung	..	..	1	..	..	..	..	..	..	..	18	7
Rabong Rugo L camp (Hamlet)		..	..	..	..	..	..	..		..	1	1
Ramdagonia	..	..	..	..	..	..	8	1	..	..	12	16
Sakrin	..	..	..	..	..	..	3	..	..	..	69	105
Saljipam (Hamlet)	..	..	..	..	..	..	..	..	..	..	3	7
Sapung	..	..	..	..	..	..	..	..	..	..	11	13
Sessa	68	12	16	1	2	..	106	..	..	..	25	34
Sobu	..	..	..	..	..	..	3	..	..	..	45	89
Thesa	..	..	1	..	..	..	2	4	..	..	113	202
Thrizino (H.Q)	25	12	10	11	..	..	106	16	1	1	145	244
Tipi	2	..	2	1	1	..	247	41	..	..	110	171
Tuluhui	..	..	..	..	..	..	1	..	..	..	15	42
U. Bhalukpong (H.Q)	64	21	18	1	8	..	424	18	..	..	229	367
Yangse	29	3	12	2	1	..	2	..	..	..	73	147
Yayung	..	..	..	..	..	..	2	..	..	.	22	40
Total	406	90	179	33	88	1	1456	183	1	4	2033	3156

Source: Census of India, 1991.

NB: Mining and Quarrying 1 at Lower Bhalukpong.

Table 7.14

Table Showing Total Workers and Non-workers of the Aka Villages 2001

	Total Working Population		Cultivators		Agricultural Labourers		Household Industry		Others		Marginal Workers		Non - workers	
Villages	Male	Female	Male	Female	Male	Female	Male	Female	Male	Female	Male	Female	Male	Female
1	2	3	4	5	6	7	8	9	10	11	12	13	14	15
Baliphoo	19	22	0	0	0	0	0	0	6	1	13	21	26	31
Bana Camp	55	43	15	37	1	0	0	0	38	6	1	0	99	78
Bana Village	55	56	44	49	5	4	0	0	4	0	2	3	82	64
Buragaon	74	64	43	53	0	0	0	3	30	8	1	0	83	87
Chijang	33	35	30	32	0	0	0	0	1	0	2	3	30	30
Dedza	40	11	0	0	0	0	0	0	40	11	0	0	16	38
Dizangania	6	6	6	6	0	0	0	0	0	0	0	0	9	8
Elephant Flat	48	18	2	0	0	0	0	0	37	4	9	14	29	40
Giziri	16	15	8	15	0	0	0	0	8	0	0	0	15	21
Gohainthan	12	16	11	15	0	0	0	0	1	1	0	0	7	12
Hussigaon	10	8	8	8	0	0	0	0	2	0	0	0	16	16
Husago	19	19	13	17	0	0	0	0	5	2	1	0	29	29
Humethu (Humethu under Jamiri)	18	16	9	10	0	0	0	0	8	4	1	2	13	17

Table 7.16 (Contd. . . .)

1	2	3	4	5	6	7	8	9	10	11	12	13	14	15
Jamiri H.Q.	37	13	6	6	0	0	0	0	31	7	0	0	25	41
Jamiri Point	66	36	7	14	0	0	0	0	58	21	1	1	54	61
Jamiri Village	24	21	15	12	0	0	0	0	8	9	1	0	48	48
Kamsiri	4	3	4	0	0	0	0	0	0	0	0	3	4	10
Karangonia	24	34	22	32	0	0	0	0	1	1	1	1	36	42
Kararamu	14	15	9	15	0	0	0	0	3	0	2	0	9	22
Kaya Valley Village	18	23	17	23	0	0	0	0	1	0	0	0	36	23
Khupi Forest Office Complex	13	7	4	7	0	0	0	0	9	0	0	0	9	11
Khupi Model Village	74	53	25	32	0	0	1	1	46	17	2	3	49	38
Kimi Village	53	28	9	8	0	0	0	0	43	18	1	2	19	15
Kitchang	21	17	20	17	0	0	0	0	1	0	0	0	21	20
L. Bhalukpong	688	87	3	2	1	1	11	1	638	80	35	3	496	744
Maraka	5	5	5	5	0	0	0	0	0	0	0	0	5	4
Nechiphu	32	22	3	3	0	0	0	0	29	19	0	0	27	22
New Sapong	32	27	19	22	5	2	0	0	8	3	0	0	28	35
Palatari	38	34	36	32	0	0	0	0	2	1	0	1	42	34
Palizi	219	102	49	56	3	1	8	0	142	42	17	3	148	183

Table 7.16 (Contd. . . .)

1	2	3	4	5	6	7	8	9	10	11	12	13	14	15
Pharizin	18	19	18	19	0	0	0	0	0	0	0	0	28	20
Pitchang	35	40	27	37	5	1	0	0	2	1	1	1	38	35
Pochung	16	16	16	16	0	0	0	0	0	0	0	0	23	16
Ramdagania	25	20	22	19	1	0	0	0	2	1	0	0	30	25
Sakrin	57	50	56	50	0	0	0	0	0	0	1	0	73	62
Sapong	17	15	17	15	0	0	0	0	0	0	0	0	12	26
Sessa	50	11	0	0	0	0	0	0	21	5	29	6	22	41
Sube	30	34	0	0	0	0	0	0	12	3	18	31	35	32
Tania	15	13	0	0	0	0	0	0	0	0	15	13	10	21
Thessa	43	41	42	12	0	0	0	0	1	1	0	28	56	60
Thrizino (H.Q)	178	74	31	43	0	0	0	0	147	27	0	4	208	355
Tipi	315	70	3	0	0	0	2	0	296	52	14	18	214	367
Tuluhi	17	19	17	19	0	0	0	0	0	0	0	0	11	26
U. Bhalukpong	370	115	0	3	0	0	4	1	351	100	15	11	447	623
Yangse	110	74	69	56	1	1	0	0	37	15	3	2	144	190
Yayung	22	15	22	7	0	0	0	0	0	1	0	7	24	29
Total	3085	1482	782	824	22	10	26	6	2069	461	186	181	2885	3752

Source : Census of India, 2001.

In addition to this there were 68 marginal workers (11 male and 57 female). A total of 2442 people were categorized as non – workers with 1111 male and 1331 female. Out of the total main workers, cultivators comprise the highest number of population i.e. 1578, which is followed by the other workers category comprising of 1493 workers.

The other categories of workers like agricultural labourers, forestry, fishing, hunting, and plantation, orchards and allied activities, mining and quarrying, household industry, etc. were very less and insignificant. In 1991 census the total main workers was recorded to be 4128, out of which 3186 were male and 942 female. There were only 5 marginal workers that include 1 male and 4 female. Large share of the population was under non–workers category i.e. 5189 (2033 male and 3156 female). Out of the total main workers the highest workers were categorized as other services i.e. 1639 (1456 male and 183 female). It was followed by the cultivators numbering 1303 workers with 724 male and 579 female. Constructions, business and contract, forestry, fishing, hunting and other allied activities also possessed better share of workers in 1991.

The 2001 census estimated the total main workers of the study area as 4567 (3085 male and 1482 female). There were 367 marginal workers with 186 male and 181 female. More than 50% of the total population belongs to non – workers, out of which 2885 are male and 3752 are female. The share of other workers was more than 50% of the total main working population. The other workers were estimated to be 2530 with 2069 male and 461 female. A total population of 1606 was categorized as cultivators that include 782 male and 824 female. The area recorded only 32 agricultural labourers and 32 household industries in 2001 census.

Occupation and Income

The whole Aka population is categorized under the occupations as found during the field survey presented in Table 7.15. The table shows still maximum people are occupied in agricultural sector. A small number of the population is

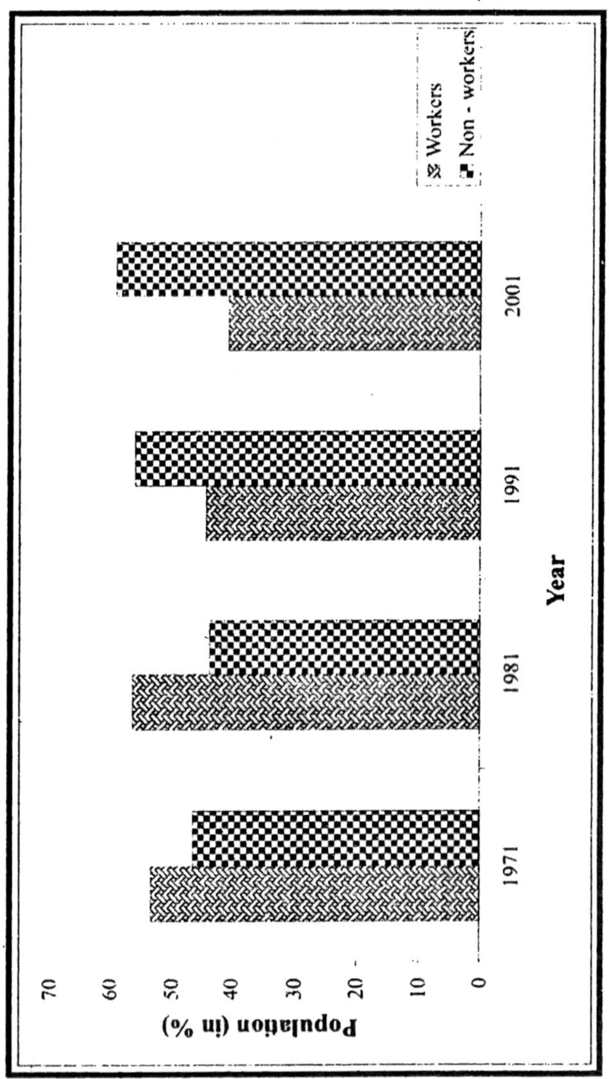

Fig. 7.4 : Comparison of Workers and Non-workers (in %) from 1971 to 2001.

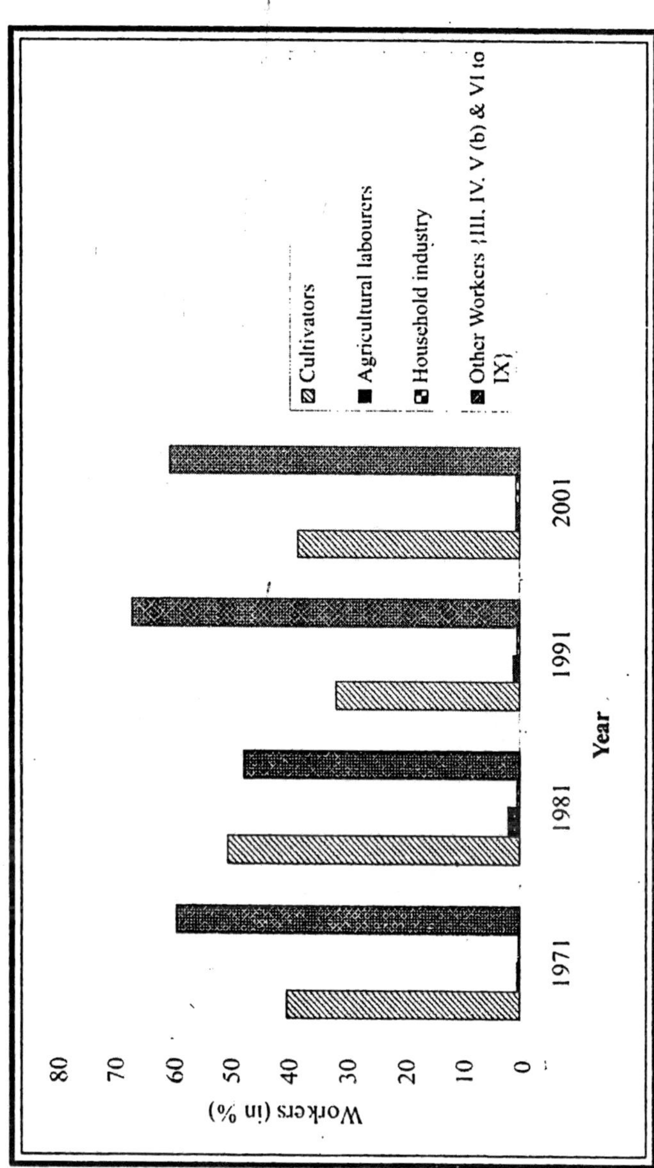

Fig. 7.5 : Percentage of Workers in various categories (1971 to 2001).

Table 7.15
Occupation and Income

Occupation	*Population*	*No. of Households*	*Income (in Rupee)*
Agriculture	1505	216	Less than 2000
Labour	79	253	2001 - 5000
Teacher	30	89	5001 - 10000
Other Services	195	79	10001 - 50000
Business	70	54	100000 and Above
Contract	172		
Private Enterprise	1		

engaged in government service. In business (contractor, shopkeeper) also a small number of person are involved. During field survey each of the household was asked for their income. It was found that almost all necessary items are produced at home. However, to buy salt, edible oil, cloth and other day to day items they manage cash amount by selling some of their produced or employing themselves in some seasonal work available in and around their villages. The cash amount earned declared by them is given in Table 7.15. Therefore, this tabular information should not be taken as total income per household.

8 SUMMARY AND SUGGESTION

The study of tribals in transition is significant to understand the level of change and transformation undergoing in a society with the passage of time. In this work an attempt has been made to carry out a comprehensive work on the Aka tribe of Arunachal Pradesh who had not also been spared by the agents of social, economic and cultural change. Thus, a research problem entitled, "Tribals in Transition: A Geographic Study of Society, Economy and Culture of the Akas of Arunachal Pradesh" is selected. In simple words tribe refers to a group of families or communities, linked by social, economic, religious, or blood ties, and usually having a common culture and dialect and a recognized leader. Whereas transition refers to the change from one place, state, condition, etc. to another.

Akas are the tribe who inhabits the south eastern part of West Kameng and western part of East Kameng district. They are divided into two sub-tribes namely *Hrusso* and *Kora*. They have no script of their own and speak the Aka dialect, which is grouped under the Tibeto-Burman family of language. The area is located in between 27° 0′ N to 27° 30′ N latitudes and 92° 30′ E to 92° 55′ E longitudes covering an area of about 1262. 21 Sq. km. It comprises 38 (thirty-eight) villages. Earlier workers (Sinha 1962, Elwin 1968, Kholey 1997) studied Akas from historical and anthropological point of view by selecting a few villages. This work is focused considering all Aka villages on their transition from post independence to recent. The study is aimed to identify geo-environmental characteristics; social, economic and cultural aspects; demographic features;

and the changes taken place. The area inhabited by Akas is delineated on Survey of India topographical maps as narrated by the elderly people during field study. Using questionnaires each and every household is surveyed. A comparative study is made by using census data of 1971, 1981, 1991, 2001 and field survey during 2006. The whole work has been divided into 8 (eight) chapters.

The altitude is ranging from 200 to 2,936 meters above mean sea level. Geologically this area is covered by Siwaliks (Outer Himalaya) and Lesser Himalaya. The main rock types found in this area are sandstone, conglomerate, shale, quartzite, dolomite, gneiss and schist. This area is crossed by Himalayan Frontal Fault (HFF), Tipi Thrust (TT) and Main Boundary Thrust (MBT) from east to west. The average slope calculated for the area ranges from level to 42°. The study area is drained by Kameng river and its tributaries. The main tributaries are Tenga and Bichom rivers. The temperature of the study area ranges in between 1° to 30° C. However, higher reaches experience snowfall during winter. The annual rainfall received by the study area is about 235 cm. The area is located in a mountainous tract with deep gorges, valleys, hills, etc. So it is obvious that the soils are of mountainous type. The soil is not much fertile, except the small patches of valleys and river terraces. The study area is rich in its flora and fauna. In general three types of forests i.e. tropical rain forest and semi-evergreen forest, subtropical forest and pine forest are available in the area.

A change in a society is inevitable as with the passage of time society adopts new things to cop up with the newly emerging necessities. The Akas are also one of the tribal groups of the state, who have been exposed to changes in their social, economic and cultural life. Societal changes seem to be more prominent among the Akas. The Aka society has experienced remarkable changes with the passage of time. Traditionally, there was a joint family system in Aka society where all the members lived together with separate fire places. The study reveals that the family in the society at present is more individual than joint system. The separation of sons from their parents is much more frequent than the past in the recent years that has led to the emergence of more and more individual families. The composition of the family is also changing due to the change in the family type. During the past a family consists of Grand Parents, Parents, Children and Grand Children. Nowadays families consist of Parents and Children only, which shows the emergence of individual type of family. The Parents preferred to live with the youngest son during the past days due to tradition and emotional attachment. In some rare cases they used to live with the eldest son if he is capable enough to take care of them. The Parents living with the intermediate son or the daughter is almost negligible in the society. In the recent days the strictness of traditional system is decreasing as a result parents select any son or the daughter to stay with, keeping in view the ability, love and care provided during their old age. Marriage institution is one of the aspects, where changes are taking place rapidly. The concept of marriage among the younger generation is becoming different than the meaning of the traditional marriage. The traditional marriage practices are loosing their effectiveness in the present context. The time duration of marriage ceremony is shortened in recent years due to less time availability as people are involved in government jobs, business and education. It may be the result of the influence of marriage systems practiced by other surrounding tribes in which less time is involved. The number of *mithuns* to be gifted is also reduced to 5 or less. Maximum impact on the traditional marriage institution is caused by the conversion of people into other religions in the recent times. Changes in religion lead to changes in the societal aspects of a community. Nowadays marriages are taking place in churches, temples, etc. Such changes are influencing the valued traditional marriage system of the tribe.

The traditional village council is also losing its importance in the society due to the introduction of Panchayati raj system. The constituents of the council are mostly filled up with the elected/selected members of PRIs instead of the appointed members of the village council. The induction of the younger generation as a member of Zila Parishad, Anchal Samiti, Gram Panchayat has also reduced the importance and active role of the village elders in the decision making process of the village. The function of village council has also taken a different form. The functions which were necessary during the past like war, defence, etc. are being replaced by other developmental works. The changes in the constituents and functions of traditional village council have profound impact on the social organization of the village as a single entity. The villagers are becoming more and more individualistic than a group. The village as a community has significant role in the house construction, hunting, fishing, festivals, rituals, etc. but, the modern political system has forced the villagers to remain aloof from each other even within the village.

The literacy rate was very low in the past, but now it has increased to 63.57% with 71.26% male and 55.74% female respectively as per the survey 2006. But, the level of education is disproportionate as majority of the literates belong to the primary and secondary level of education. The number of graduates and post graduates are very less. The status of women in the Aka society is better than many communities in the world because they are allowed to participate in all activities ranging from social, economic, cultural and political. The past years reveal some kinds of exploitation of women i.e. marriage by capture, child marriage, polygyny and torture. Such incidences are very rare in the present days, though some kind of child marriage, polygyny and torture is still evident amongst the people. More and more women are becoming educated and employed in different jobs, which has improved the status of women at present. The division of labour in the society has tremendously changed in comparison to the past. Day to day activities of a family is also changed due to the introduction of modern amenities. The harsh environment has made them to derive a mechanism of work division among themselves to sustain but the introduction of education, medical, and other infrastructural facilities has encouraged them to leave those arduous tasks. Nowadays education has been given more emphasis and the children are being sent to schools irrespective of sex.

The absence of good infrastructural facilities in the area was one of the major factors in the underdevelopment of the area. Educational institutions were introduced very lately in the area. There were few public schools in the 32 villages during 1971 with little infrastructures. Consequently, the literacy rate of the area in that particular year was only 12.11%. However, the number of educational institutions has increased rapidly since then and as per the recent survey there were nine (9) community schools, fifteen (15) primary schools, four (4) middle schools, two (2) government secondary schools and eleven (11) adult literacy class centers attached to some of the schools in 39 villages. Some more private schools started by the missionaries and individuals have also come up at Palizi, Thrizino, Buragaon, Bhalukpong and Yangsey villages. The Christian missionaries had established St. Xavier secondary school at Palizi village. Their branches are also spread to Thrizino and Buragaon, though these schools are at their initial stage of development. Apart from this there is a Navajyoti school and a primary missionary school at Bhalukpong. The impact of the increase in number of educational institution is the abrupt rise in the literacy rate to 64%. The area requires some good educational institutions in the form of private, semi-government schools like VKVs, JNVs, etc. for qualitative education. Apart from this some of the schools in the area are not functional and exist by name only. The instances of such schools are the Government Primary Schools of Yayong and Thissa, where there is no teacher, enrolments, desks, benches, etc. since 2004. The area do not improved much in the medical amenities. As per the survey conducted in 2006, there was no increase in the number of Physical Health Sub-Centre since 1991. It remained three and out of these the PHS of Thrizino has been taken up by an NGO Voluntary Health Association of India (VHAI). There were 3 (three) Physical Health Centre, 1 Others and 1 Health Centre of military at Sessa. The hospitals are also not equipped well to cater the needs of the people. Every year there is an outbreak of epidemics of one form or the other. Apart from the villages located in the accessible areas the other villagers are facing acute shortage of medicines during epidemics. The villagers of Thissa, Yayong, Karangania, Kararamu, Palatari, Morkha, Pichang, Chijang, etc. have to cover 10 to 20 kms on foot to avail the medicines and doctor. The area enjoys good connectivity of pipelines of drinking water and the villages which do not avail the pipelines are located near to water sources. Therefore, the area has good drinking water connectivity but, there is no treatment of water which causes water borne diseases. Water treatment system and awareness programme could play significant role in reducing the occurrences of water borne diseases. The banking facility is being provided by the only bank i.e. State Bank of India (SBI), Bhalukpong. However, the SBIs situated at Chindit top, Bomdila and Seppa are also catering the needs of the people. A branch of SBI at Thrizino, the headquarters of the sub-divisional office as a central place could be helpful for the villagers. Post and Telegraph facilities are available at Thrizino, Bhalukpong, Bana and NEEPCO at Kimi that cover the all villages. The other villagers have to travel more than 10 kms to avail such facilities. Poor transport and communication is one of the hurdles in the proper development of the area. The majority of the villages are connected by footpath only. There are few villages located along the metalled roads. The two important concentration of the population i.e. Buragaon and Thrizino are connected by unmetalled roads, which are not motorable in the summer season. There is overall lack of transport infrastructure in the area. The number of buses and bus stands are also very less in comparison to other parts of the district and state. Though all the villages are electrified but, power supply is availed during one season of the year only for domestic use. In Thrizino and Bhalukpong power supply is available throughout the year because of the arrangement of generators in case of main power supply failure. Bhalukpong located at the border with Assam is a main market centre. Therefore, the villagers are dependent on the market of Bhalukpong only. Some minor day-to-day requirements are acquired from the market at the district headquarters. Major commodities are availed from Bhalukpong, Balipara and Tezpur (Assam).

Forests and forest products have profound impact on the economy of the Akas. Their traditional economy revolve around forests which includes various occupations such as agriculture (*jhum*/shifting cultivation) and subsidiary means like hunting, fishing and food gathering. The products of jhum field such as vegetables, cucumbers, fruits and maize are sold for the requirement of money. Farmers personally do not sell their product in the market. Usually, they deliver the products to the owner of a shop to sell. The shopkeeper gets some money in form of reward for selling those products. Likewise wild vegetables, mushrooms, wild fruits, bamboo, etc. are collected from the forest for self-consumption. But, if it is excess, they give it to a shopkeeper for selling. The flesh of wild animals and fish are also sold in exchange of money. Whenever they kill a big wild animal, they use to sell the half portion in exchange of money and keep the remaining portion for the family members. In case of excess fish catch some portion is sold and rest retained for the family members. The *jhum* cycle, which was 5 to 10 years during the post independence period, has declined to less than 3 years at present due to increase in population. Proper suggestions and alternatives to *jhuming* could help in mitigation of adverse linkages emerging out of man-nature interaction in the area. The inhabitants along the main road or the settlements having good transportation facilities have mostly changed their economy from *jhuming*, hunting, fishing and food gathering to timber extraction. The villagers of Jamiri, Khuppi, Bhalukpong, Tippi, Palizi, Bana, etc. became more or less timber contractors and heavily depended on it. Saw mills at Bana, Palizi, Tippi were established. A plywood mill was also established at Tippi. In addition to timber extraction the other business activities were cane, herbs for medicine and dye extraction, etc. But, the ban on timber operations by the Hon'ble Supreme Court has badly affected the economic life of the people. This ban has created such a situation for them that neither they can continue their business nor they can go back to their traditional economy. For a period of about 5 to 10 years they had forgotten their traditional economy and shifted themselves towards timber business. The ban on timber extraction had slowed down the pace of timber extraction to certain extent but still for personal use extraction is going on. Along with the timber operations, the extraction of cane, herbal/medicinal plants, etc. are also gaining momentum. The abundance of different species of trees, bamboo groves and plantain leaves plays important role as these provide them variety materials for house-building, hunting/fishing implements, agricultural tools, dress and ornaments, domestic utensils and other implements. These people extract only the required parts/items from the forests and make use of them. They do not kill some animals and birds, which maintains the ecological balance. A number of social restrictions and customs have been in vogue, which every man and women has to be abided by. They do not fell some trees because there is a strong belief behind the felling of these trees e.g. to fell banyan tree causes illness to the person. The Akas as a forest people has age-old tradition of conservation, preservation, protection, management and optimal utilization of the forest resources. These people have a great role in protecting their nearby forests, since from their existence on this earth. They worship the forests as feeder and rearer to the human beings. They utilize forest-based resources and are also careful about its management that is evident from the indigenous beliefs, practices and the traditional mode of forest conservation adopted by them. These include the protection of sacred-groves that are not intruded as plucking of even single leaf from such areas is strictly prohibited. The interaction/inter linkages of the people with their immediate forest is harmonious and quite congenial that has preserved the present green forests in this area. However, the rapid growth of population and scientific and technological advancement had increased the momentum of people's interaction with the forests. The study reveals that some animals such as deer, bear, monkey, wild pig, etc. have become endangered one. It is also found that the forest cover around the settlements has degraded up to a distance of 30 to 40 km. The forest policy makers/Authority concerned of Anchal forest may invite the villager's views and their participation to avert the adverse impact on the forest ecology and adopt mitigation measures to certain problems of the surrounding forests. Some specific fund should be provided for creating awareness in remote villages concerning various issues and significance of the forest ecology. The planning for tribal development must take forest resources as the base on which tribal economy can progress with greater confidence. The tribal people should become not only co-sharer in the new wealth created in those areas but should also have active role in participation of its management. Their existing knowledge base, which is popularly termed as 'Indigenous Knowledge System' (IKS) in relation to their ecosystem may facilitate a movement to preserve and protect huge forest resources.

The total Aka population was 5027 (Survey, 2006) with a natural increase rate of 0.04018 or 4.018%. There is a rapid increase in the population in the recent decades. The crude birth rate was 49.73 and the crude death rate was 9.55. By putting the value in the exponential population growth equation it is found that the Aka population will double in approximately 17 years i.e. 10000 in 2024. The Aka population has a share of 44.87% to the total population and 78.46% to the total Scheduled Tribe population. The Infant Mortality Rate was estimated to be 92 per 1000 live births (Survey, 2006). The demographic statistics reveals that the population has entered the stage 2 of demographic transition characterized by high birth rate and low death rates. The total population in the age group of below 14 years is very high due to the high crude birth rate. Hence, the age sex pyramid of the population shows the model of an area under the stage 2 of demographic transition. The sex ratio of the total population was 876.72 females/1000 males as per 2001 census. The sex ratio of the scheduled tribe population was 1017.30 females/1000 males (2001 census) and the sex ratio of the Aka population as per the survey 2006 was estimated as 1006 females/1000 males. The work participation rate was

40.82% to the total Aka population, which shows higher dependency ratio.

Nowadays the rituals are declining due to conversion into other religion and the advancement/developmental activities in the area. Change is inevitable, but change or transformation has two aspects; some changes sound healthy and some changes sound unhealthy for the society. The changes in marriage system (especially marriage by capture) sound good to check the exploitation of the women. However, the abandonment of the practice of rituals in marriage sounds unhealthy, because they are losing their culture. They are very much attached to the priests and the rituals that even in this age of science and technology; they are still practicing number of rituals in marriage ceremonies. Though, the rituals performed in the marriages through capture acts as a restriction forbidding the girl from running away, it has got some social importance during the olden days.

In recent days there is a rapid decline in the number of priests in the Aka area. In some villages it has depleted so fast that even a single priest is not available throughout the village. Lack of interest among the younger generation is one of the important causes for rapid decline in the number of priests. The scientific knowledge, medicinal development and other related developmental activities had reduced the belief and faith of the people on the priests. However, the conversions of the people towards different organized religions as well as the forces of modernity are responsible for the decrease in the number of priests. The decrease in the number of priests as well as the changing attitude of the localities with the development of the society has led to decline in the practice of rituals in all the fronts, such as marriage, sufferings, construction of house, hunting, fishing, etc. Besides, the priest in the recent days has lost their importance by leaving their works half done during the performance of rituals. These days the priests are guided by the motives of earning and gaining some good materials as gift for the performance of rituals. Such motives of the priests had led to the degradation in the qualitative rituals in the area (The quality of a priest is determined by the people's faith on the priest). Any kind of realization among the people regarding the importance of rituals is very much essential in this particular period.

In the Aka society the oldest religion, which prevails from the earliest times is only the *Nyezino* or *Nyezi aou* (sky the father), *No ain* (earth the mother). Though, there is not any form of statue or idol for worship like other religions, the word *Nyezino* has such a place in the minds and souls of the Akas that they use to take the name of *Nyezino* at every moment of grief, problems or sufferings. The penetration of the scientific knowledge and technology into the land of this forest people had caused deep impacts on their lives. Due to the assimilation of knowledge and the early adaptation by the local people, there are lots of changes in the sphere of religion as well as festivities. People are converting to Christianity, Hinduism, etc., which may be the outcome of either the local people's inclination towards new faiths or for getting better facilities from various organizations of the other recognized religions. During the field survey, out of total Aka population (5027), 3905 are still continuing their own cultural practices i.e., *Nyezino* and *Mene Alan,* whereas 1117 persons have abandoned their own cultural practices and adopted Christianity. However, only 5 persons declared themselves as Hindu. They consider the existing Aka cultural practices were among the Hindu believers during Vedic period.

The Aka area has not progressed impressively during the post independence period. The tribe is one of the old and recognized tribe of Arunachal Pradesh. But, the region is still legging behind in terms of the indicators of development. There are many factors behind such underdevelopment. The lack of efficient and effective transportation system and the inadequate means of communication are the major hurdles of development. The whole area is located in between the two district headquarters i.e. East Kameng and West Kameng. Both the headquarters are linked with mettaled roads. Excluding the settlements situated along this metalled road, most of the settlements are not linked by road. Low literacy rates as well as low per capita income are the other indicators of development, which are responsible for the underdevelopment of the area. Their social customs, beliefs, faith, tradition, etc. reflects a deep imprint of the nearby forests. They worship the forests as gift of god to them. Their folktales, folklores, myths and festivities are highly influenced by the nearby forests. Besides, they practice a numerous modes of traditional conservation and management of plant and animal resources. These include the protection of sacred-groves from which no plant material is extracted. The economic organization, material culture, food habits, social, cultural and religious practices are largely determined by the existing forest resources.

REFERENCES

Abbink, J. 1995, Medicinal and ritual plants of the Ethiopian Southwest: an account of recent research. *Indigenous knowledge and Development Monitor*, 3, pp 6-8.

Ansari, W. A. 1980, The Changing Village India, Chetana Publications, New Delhi, p. 341.

Balan, K. 1992, Socio-economic Change in India, Ashish Publishing House, New Delhi, p.73.

Bhargava, G. 1992, *Environmental Challenges and Ecological Disaster*, Mittal Publications, New Delhi.

Bongaarts, J. 1994, "Population Policy Options in the Developing World", Science 263, pp. 771 - 776.

Bose, N. K. 1971, *Tribal Life in India*, National Book Trust, New Delhi.

Chaudhari, B. 1992, Changing Religion and Festival Cycle of the Mundas, (Ed.), B. Chaudhari in Tribal Transformation in India, Vol. V, New Delhi.

Cheong, M. 2001, "Aspects of Human Geography", Pekoe Books: Singapore.

Choudhary, S. D. 1996, Arunachal Pradesh District Gazetteers, East Kameng, West Kameng and Tawang Districts, Gazetteers Department, Government of Arunachal Pradesh, Shilong, p. 272.

Cunningham, A. B. 2001, *Applied Ethno botany: People, wild plant use and conservation*. London and Sterling, VA: Earthscan Publications Ltd.

Dasgupta, S. 1992, Role of Forest in the Socio-cultural Life of the Birjia - Some Observations, *Journal of Indian Anthropological Society*, (27) pp. 1-6.

Gadgil, M. 1998, Conservation: where are the people? *Survey of Environment*, The Hindu.

Gadgil, M. and Guha, R. 1992, *This Fissured Land*, The Book Review Literary Trust, New Delhi, p.

Ghosh, A.K. 2000, Traditional Knowledge in Biodiversity: Past trend and future perspective, Journal of Indian Anthropological Society, (35) pp. 179-184.

Ghosh, G. K. 1992, Tribals and their Culture, Ashish Publishing house, New Delhi.

Gohain, B. K. 1994, Continuity and Change in the Hills of Assam, Omsons Publications, New Delhi, p. 22.

Halley, E. 1693, "An Estimate of the Degrees of the Mortality of Mankind", *Philosophical Transactions*, published by the Royal Society (International), London, 196 (1692/3), pp. 596 – 610.

Hillard, K., et.al, 2000, "A Theory of Human Life History Evolution: Diet, Intelligence, Weed Knowledge and Longevity", in Evolutionary Anthropology, pp. 156 – 185.

Joshi, R. C. and Rawat, A. S. 2001, Morphotectonic observation along Main Boundary Thrust in between Dikrong and Ranga river, Eastern Himalaya, Arunachal Pradesh, Final project progress report submitted to the Dept. of Science and Technology, New Delhi, p. 71.

Joshi, R. C. 2006, Physiography of Arunachal Pradesh, (ed.), N. Nagaraju and B. Tripathy in Cultural Heritage of Arunachal Pradesh, Indus Publishing Company, New Delhi, pp. 19 – 31.

Joshi, V. 1997, Genesis of Tribal Problem, (ed.), G. Shah in Social Transformation in India, Vol. 2, Rawat Publications, New Delhi, p. 465.

Kar, P. C. 1982, The Garos in Transition, Cosmo Publications, New Delhi, pp. 264-5.

Kholey, R. N. 1997, Aspects of Customary laws of Arunachal Pradesh, (ed.), P. C. Dutta and D. K. Duarah, Arunachal Government Press, Naharlagun, p. 16.

Kumari, P. and Sinha, A. K. 1994, *Role of Minor Forest Produce in Tribal Economy (ed.)*, B. Chandari in Tribal Transformation in India, Inter- India Publishers, New Delhi p. 348.

Kuppuswamy, B. 1989, Social Change in India, Vikas Publishing House, New Delhi, p. 42.

Mann. R. S. and Mann, K. 1989, Tribal Cultures and Change, Mittal Publications, New Delhi, pp. 9-10.

Macharia, P. N. and Ekalaya, W. N. 2001, Masai Indigenous Knowledge on Range Vegetation Analysis, Utilization and Management, *Journal of Human Ecology*, 12(4) pp. 287-288.

Malhotra, K. C. 1996, People and Biodiversity, *Arunachal University Research Journal*, (1) pp. 98 – 112.

McLennan, J. F. 1888, "The Origin of Exogamy", *The English Historical Review 3*, pp. 94 – 104.

Nair, P. T. 1993, Tribes of Arunachal Pradesh, Spectrum Publications, New Delhi, p. 36.

Nakata, T. 1972, Geomorphic History and Crustal Movements of the Foothills of the Himalayas, Tokbu University, Sendai, Japan, p. 177.

Nimachow, G. 2001, Akas of Arunachal Pradesh and their Impact on Environment, Unpublished M. A./M. Sc. Dissertation submitted to Arunachal University, Itanagar, p. 67.

Nimachow, G. 2002, Forest and Tribe: A study on the Akas of Arunachal Pradesh, Unpublished M. Phil thesis submitted to Arunachal University, Itanagar, p. 87.

Nimachow, G. 2003, Akas and their forests: A study on traditional management of forest resources in Arunachal Pradesh, *Arunachal University Research Journal*, Itanagar, pp. 79 – 92.

Nimachow, G. 2003, Towards the sustainability of forest resources: A case study of Akas of Arunachal Pradesh, *Resarun*, Itanagar, pp. 75 – 81.

Nimachow, G. 2003, *Sacred Places, beliefs, festivals and rituals of the Akas of Palizi Village*, (ed.), T. Mibang and M.C. Behera in Dynamics of Villages in Arunachal Pradesh: Emerging Realities, Mittal Publications, New Delhi, pp. 199 – 225.

Nimachow, G. 2006, *A Note on Marriage practices in the Aka community of Arunachal Pradesh*, (ed.), T. Mibang and M.C. Behera in Marriage and Culture: Reflections from tribal societies of Arunachal Pradesh, Mittal Publications, New Delhi, pp. 45 – 54.

Nimachow, G. 2006, Linkages between bio-resources and human livelihood: (A study on the Akas of Arunachal Pradesh), *The Deccan Geographer*, Pune.

Nimachow, G. 2007, *Significance of rituals in Marriage systems of the Akas of Arunachal Pradesh,* (ed.) T. Mibang and M.C. Behera in Marriage in Tribal Societies (Cultural Dynamics and Social Realities), Bookwell Publishers, New Delhi, pp. 213 – 219.

Nimachow, S. 1995, Nyetshhidow (Nechidow) Festival of Hrussos (Akas) in *Arunachal Review*, Published by the Directorate of Information and Public Relations, Government of Arunachal Pradesh, pp. 10 – 12.

Pandey, M. C. 1990, *Some Measures to Control Environmental Degradation in the North Eastern Region (ed.)* P.K. Rai, A. C. Mohapatra, S. K. Mitra, D. K. Nayar and B. S. Butola, In Hill Area Development, Geographical Society of North Eastern Hill Region (India), Shillong.

Parihar, V. 1989, Society in Transition, Printwell Publishers, Jaipur, p. 36.

Prasad, K. 2001, Indian Tradition of Ecological Protection and Religion, *Man and Development*, Vol. XXIII, No. 4.

Raha, M. K. 1989 (ed.), Tribal Life in India, Problem and Development Prospects, Gyan Publications, New Delhi.

Ramamani, V. S. 1988, *Tribal Economy*: *Problems and Prospects.* Inter-India, New Delhi.

Raza, M. and Ahmad, A. 1990, An Atlas of Tribal India, Concept Publishing Co., New Delhi, p. 1.

Raza, M. and Thakur, D. N. 1994, *Tribal Life in India*, Vol. I in Tribal Life and Forests, Deep and Deep Publications, New Delhi.

Riba, T. 1997, The Tribes and their Changing Environment: A Case Study of Galos (Adi) of West Siang District, Arunachal Pradesh: Project Report, Department of Geography, Arunachal University.

Roy, S. B., Mukhopadhyay, D. and Das, S. 2001, Strengthening Institutions in Joint Forest Management: Systematic Approach to Forest Conservation, *Journal of Social Sciences,* 5(192) pp. 109 – 117.

Roy, S. B. Mukherjee, R. S. and Chatterjee, M. 1992, Indigenous Development in Participatory Forest Management, *Journal of Indian Anthropological Society,* (27) pp. 48 – 55.

Rubenstein, J. M. 1992, The Cultural Landscape: An Introduction to Human Geography, Macillan Publishing Company, New York, p. 580.

Satyanarayan, M. 1990. *Tribal Development in India: A Trend Report*. Inter-India, New Delhi.

Singh, K. S. 1994, The Scheduled Tribes, Vol. III, Oxford University Press, New Delhi, p. 57.

Sinha, R. 1962, The Akas, Published by Dr. P. C. Dutta, Directorate of Research, Itanagar, p. 143.

Soumen, S. 1988, Between Tradition and Change, B. R. Publishing Corporation, New Delhi, p. 16.

Thornhill, N. 1993, The Natural History of Inbreeding and Out breeding: Theoretical and Empirical Perspectives. The University of Chicago Press, Chicago.

United Nations Organization, 1999, "*World Population Prospects: The 1998 Revision*", Vol. I: *Comprehensive Tables*. New York: Population Division, Department of Economic and Social Affairs, United Nations.

Verrier, E. 1968, Myths of the North-East Frontier of India, Research Publications, Shillong, pp. 116 – 17.

GLOSSARY

Aa	one in Aka (Hrusso) dialect
Adii	local name for chili
Ain	descriptive term of address for 'mother'
Ajyoyi	beads of silver/other coins
Anh-Anh	masked dancers for driving away evil spirits
Aou	descriptive term of address for 'father'
Aao Tsase – Anyi Tsase	pigs given the parents of bride
Atchii	local name for elephant
Bagha – Giiba	permanent constituents of traditional village council
Basha	cloths given to the parents and relatives of bride
Bela	plate, especially brass plate
Biyo	a type of bamboo basket
Bjechi	a kind of bamboo used for vegetable
Bjiga-go-hutu – Ksum-go-nyetrii	the place from where the Akas believe to originated
Bjiva	a musical instrument
Bjivu	a form of making relationship for trade
Buslou aou	local name for ancestor (Hrusso)
Chibiu	local term for eel
Chimso	local name of a variety of fish
Dilephu	name of the highest mountain peak in Aka area

Drubji	local name of pumpkin
Duonyo	essential materials for ritual performance
Eche	one in Aka (Koro) dialect
Ekri - edro – jumyong	tying the root of life of bride and groom together
Fachosum	a kind of ritual dance
Fokki	a thread made of wool
Fomkrii	a thread with knots for fixation of dates
Froh-Froh	masked dancers for driving away evil spirits
Fu	mithun
Fumpem	a small edible plant gathered from the forest
Fusva	small bamboo ear-rings
Ghao/Khayiw 'etrii	local concept for migration
Ghaz	village members
Ge atra	a large piece of cloth given in bride-price
Gemso	a small piece of cloth given in bride-price
Giisen	local name for beads
Gudu	a kind of cover worn over the legs for protection against flies
Ghzee	local term for marriage
Hazarikhawo	a term used for a section of Akas in old writings who used to collect tax from the Assam
Huji dow	local term for addressing the process of community fishing
Humo	son-in-law
Humtru	local term used for Bichom river
Jajulaye	name of a mountain near Pichang
Jechi khruw	a ritual for selection of suitable girl for marriage
Jenye	a resting place in the top of hills and mountains

Khchan Chan Pro	a special type of dance in marriage parties
Kheo – nyeo	village elders
Kiistradu	a medicinal tuber
Kiyi	local term for bow
Kotocovo	a kind of wild fruit
Ksum	local name for Kameng river
Laprapra	french bean
Lasa-sigyeng	a place where aconite poison plant is found
Liimu	silver
Luchogo	name of a stream
Lumyo	local name for mushroom
Mdjeo/Mdjem	a man or woman who do not marry throughout the life
Mene – Alan	the sky and the earth (Koro)
Meye	traditional village council
Miidruw jiew	local term for barter trade
Mipesha	reception of the marriage party outside the village
Moo	local term for arrow
Miyan	10 pieces of brass plates
Mugow	local name for a priest
Mufo-uhu	a special blackish paint prepared from pine
Mukhow	the go-between or mediator
Mükho kiinye gzeeu	marriage by negotiation
Muksung	tobacco pipe
Muku	aconite poison
Miisanga	a kind of ring-cap of bamboo
Nearma husu	name of pond
Noke	dense forest land
Nowdii	fallow land left for at least five years
Nugou	local term for rich man
Nugom	local term for rani or rich women

'Nye	house
Nyechi	granary
Nyemkho	a small enclosure in the house serving as the main entrance
Nyepsiw	local name of stinkbug
Nyetriidow	local festival of Akas (Hrusso)
Nyetrii psigah	platform for holding meetings of a village
Nyetrii-Sao	the procession of driving away the evil spirits from village
Nyezino	local term for the religion of Akas (Hrusso)
Nyetro Do	separation of a son from the parent's house
O	paddy
Palo	an agricultural instrument
Pesa	a small edible plant used for vegetable
Pulbji	local term for peas
Puwje	local term for axe
Pyen	local term for a creeper consumed as vegetable
Sarok	local term for major festival (Koro)
Saslon	local name for ancestor (Koro)
Shashi-ge	a traditional garment of the Akas
Shii	gold
Sinsi	brass cups
Siibe	the local term for addressing maize
Siim-nyeksii	an edible wild plant
Syobotro	small sticks used by the village elders for counting
Syowum	a medicinal herb for curing coughs and fever
Syojyo-gin	a small enclosure made in the wall to keep firewood
Sujum	local term for a fly known as dam-dum
Tsum	a valuable beads
Thumona	guests

Thuvo	local term for quiver
Tiikrin	local term of expressing ginger
Trasgha – jiw	an ordeal for administering justice
Trasgha – nye	an altar prepared for the ordeal
Tsastrii dow	tradition for lowest marriage rule and seperation of a son from parental roof
Tro	local name for Arum (Commonly known as Kochu)
Tromo	local name of fishing net
Truka	local name of comb
Tsilanye Gzeeu	marriage by capture
Tumona	a term for addressing guests
Tuwonye	temporary huts made on the jhum field
Shhthwo/Ukro	iron made heart stand
Uluyi	the main hall or compartment in the house
Umkhyo	big size of cloth
Umnyo	small size of cloth
Vetsfa	medium size dao used for all purposes
Vetsii	dao or sword
Vetsiipsii	a long dao or sword for decoration and material wealth
Vee cheo	local term for addressing shifting cultivation
Veenyeksii	a kind of wild plant gathered from forest
Veeto	continuation huts made on the jhum field
Vo	pig
Vojopnu	name of a sacred mountain near Palizi
Womsey	leaves used for keeping edibles and storing rice for local wine
Wulo – do	a ritual for tying the souls of bride and groom in a knot
Wulo – kiw	ritual for freeing up the soul of a death person

Index

E

F

G